THE ULTIMATE MICROSOFT OFFICE BOOK!

Microsoft
PRESS

ERIC STROO

PUBLISHED BY
Microsoft Press
A Division of Microsoft Corporation
One Microsoft Way
Redmond, Washington 98052-6399

Library of Congress Cataloging-in-Publication Data
Stroo, Eric E.
    The ultimate Microsoft office book / Eric E. Stroo.
        p.   cm.
    Includes index.
    ISBN 1-55615-659-6
    1. Microsoft Windows (Computer file) 2. Microsoft Word for
Windows. 3. Microsoft Excel 4 for Windows. 4. Microsoft PowerPoint
for Windows. 5. Microsoft Mail for Windows. 6. Microsoft Access.
7. Business--Computer programs. I. Title.
HF5548.2.S83372   1994
650'.0285'5369--dc20   94-29761
                                                         CIP

Printed and bound in the United States of America.

2 3 4 5 6 7 8 9 QEQE 9 8 7 6 5 4

Distributed to the book trade in Canada by Macmillan of Canada, a division of Canada
Publishing Corporation.

A CIP catalogue record for this book is available from the British Library.

Microsoft Press books are available through booksellers and distributors worldwide. For further information about international editions, contact your local Microsoft Corporation office. Or contact Microsoft Press International directly at fax (206) 936-7329.

Acquisitions Editor: Casey D. Doyle
Project Editor: Jack Litewka
Manuscript Editor: Ina Chang
Technical Editor: Jerry Joyce

Contents

Preface

Much as I enjoy writing about software, I still consider most computer books to be a necessary evil. Suits me fine if you see them the same way. In a better (but perhaps unattainable) world, software would conform so intimately to the work we want to accomplish that the interface would anticipate our every aspiration. The documents we assemble would readily contain whatever types of data we chose to import or create—and with help from the operating system, they would be smart enough to keep track of their components, as well as updates, changed filenames, and all that baggage.

Microsoft Office is headed in the right direction. It helps you venture into the information landscape and create documents using the combined resources of Microsoft Word, Excel, PowerPoint, Access, Mail, and another handful of smaller, specialized helpers. Office has reached the stage at which a book about how the applications and their components interact can be extremely helpful—not so much as a necessary evil, but as a handy guide to the powerful integrated features of Office and its easy-to-use, built-in work-savers: wizards, templates, and the like.

Since the software suite has such high goals, it seems fair to set high goals for this book as well. It, too, should try to conform to your needs and anticipate your aspirations and exasperations. Here's how it will try to do so:

- It assumes that you know the basics of navigating in Microsoft Windows. For the sake of efficiency and a clear focus, this book does not explain the basics of how to make choices in dialog boxes, resize windows, or open files.

- It focuses on interoperability and on achieving streamlined results. It doesn't try to teach you the fundamentals of using the various Office applications (although it does supply some broad summaries of tasks and key features, and it patiently lays out a strategy for using the online Help resources). It saves the spotlight for application features that come into play when you use applications together.

- It stops shy of macros and advanced customization. People are increasingly using the macro capabilities and customization options to draw upon the well-crafted features of the Office suite and to build ingenious custom solutions. These are deservedly hot topics, and ones that many readers of this book will progress to, but they're clearly a separate subject.

- It uses various signposts to present information in categories. To help you zero in on the facts you need and to skip explanations that lie beyond (or beneath) your concerns, the book sorts information into tips, definitions, "power plays," troubleshooting suggestions, and other elements—set off by colorful boxes and icons.

- It goes to the source—software consumers—to discover the most persistent problems. The final chapter, contributed by the pros at Microsoft's vigilant Product Support Services (PSS) division, lays out the answers to common user questions—some broad, some narrow, and some (to me) unexpected.

As I mentioned, I enjoy writing about software. But that vocational quirk does not, in itself, produce a first-class book. No, you need first-class associates, only a fraction of whom I have the space to thank, but here's a swat at it.

The writers of Chapter 15, "Real Questions, Real Answers," Lola Jacobsen and Tonya Wishart, applied their years of insight about customers and products to the selection of questions and answers that match the mission and scope of this book. Others at PSS assisted me in uncovering material, among them Lydja Williams, Jon Perera, Michael Maxey, Kevin Chang, and Pam Biallas. The whole group churns up gigabytes of great data and problem analysis—a tremendous boost to the product teams at Microsoft and to info-feeders such as I.

I tapped many other people at Microsoft for their perspectives and suggestions on everything from spreadsheet examples to training experiences. I hope they don't mind being lumped together: Camille Wagner, Jerry Smith, Brad Hastings, Todd Hager, Mark Dodge, Carl Chatfield, Russell Borland, and Teresa Anderson. For technical refinements, I am grateful for contributions from Eric Yamada, Larry Tseng, John Tafoya, and Starlene Burgett. In the Office product group, I owe special thanks to Scott Raedeke for his support, as I do to Casey Doyle (acquisitions editor) and Suzanne Viescas (editor-in-chief) at Microsoft Press.

My mother is fond of the saying "Don't believe what you hear—and only half of what you read." Thanks for the skepticism, Mom; it made me a more careful writer. But if the facts in this book are to be believed, I owe an equal share of thanks to the book team that read the manuscript and responded so capably. Dori Shattuck, David Rygmyr, and Sally Brunsman all read and improved the outline. Ina Chang, the manuscript editor, exercised a thoughtful and nimble pen; she elevated the text, managed a swarm of details, and generally advanced the project wherever she turned. Jerry Joyce, the technical editor, deserves tremendous credit for ironing out procedural details, spotting useful tips, cleaning up screen shots, and generally helping to keep the multitude of applications from overwhelming what talents I could offer. Sally Anderson (principal proofreader/copy editor) and her cohorts—Therese McRae, Jennifer Harris, Patrick Forgette, and Alice Copp Smith—scrutinized the book well and often with their rigorous standards of correctness and clarity; I am in their debt. John Sugg, the compositor, inspired confidence with his mastery of his job and his unflappable manner. I've had the pleasure of working with indexer Lynn Armstrong in the past, and I appreciate the judgment and experience that he's brought to this book's index.

For making the book a pleasure to look at, several clever and knowledgeable people deserve credit. Illustrator David Holter has a fine gift for simultaneously informing and dazzling; I was lucky to work with him. To Wallis Bolz, photo editor, and Van Bucher, photo researcher, a tip of the hat for their energetic performances and their appreciation of the offbeat. Likewise to Sandi Lage, who oversaw the scanning and the refinements that transported the photos onto the printed page. Kim Eggleston assisted in the selection of photographs and was involved in all of the art- and design-related decisions. Brett Polonsky took charge of layout, working with a fine interior look from Hansen Design Company. His exceptional layout finesse was compounded by the talents of Jack Litewka, project editor. Jack is a gentleman and a scholar, as they say. He's also an appreciative reader, with pedigreed herding instincts and a rare sense of accountability. Rebecca Geisler, Gina Sullivan, and Christy Gersich made fine and distinct contributions to the cover.

Finally, a personal thank-you to my family—Cindy, Sarah, and Hans. Book lovers all, they cheerfully endured the slights and shared the sacrifices that brought this one to light.

—*Eric Stroo*

① A Window with an Office

Chapter 1

Small Step, Giant Leap

Information at the Center

Microsoft Office is part of an evolving vision for using software on our personal computers. Those who spin the vision—including the folks at Microsoft—have long recognized the obstacles that we face when using specialized but unneighborly applications. Most of these programs have

handled tasks differently (even identical tasks), and each has packaged its results in a different file format, mysterious to other applications. The result? A fragmented workspace—an "application-centric" universe in which information has remained more or less captive to the application it orbits.

To combine results from different applications, your intrepid information-gathering spacecraft has had to limp and lurch from one application to the next. And to use the same information for two purposes—say, a quarterly shareholder report and a slide presentation for analysts—you've had to enter the data in one application and then reenter it in the next one, with little or no opportunity for sharing.

In the new vision, you trade in the commuter craft for a space station. This is the "docu-centric," or information-centered, model: Your information is in the center, served by applications that modify, analyze, enhance, and present it. If your document combines information from a handful of application formats, the various applications orbit your document, waiting to be summoned. The information you want to work with is principal; the tools that you use to create or modify that information are subordinate.

The ways of presenting the information—printed copy, slide show, electronic mail, etc.—are likewise subordinate. If the information you've gathered exists in a data table, it isn't stuck there. You can analyze it and chart it with a spreadsheet, you can include the chart as an illustration in a printed training document, you can attach the spreadsheet to an e-mail message or insert the chart into a slide or transparency for a public presentation—and so on. The information in your document remains central, regardless of which application you use to modify it and which vehicle you use to distribute it.

You Say You Want a Revolution?

OK, it doesn't sound quite like a revolution. In fact, software developers have tried various strategies over the years for ushering in the new work style. In some cases, they have tacked an ever-widening assortment of capabilities onto existing applications, with the result that key applications have become sophisticated and complex. Word processors can now routinely do math, create tables and graphs, draw pictures, sort lists, and create form letters. Spreadsheets can generate 3-D charts, double as databases, and produce colorful, elaborately formatted reports.

And then there are the so-called integrated software packages. These packages usually include limited-feature versions of the most common applications: a basic word processor, a spreadsheet for computations, a simple database, and maybe a simple drawing utility or a communications component for sending and receiving files with a modem. Generally, these components lack the specialized bells and whistles of the stand-alone programs, but they share a design strategy so that they can work together. And hey, the price is right—an integrated package generally costs less than a single big-name solo application, and it frequently comes preinstalled on new computers.

To better integrate these all-in-one packages, developers have improved the ability of the components to shuttle information back and forth. You can cut and paste from the spreadsheet to the word processor, copy a list from the word processor to the spreadsheet, merge fields from your database into a form letter, and so on.

All This and OLE Too

Microsoft Office takes these advances in integration one step further. The industry calls Office and its competitors *software suites*. The components are all full-scale professional applications, and they're integrated and standardized in significant ways to function as a unit. They work alike and share information readily. And they ought to, since they are billed as an interrelated set of applications and not just a bunch of all-stars that happen to be wearing the same uniform.

What distinguishes Office even more is the adoption of OLE, an advanced technology that lets you nest information from one application inside a document created in a second application. This might sound like pasting, but it isn't, and the difference makes, well, all the difference. With OLE, the nested information need not sacrifice its file format to merge into the new document; as a result, you can still edit the information using the original application. This new type of document, with its nested components from other applications, is known as a *compound document*.

Designing applications to support the OLE technology is not a trivial matter. Even within Office, the applications differ in their need for and receptiveness to OLE. But as you'll see when you come to individual tasks, such as inserting a block of spreadsheet cells in a word processed project summary, *using* OLE is relatively simple.

Let's start with a quick who's who to introduce the players, large and small, in the Office suite. Afterward, we can look at how they combine their capabilities to let you adopt an information-centered way of working.

The Key Players

The four major Office applications—Microsoft Word, Excel, PowerPoint, and Access—plus a Microsoft Mail license are sold separately in addition to being sold as part of the Office suite. There are two current versions of Office: Version 4.2, the Standard Edition, contains Word, Excel, PowerPoint, and a Mail workstation license; version 4.3, the Professional Edition, contains the applications in the Standard Edition plus Access.

Beyond the major applications is a set of smaller applications, or *applets*, identified within Office as *shared applications* and *utilities*. The items in this group are available to the major applications—that is, the major applications share them. The shared applications let you introduce specialized chunks of information into your document files—drawings, graphs, equations, sound

OLE

OLE is the technology at the heart of Microsoft's document-centered strategy. OLE allows applications to share information and capabilities. What can be shared and how it can be shared depend on the design of the applications.

OLE1 and OLE2

There are two versions of OLE: OLE1 and OLE2. The more recent version, OLE2, provides all of the capabilities of OLE1 plus many more.

Although applications that use OLE1 can create compound documents and work with applications that support OLE2, you'll find that compound documents are much easier to work with if your applications support OLE2.

All of the major Office applications support OLE2.

clips, animation segments, and so on. Utilities are helpful in their own way—they check for misspelled words, modify your installation, help you trouble-shoot your system, and the like.

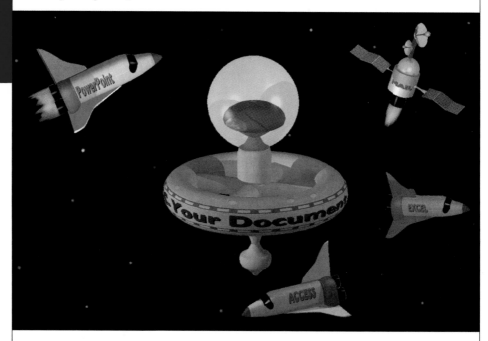

If you're a new user of the Office suite, you're probably not familiar with some of the applications, or at least not with their latest versions. The summaries that follow will help: You need to learn enough about the applications to decide which of them (individually or in combination) will best meet your needs. Would you be better served if you created a database to pool the information in some of your worksheets? Could you create transparencies for a presentation with PowerPoint more effectively than you've always done with your word processor? When you're comfortable with each of the applications, you'll start to recognize when and how to mix information from two or more of them.

To get some additional pointers about learning how to use the major applications, see Chapter 3, "Learning on the Job."

Microsoft Word 6

 The most widely used application for personal computers is the word processor, and Microsoft Word is a standard, if not *the* standard. For both Macintosh and Microsoft Windows operating environments, Word is known for its broad set of features and for the ease with which it lets you accomplish the most common tasks. Word's toolbars simplify formatting and editing, and zip you through the process of creating tables, numbered lists, and bulleted lists.

As you probably know, modern word processors do a lot more than process words. They have evolved into document processors: Word lets you enter, edit, format, and arrange text, and it lets you automate many parts of the process in dramatic ways. As you work with Word, you'll appreciate more and more the variety of documents you can create—reports, memos, résumés, forms, newsletters, screenplays. With each successive version, Word has refined its layout capabilities, so you can now put together multiple-column documents, create special-effect headlines, and flow text around graphic elements (just as the text above detours around the Word 6 program icon).

Word 6 includes numerous special features that boost its value in the Office suite:

- Wizards accomplish complex tasks for you, such as constructing a document template. Wizards step you through a series of questions and simple choices, allowing you to guide the process and learn the key terms.

- AutoFormat applies formatting to a document automatically. This feature is worth noticing because formatting can be a huge sinkhole for your work time—more than you might realize. It's also customizable, so your documents can still be distinctive.

- Shortcut menus, which you display by clicking the right mouse button, can become a big part of your routine editing and formatting (in Word and in the other major Office applications). The shortcut menus are "context sensitive"—when you click a particular screen element, the commands that are relevant to that element are collected from different menus and are shown on the shortcut menu. If you click the right mouse button while pointing at a toolbar, for example, the shortcut menu contains commands that let you choose which toolbars are displayed and how the toolbars work.

- Word lets you create professional-looking business forms and provides a set of commonly used forms, such as invoices and purchase orders, which you can customize as you see fit. Creating forms is much like creating templates, with some additional tinkering. Forms are an efficient vehicle for gathering data—particularly over electronic mail.

TEMPLATE

Templates provide the framework for any document you create. In Word, a template is a customized application environment for a certain kind of document, such as a monthly update for the field reps or a press release.

A template specifies styles of headings and text in the document, tabs and margins, customized arrangements of tools and menus, macros, and any standard content (such as logos or other graphic elements).

- Envelope printing and label printing are tasks that seem to defy automation, but Word's current approach helps you take control. Chapter 13, "Winning Those Skirmishes with Your Printer," explores this approach in more detail.

- Word gives you control over the process of merging information directly from a database into your document. You can choose what information is extracted and which records are used through simple query commands. This is encouraging news if your job includes creating form letters, catalogs, or other documents that need to draw content from an outside source.

Word provides numerous layout options and simple ways of including spreadsheets, voice recordings, and other information in a document.

North Wind Traders

REPORT OF OPERATIONS

I N V E N T O R Y

"Eu feugial nulla facilisis at vero eros et acumean et iusto oldio dignissim qui blandit present lupptatum zzril delenit augue. Duis autem vel eum iriure dolor in hendrerit in vulputate velit esse molestie consequat."

DARK ROAST ● Hendrerit in vulputate velit esse molestie conspeat, fnulla facilisis at vero eros et acumsan et iusto olldio dignissim qui blandit prasent lupptatum zzril delenit augue duis dolore te feugait nulla facilsi. Sit amet consectetuer adpisicing. Lorem ipsum dolor. Nulla facilisis at vero eros et acumsan et iusto olldio dignissim qui blandit prasent lupptatum zzril delenit augue duis dolore te feugait nulla facilsi. Eu feugial nulla facilsis at vero eros et acumean et lusto oldio dignissim qui blandit prasent lupptatum zzril delenit augue. Duis autem vel eum iriure dolor in hendrerit in vulputate velit esse molestic consequat, vel illum dolore eu feugial nulla facillsis at vero eros et acumsan et lusto oldio dignissim.

NORTHWEST BLEND Hendrerit in vulputate velit esse molestie consequat, nulla facilsis at vero eros et acumsan et iusto olldio dignissim qui blandit prasent lupptatum zzril delenit augue duis dolore te feugait nulla facilsi. Sit amet consectetuer adpisicing. Lorem ipsum dolor. Nulla facilisis at vero eros et acumsan et iusto olldio dignissim qui blandit prasent lupptatum zzril delenit augue duis dolore te feugait nulla facilsi. Eu feugial nulla facilsis at vero eros et acumean et lusto oldio dignissim qui blandit prasent lupptatum zzril delenit augue. Duis autem vel eum iriure dolor in hendrerit in vulputate velit esse molestie consequat, vel illum dolore eu feugial nulla facillsis at vero eros et acumsan et lusto oldio dignissim.

COLOMBIAN ● Duis autemvel eumed iriure dolor in hendrerit in vulputate velit esse molestic consequat, nulla facilsis at vero eros et acumsan et iusto olldio dignissim qui blandit prasent lupptatum zzril delenit augue duis dolore te feugait nulla facilsi. Sit amet consectetuer adpisicing. Lorem ipsum dolor. Nulla facilisis at vero eros et acumsan et iusto olldio dignissim qui blandit prasent lupptatum zzril delenit augue duis dolore te feugait nulla facilsi.

"Eu feugial nulla facilisis at vero eros et acumean et lusto oldio dignissim qui blandit present hendrerit in vulputate velit esse eu acumsan et lusto oldio dignissim qui blandit."

SUMATRAN ● Lorem ipsum dolor. Duis autem vel eum iriure dolor in hendrerit in vulputate velit esse molestie consequat, nulla facilsis at vero eros et acumsan et iusto olldio dignissim qui blandit prasent lupptatum zzril delenit augue duis dolore te feugait nulla facilsi. Sit amet consectetuer adpisicing.

M A R K E T I N G

	1st Q	2nd Q	3rd Q	4th Q
DARK ROAST	886	892	952	897
NORTHWEST BLEND	567	524	532	583
COLOMBIAN	458	510	654	602
SUMATRAN	369	425	405	485

Eu feugial nulla facilisis at vero eros et acumean blandit present lupptatum zzril delenit augue. Duis autem vel eum iriure dolor in hendrerit in vulputate velit esse molestic consequat, vel illum dolore eu feugial nulla facillsis at vero eros et acumsan et lusto oldio dignissim.

Microsoft Excel 5

Microsoft Excel is the number processor in the Office suite. Excel is a spreadsheet application—a comprehensive tool for juggling and calculating numeric information. For all its number-crunching and charting power, however, Excel is often used simply as a way to maintain information in tables that have no built-in computations and little or nothing that's chartable. Once you've seen what Excel can do to analyze numbers, using it to set up a car-pool schedule will seem like wielding the royal scepter to crack walnuts. But so be it.

Excel becomes invaluable when you have numbers to analyze, and later when you want to demonstrate what you've learned from analyzing the numbers. Do you want to know which issues in a given group are outperforming the Dow industrials, which regions are responding well to a product promotion, or what effect a price change might have on revenue in the coming quarter? If you've got the data, Excel can help you analyze it.

After you extract the results you need, Excel can isolate the important information for clear presentation. Better yet, it can represent the figures in clearly labeled graphs and charts that expose the trends and comparative values you want to reveal. You can create dozens of chart variations, including line and scatter charts, bar charts, pie charts, and area charts. Of course, the point here is that pictures can say what words and numbers often cannot. Here's a modest sample:

CHART POWER
The various Office players can also create charts using Microsoft Graph 5, but you'll probably want to use Excel's charting capabilities when you need the broadest choice of chart types, the cleanest presentation, and precise control of visual details.

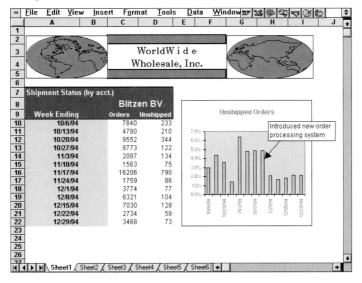

Like Word, Excel has wizards that help you get your work done. Among the most valuable of these is the Function Wizard. With the Function Wizard, you can use a function in a formula by choosing it from a list and then identifying each of the arguments as the wizard prompts you for them (defining each one as it goes). Other Excel wizards to explore include the ChartWizard and the Text Wizard, which help you create charts and transfer text into a spreadsheet. And then there's the TipWizard. You probably won't have to go looking for it—it will find you. If Excel notices that you are accomplishing a task in an unnecessarily tedious or roundabout way, the TipWizard suggests a more efficient method.

Microsoft PowerPoint 4

Once you see an electronic presentation created with Microsoft PowerPoint, you'll have a good sense of what PowerPoint can do for you. But the program also does a lot that you don't see on the slides, with all their nifty and colorful fading, wiping, and dissolving. For example, it offers a great outlining resource and an AutoContent Wizard that can steer you very productively through the content-generating phase of your presentation. And PowerPoint delivers much more than electronic slide shows. It can tailor its output to produce a printed outline, speaker's notes, audience handouts, 35-mm slides, or transparencies for an overhead projector.

Behind most PowerPoint presentations is an important feature that you can't see (although you might suspect that it's there): a built-in presentation template. Each PowerPoint template includes masters for slides, handouts, and

This PowerPoint slide is based on the DBLLINES template.

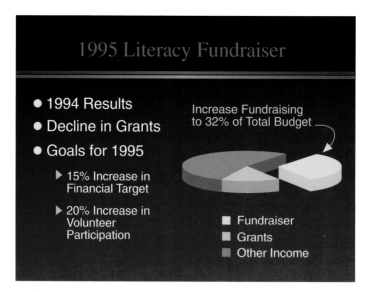

other elements, as well as a color scheme that's coordinated with the look of the slide master. The program comes with 165 certifiably tasteful templates, and you can create your own simply by modeling the new template on an existing presentation.

With version 4, PowerPoint has become an entrenched part of the Office suite, with its toolbars, menus, and command structure closely resembling those of Word and Excel. PowerPoint has features that let you draw and graph and enter text on your slides, and it readily accepts tables, charts, and clip art from other applications. You can also transfer the outline of your PowerPoint presentation to Word to expand it into a written report.

POWER PLAY

Sharing Your Slides

PowerPoint comes with a separate application, PowerPoint Viewer, which lets you distribute a slide presentation to people who don't have PowerPoint. Your software license restricts you from passing out the complete PowerPoint application freely, but you can give out copies of the PowerPoint Viewer disk to anyone. PowerPoint Viewer is sufficient for stepping through (but not modifying) slide presentations.

PowerPoint Viewer appears in your Office program group as a separate icon. If you share copies of the PowerPoint Viewer disk, keep in mind that the program must be installed on a hard disk. Because presentation files are typically large, sharing them across a network is often preferable to passing numerous floppy disks from hand to hand.

Microsoft Access 2

If you have the Standard Edition of Microsoft Office rather than the Professional Edition, don't spend your time looking for Access 2. You don't have it, unless you bought it separately.

So what do you have (or not have) in Access? Access is, broadly speaking, a *relational database management system,* or *RDBMS.* This name is more self-explanatory than it might seem: Access is a software system that helps you manage large stores of data. It can take the broad base of data that tracks—or constitutes—your business, and relate the various natural groupings of information you use. These groupings might include customer records, vendor information, transactions, employee data, and production details.

Electronic management makes your information more accessible and more comprehensible. Access enables you to design forms and reports to display or print your records, and you can define a set of conditions, called a *query,* that determines which information from which records you want to focus on. In fact, you can define numerous queries, and you can save and reuse them. Routine activities can even be defined as macros (as in Word and Excel), to automate what would otherwise be repetitive and more time-consuming work for you.

Access was developed expressly for the Windows environment. You not only benefit from the familiar Windows interface and controls, but you can also design your forms to contain buttons, check boxes, and other standard controls from a handy design palette. Version 2, in fact, provides Control Wizards to speed up and simplify the process of adding controls.

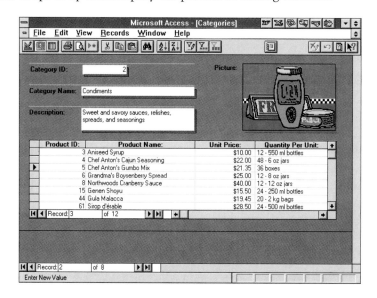

Once a bit aloof, Access has gotten tighter with the rest of the Office gang. Its toolbars are now customizable and movable, its menus and commands align more closely with those of its suitemates, and with OLE, its ties to the other applications are more conveniently integrated into the product. For example, a new Output To command lets you transfer information *and* formatting from Access to other Office applications. You can also attach Access information to a Mail message or merge names and addresses from Access into a mass mailing you've developed in Word. More on these two topics in Chapter 10, "Collaborating."

Access has one other trait that you should be aware of, especially if you work in a networked environment. Unlike the other Office players, Access is a multi-user application. The value of this trait lies in the fact that data can be read and updated by many people at once by means of a single shared database. If many employees use a large body of information that needs to be up-to-date and easy to get at, multi-user access makes a lot of sense.

Microsoft Mail

The Office package includes a workstation license for Microsoft Mail, but it does not contain the software for the workstation. The license *entitles* you to install and use the software on your computer; you (or your organization) must acquire and install the software—Microsoft Mail for PC Networks, Server Version—separately. That package contains the server software as well as the workstation software, which can be installed only on a licensed workstation. That's where your Mail license comes in.

Microsoft Mail offers some attractive ties to other Office applications. You can paste text and graphics into a Mail message from other applications. Text formatting is lost in the process, but if that's a key factor, you can attach a formatted document to a Mail message. The document appears as an icon in the message itself. Not only can the people who receive the message open and read the document that's "tucked inside" the icon (provided they have the associated application), but they can also edit and return the document—or pass it on to the next person on a preset routing slip. Chapter 10, "Collaborating," looks at this Mail feature and some of the possibilities it introduces.

DIRECT MAIL
The integration of Mail with the other Office applications allows you to send information directly from the application. You might send a PowerPoint presentation, for example, as an attachment to a Mail message simply by choosing the Send command from the File menu in PowerPoint.

Lauren's message to Sam includes an attached Excel spreadsheet.

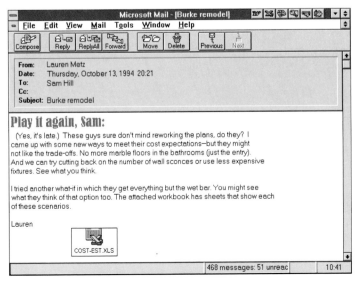

Although Mail is part of the Office suite, here and in much of the discussion that follows Mail is often an exception. Don't expect OLE to apply to Mail in the same ways that it applies to the other members of the Office suite. Mail is a messenger—it can carry sophisticated documents, but it's not designed as a tool for creating them.

Shared Applications and Utilities

The shared applications and utilities are fairly numerous, but easy to miss. Unlike the key applications, most of them don't show up as icons in Program Manager. Instead, you start them from within one of the major applications; in most cases, you launch them from a dialog box that appears when you choose Object from the Insert menu. As you'll see in later chapters, the objects (drawings, graphs, and so on) created by the shared applications ultimately reside in a document that you save in one of the major applications. Many of the shared applications are discussed in more detail in Chapter 12, "Graphics and Other Gizmos."

Microsoft WordArt 2   With Microsoft WordArt, you can stylize text using a palette of shadows, colors, spacing, and alignment variations. This is the sort of thing you might do to call attention to a headline or produce a logo or design component. In the document at the top of the facing page, WordArt was used to create the BULL-ETIN heading. For more details on WordArt, see Chapter 12, "Graphics and Other Gizmos."

Microsoft ClipArt Gallery   The Office applications supply over 1000 pieces of clip art—images with a wide variety of subjects and styles that you can intro-duce into your documents. Add to those your clip art from other applications and third-party libraries, plus any images you've created or modified, and you can make yourself crazy locating the appropriate image for a given purpose. The Microsoft ClipArt Gallery can assemble your scattered holdings into a flexible set of easy-to-browse categories, such as Banners, People, and Special Occasions. You can search for an image by category, filename, description, or file type, and you can preview thumbnail versions of the art to verify that a file contains the image you want to use.

The document at the top of the facing page includes an image of a bull from the ClipArt Gallery. (The image is supplied with Word.) See Chapter 12, "Graphics and Other Gizmos," for a complete example.

Microsoft Organization Chart   Microsoft Organization Chart offers a quick way to diagram the groupings and relationships in an organization, corporate or otherwise.

Equation Editor   Let's face it: You don't need to be a nuclear physicist to find yourself struggling to represent mathematical expressions that go "over the head" of your word processor. Equation Editor is a specialized application

CLIPPED ART

If you choose the Typical installation when you install Office, the Setup program omits some of the clip art from the files on your disk. This is all for the best if you rarely use clip art—it can consume a lot of disk space. But if you want every piece of clip art to be available in your gallery, you can install the holdouts by running Office Setup and Uninstall from your Office menu. See the next chapter, "Installing Office and Getting to Know MOM," for details.

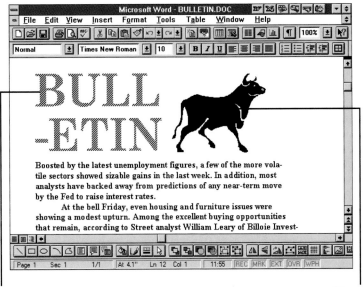

WordArt   Clip art

that's equipped to deal with the special characters and the unusual spacing requirements of fractions, integrals, radicals, set notation, and the rest. Help is available, but you might not need it. Most of what you want to do is easy to learn on the fly.

Microsoft Graph 5   Microsoft Graph gives you the ability to represent a table of values as a chart. You can enter the numbers and headings in a datasheet or transfer them from another source. Be aware that the datasheet holds the information, but unlike an Excel worksheet, it contains no formulas and makes no calculations. Graph offers a healthy variety of chart types—bar charts, pie charts, and line graphs of many types—but it lacks the formatting sophistication of Excel. It's a solid tool, but it's not the best choice when the data is dynamic or the formatting is crucial.

Media Player   Media Player is the application that Office launches when you insert a multimedia file. It plays files such as sound or animation files, and it lets you control hardware devices, such as videodisc players. See Chapter 12, "Graphics and Other Gizmos," for a more detailed look at both Media Player and Sound Recorder.

Sound Recorder   Sound Recorder, as the name indicates, lets you record a sound and insert it into your document as an icon. You can also insert previously saved sound (WAV) files, edit them, and alter their playback qualities: volume, speed, and direction.

Among your other Office supplies, you'll find an assortment of utilities. Some of these are likely to prove useful every day. Most apply to the entire Office; a few work with only one or two applications.

Spelling   The Spelling utility is handy for detecting misspelled words and suggesting replacements—whether in a small selection or an entire document. In Office, Spelling is a shared resource: You can use the standard dictionary and any custom dictionaries saved in Word, Excel, PowerPoint, or Mail.

Setup (Maintenance)   The Setup program is also a shared resource. Of course, Setup handles the initial Office installation. But as you'll see in the next chapter, Office installs a maintenance version of Setup that you'll need for making changes to your installation. If you uninstall (remove) or modify any Office

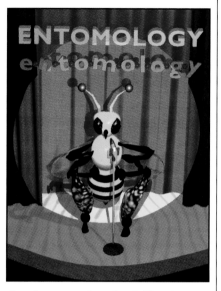

components, you'll generally want to make the changes using the Office Setup and Uninstall command (on the Office menu).

ODBC Drivers   The ODBC drivers are utilities for accessing external databases for mail merge, data analysis, and other activities. Among the databases you can talk to with this set of drivers are Access, dBASE, FoxPro, Paradox, and SQL Server. ODBC drivers conform to the Open Database Connectivity standard, developed by Microsoft.

Microsoft System Info   A valuable troubleshooting aid, System Info is a small application that displays configuration information about your operating environment. You'll see it in action in Chapter 15, "Real Questions, Real Answers."

Docu-centric Application Surfing: A Scenario

With all that we've covered, you might still be wondering what is so different about Office and its document-centered approach. What follows is a truly modest example that could start you thinking. Don't worry about how to carry out the specific procedures. You'll learn these procedures, and many more, in the following chapters.

Preparing a Quarterly Report

You are working in Word on a quarterly report to the board of directors of The Foundation when an electronic mail message arrives in your Inbox. You click a button on your Microsoft Office Manager (MOM) toolbar to switch to Mail. The message, from Hilda, contains a summary of administrative expenses for the previous quarter. The summary is conveyed by an Excel worksheet that is attached to the message.

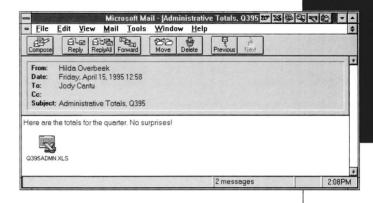

The worksheet appears in the message as an icon. You double-click the icon to open the worksheet and review the expenses. The breakdowns seem reasonable, so you copy the totals to the Clipboard.

Updating the Report

Next step: pasting the new expense data into the financial summary of your quarterly report. Click the Microsoft Word button on the MOM toolbar and you're back to your quarterly report, where you've been leading into an overview of the recent Grants Committee deliberations. You jump to the financial section of the report and double-click in a table of figures, and the tools at the top of the screen change. The table, actually a linked block of cells in an Excel spreadsheet, is available for editing with Excel tools.

With the spreadsheet active, Word's tools and menus are replaced by those of Excel.

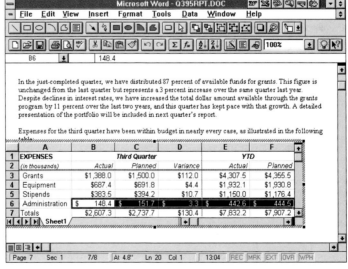

You paste the values from the Clipboard into the appropriate row and compare the recalculated expenses with the budgeted values. The comparisons are all favorable—a nice fact to illustrate with a chart, you think, but you haven't had much experience creating charts with Excel. No matter. You highlight the expenses, actual and budgeted, and you click the ChartWizard button on the toolbar. After you select an area on the sheet for the chart, the ChartWizard asks for your preferences in a series of dialog boxes, and there's the chart.

Adding a Chart to the Report

Next, you'd like to paste the chart into your report but still be able to edit and reformat it in Excel. Unsure exactly how to proceed, you look at the Office Cue Cards and find a set of cards to step you through precisely this task. (Nice when that happens.) Add a caption below the chart, and you're satisfied with the financial summary.

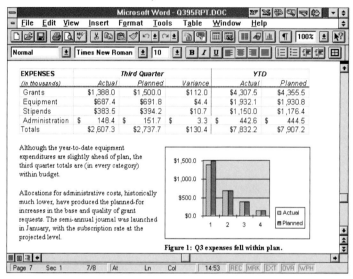

Now back to the Grants Committee section. Last week, you downloaded a file from the committee chair. The file was not created using Word—or even another Microsoft application—but you try the Insert File command anyway. To your relief, Word inserts the text after converting it from the foreign file format.

Creating a Slide Show for the Board Meeting

Fast-forward a bit. With your written report for the board complete, you prepare for your oral presentation at the upcoming board meeting. The boardroom is equipped with a large display monitor and a jack for electronic presentations, so you decide to prepare a set of PowerPoint slides. But you don't start from scratch. Instead, you use the PresentIt macro in Word to export your report to PowerPoint: The main headings in your Word document automatically become slide titles, with the lesser headings arranged below them as bulleted items. At the top of the facing page is a sample slide from your report, after you choose a template and color scheme.

You prepare a few detailed handouts to accompany your slides, primarily by copying and pasting text highlights from your report, you drop in some clip art, and you call it good.

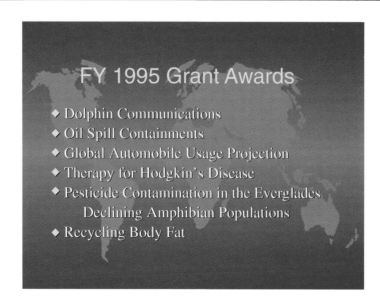

Preparing a Meeting Agenda

Now for a meeting agenda. You open a new Word document with the template you created last quarter using the Agenda Wizard—the board's agenda has a lot of standard items. Switching back and forth between the agenda document and Mail, you paste in a few new agenda details that you received from board members. For safety's sake, you use the Spelling utility, which is customized to include the correct spelling of the board members' names. Finally, you choose Word's Send command to distribute the agenda to members who use electronic mail. You fax copies to the other members, and you might as well print one for yourself. Seems like it should be lunchtime by now.

The Office Advantage

The above scenario highlights a number of the strengths of the Office suite. There are many others, of course. Let's run through some of the most compelling qualities of Office, which you'll encounter many more times later in this book. For one thing, the Office suite represents a sizable savings over the combined prices of the component applications. You noticed that? OK, well, those savings are enough to sway a lot of people—assuming, of course, that they plan to use at least a couple of the Office applications anyway. But that's not the whole story.

If cost were the only reason for using the Office suite over stand-alone applications, there'd be little reason for writing, or reading, this book. You can get a broader view of the stand-alone features of the applications somewhere else. What Office can provide, cost savings aside, that you don't get with any collection of individual applications is a level of consistency and integration that multiplies the value of the components. Look at the toolbars of the various Office applications, and their menus; look beyond the standard dialog boxes to those unique to the individual applications. In any of these comparisons, the consistency of design is obvious. The Standard toolbars in all of the core applications, for example, are quite similar. In fact, the left sides of these toolbars, with buttons for the most common editing and file management tasks, are nearly identical. More differences crop up on the right side to reflect tasks that are unique to or more commonly performed in a given program.

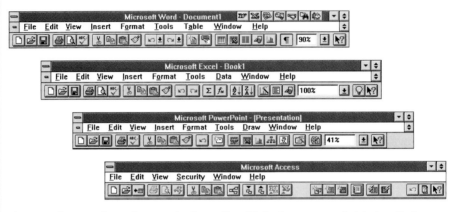

A second area of consistency is the online Help feature available in all the applications. Increasingly, the programs offer identical help features, with the same techniques for launching and navigation. Many of the Office applications have Cue Cards with step-by-step instructions that appear alongside your work area. As you saw in the scenario in the previous section, Office even has Cue Cards of its own for common information-sharing tasks among applications.

Ease of use is another attraction. In the latest Office release, this is reinforced by features that Microsoft loosely groups under the heading IntelliSense. Whatever that means exactly, it's satisfying when you see evidence of it. As you use the programs, you're likely to see examples of IntelliSense, such as Word's AutoCorrect feature. AutoCorrect automatically fixes common typing errors, such as capitalizing both the first and second letter of the first word in a sentence. You can also teach AutoCorrect to spot your own particular typing foibles or to take a few characters and expand them into one of those constantly recurring words or phrases—product names, company names, titles, and the like.

As you gain familiarity with the Office applications, you'll learn to take advantage of the way the applications work together. In a single step, a button on the Word toolbar can insert an Excel spreadsheet. Similarly, a button on the PowerPoint toolbar can export your presentation headings as a Word document. Integration techniques, as you saw in the scenario in the previous section, extend from cutting and pasting to linking a chart and importing non-Office files. You'll find integration emphasized throughout this book, as you learn new ways of combining information across application boundaries.

Finally, the Office applications have themselves become platforms on which custom solutions to business problems are built. Word, Excel, and Access use advanced forms of the Basic programming language as macro languages. Using these and other tools, a programmer can extend the applications and blur the boundaries between them even further. As these languages evolve, they will become more similar and more powerful—able to modify and enhance each application's capabilities in ways that are customized precisely to your needs.

Chapter 2

Installing Office and Getting to Know MOM

Installation Considerations

SETUP WOES

If this chapter does not speak to your setup problems, see Chapter 15, "Real Questions, Real Answers," for more advice on common installation questions.

Chances are good that you already have Microsoft Office installed, either locally (on your own hard drive) or remotely (on a server or a shared disk in your organization's network). If it isn't installed, the procedure needs a bit of explanation, so read on. If installation isn't a concern, skip ahead to "Meet MOM." MOM—Microsoft Office Manager—is the "remote control" of application flipping: It's the simplest way to start using Office as more than the sum of its parts. We'll look closely at MOM later in this chapter.

The installation process can have a few wrinkles, especially if you already have stand-alone versions of Office applications installed or if you're up-grading a particular application between releases of the Office suite. The current Setup program is equipped to iron out most of these problems, however, so we'll try to head them off.

Of course, Setup, like orange juice, isn't just for breakfast anymore. You'll probably come back to it at times other than the initial installation. With a megaprogram like Office to keep track of, and with lots of pieces that you can add or remove as your needs and skills evolve, the Setup program has quietly mushroomed into a many-leveled (and very usable) fixture on your Office menu. So this chapter will also consider your need to add, remove, and update Office components.

Is Your Computer Ready for This?

No point in sidestepping this one: Office is not a good match for that hand-me-down 286 from Uncle Clarence and Aunt Clarisse. Once you start cooking up documents that fold together information from multiple applications, you'll run out of disk space, memory, and patience—and not necessarily in that order.

To start with, you need horsepower. Your machine's microprocessor must be an 80386 or better, preferably better. The progressive improvements in the speed and capacity of today's processor chips have helped to make products like Office viable. An information-centered approach to your work would not be achievable otherwise. Using Office, especially using it with large compound documents and multiple applications loaded at the same time, will tax the best memory management techniques that Microsoft Windows has to offer. So don't underestimate the effect that processing power has on your satisfaction with Office, or with any software suite.

More important, don't underestimate the software's appetite for extended memory. Memory is a key requirement: Officially, you can get by with 4 MB of RAM, but only if you plan to run your applications one at a time. To run multiple programs, consider 8 MB the minimum, but run with 12 MB or 16 MB or more if you can swing it.

Next, you need Office space. Assuming that you already have Windows installed, the Standard Edition of Office needs another 49 MB of disk space for a typical installation. For the Professional Edition (which includes Microsoft Access), 58 MB is typical, and to go the maximum, you're staring at no less than 82 MB. And don't neglect the fact that Windows will also want to use part of your leftover disk space for its own purposes, including a swap file of considerable size.

Ponderous as all that may seem, disk space is one area in which Office adds up to *less* than the sum of its parts. According to the documentation, the applications in the Standard Edition, which typically occupy 49 MB, would need another 11 MB if they were installed separately. Office avoids a lot of the duplication that results from numerous separate installations. This is the good that comes from sharing, as MOM would say (but not about your toothbrush).

Note that Office also has minimum installations, which let you pare down some or all of the applications to fit on an easily overcrowded machine, such as a laptop computer. The Office license also permits you to install the programs on a second machine (if you do not use two machines simultaneously, and if you are the primary user of both; check your Office license for details).

Performance Matters

To say it again, running multiple Office applications will probably put your computer's capabilities to the test. Windows has to load a whole succession of programs into memory, try to meet the needs of each one as the focus shifts, and often perform other background tasks to print files, accommodate the TSR (terminate-and-stay-resident) programs that always reside in memory, and execute network duties. Hence the recommendation for a high-end machine: a fast, powerful processor and loads of memory.

Beyond the basic commandment *Thou shalt have as much RAM as possible,* you can take further steps to improve the performance of Windows. These measures, which affect both hardware and software, can increase the speed of many Office operations. Some of them affect only specific activities, such as disk access, whereas others improve performance in a broader way.

In general, the suggestions in the following list are intended for the confident and technically adept user. If you don't know how to proceed with them, see your computer dealer or a technical support professional in your organization.

- If your system has a memory expansion board, configure all the memory as extended memory (if possible). If you run non–Windows-based applications that require expanded memory, you can use EMM386.EXE to emulate expanded memory. (For information on configuring the memory on your add-in board, see its documentation. Some expanded memory boards are incompatible with EMM386.)

- If you are not running an up-to-date version of MS-DOS (version 6.2 or later), upgrade. Doing so will let you improve the efficiency of memory use. Run MemMaker to let MS-DOS make optimal use of high memory.

- Maintain your hard disk regularly. In general, fewer files on your hard disk means quicker access. Delete unnecessary files, including BAK and TMP files. (Be sure Windows is not running when you delete TMP files.) If you have MS-DOS version 6.2, you've got ScanDisk and DeFrag, two utilities that can help you get peak performance from your hard disk. Use ScanDisk to detect and recover lost clusters, and use DeFrag to consolidate the contents of your disks for more efficient search and retrieval.

- Watch for spendy memory indulgences in your Windows setup. Using a color or a pattern for the desktop background instead of wallpaper frees up memory for running applications. (Bitmaps consume more memory.) Choose the lowest-resolution display driver that meets your needs. In general, use the standard VGA driver to ensure faster display performance (although you'll get lower resolution and less color support).

- Create a permanent swap file. If you run Windows in 386 enhanced mode, it can use a swap file on your hard disk to supplement the available RAM.

This feat, which creates virtual memory, increases your effective RAM, but it's slower than if you use RAM chips. To get the greatest benefit from virtual memory, designate a subdirectory (usually TEMP) on a fast hard disk or on a RAM disk as the location for your swap file. Windows calculates a maximum size for the swap file based on available extended memory and the amount of free contiguous disk space. Use a temporary swap file if hard disk space is at a premium (and don't try to locate it on a compressed drive).

• Try 32-bit disk access. Your system will tell you if it thinks this option is available to you. (To check, click the Enhanced icon in Control Panel, and look at the virtual memory settings, as shown at right.) With this option, a program called FastDisk replaces the disk BIOS and produces faster disk access, particularly if Windows is running in enhanced mode. In some cases, alas, using 32-bit disk access 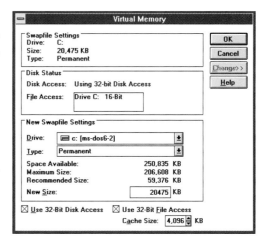 can crash your system. Often such crashes occur because the hard disk controller is not compatible with the replacement driver. On laptop machines, the cause is often a "sleep" feature that is used to conserve power. If you experience these problems, go back into Control Panel (after you restart Windows) and deselect the Use 32-Bit Disk Access check box.

Are *You* Ready for This?

Having looked at some ways to prepare your hardware and software for installing Office, you might consider your own readiness. Not that you should feel daunted, but a bit of reflection on your current work habits might help you prepare for certain situations and avoid others.

Know Windows

You need to know a fair amount about Windows to work successfully with any Windows-based application. To open and save files, for example, you should have a grasp of your directory structure and be able to navigate in it using the various lists in the dialog boxes. For that matter, you should know how to use all the standard controls in any dialog box. One of the nice things about Windows is that you can learn this stuff easily: What isn't obvious often lends itself to trial and error. For example, most people figure out that dialog boxes cannot be resized. Moved, yes; resized, no.

And it's a great moment when you discover that the button you just "pressed" on the screen by depressing the mouse button can be "unpressed" by sliding the pointer off the onscreen button before you release the mouse button. Call this one "trial and relief." When it saves you from overwriting a crucial file or accidentally discarding many hours' worth of file editing, you're not likely to forget it soon.

Learn as many timesavers as you can, as well. Some of these you can figure out through trial and error; others you can't. You might discover by trial and error that typing a few characters in a combo box (a text box attached to a list box) can save you a lot of scrolling down the list. But trial and error will probably not teach you that Ctrl+Esc brings up Task List so that you can switch tasks, or that holding down the Alt key and pressing Tab repeatedly lets you switch to any of a succession of currently loaded (but inactive) tasks. (Office improves on both of these techniques, as you'll see later in this chapter, but they can still prove useful.)

Task List provides a Windows shortcut for changing tasks or arranging multiple windows on your screen.

Use Windows Wisely

Windows enables you to keep multiple applications open, and within an application, to have multiple files open for reading and editing. With Office applications, you can drag and drop information from place to place in a document, from file to file, and even from one application to another. But each application and document that Windows keeps open costs you in available memory—the memory you need as you scroll and edit, create charts, and recalculate. Minimizing applications does not make a significant difference in this respect. To make as much memory as possible available to the applications you are using, you should close any others that you have no immediate need for.

And then there's your directory structure. Some people would rather not talk about this. They organize their hard disks like they do the hall closet: Open the door, shove in the umbrella (mittens, flashlight, ski poles, vacuum cleaner), and close the door fast. This system works until the closet is full, or until you need something out of it. Office gives you a few new reasons to pay attention to your file directories.

Not that there's one clearly better way to organize your files all of a sudden. Many different organizing schemes work, but having a system of some kind is the key. In the past, many people tended to have directories that contained only correspondence or only spreadsheets. With Office, some people find that they are creating files using a number of different applications, so they group them in directories according to the project to which they relate. But you can't sort every file by project. Some files apply to many projects, and some are more naturally grouped in some other way—by job responsibility or topic of interest, for instance.

What's more, Office makes it easy to link the contents of document A to document B so that changes made to A show up as updates within B. A nice trick, but it stops working if you move A to a new location. You can restore the connection, but if you can avoid the hassle by storing document A where you want it in the first place, so much the better.

Exit Gracefully

Under normal circumstances, quitting Windows is pretty foolproof. Dialog boxes remind you of any files that you left open with unsaved changes so that you can decide whether to save the files and exit with all your work intact. The problems come when circumstances are not normal: Your application locks up, the network goes down, the system runs out of memory or crashes. Now what to do?

The last resort, of course, is turning off your machine and restarting it, or, to be slightly less disruptive, pressing the Reset button (if your machine has one). Before you do that, however, consider a few options:

- Wait a while. Sometimes a background task, such as printing or memory swapping, causes temporary inactivity. With a network, you sometimes have to be patient during a period of heavy network use. Sharing applications over a network affects some application tasks more than others. In any event, waiting is often worthwhile, especially if you stand to lose a significant amount of work by taking another course.

- Press Ctrl+Break. This combination (particularly with MS-DOS programs) can occasionally break the program out of a prolonged or endless processing loop.

- Close the locked-up application. Encouraged by Office to use multiple applications, you might find yourself with an application that's locked up

REGAINING YOUR MEMORY

If you experience errors as a result of "insufficient memory," you can sometimes get past them by exiting Windows and re-starting it. If that doesn't help, quitting and rebooting might do the trick. See Chapter 15, "Real Questions, Real Answers," for more details.

while you still have unsaved work in one or more other applications. If you press Ctrl+Alt+Del, Windows can often close only the program that has stopped responding and you can return to Windows to save your work in other applications.

- Reboot the computer. Sometimes an error will leave you with no choice but to restart Windows. Press Ctrl+Alt+Del and then press it again to reboot. This method usually abandons a number of temporary files on your hard disk, in addition to forfeiting the unsaved work in memory. That's why it's the almost-last resort. If the system does not respond to Ctrl+Alt+Del, you'll have to press the Reset button or find the Off switch.

Installing Office

The actual installation of Microsoft Office is straightforward. The procedure has a few variations, of course, because the programs might be set up directly on the hard disk of an individual computer or on a shared disk or directory within a network. From its network location, a user might install Office to a workstation or run Office applications directly from the shared location. In any case, the installation procedures are similar and easy to step through.

Vanilla Setup

In the standard setup procedure (the only one this book will consider in any detail), you install Office on your own hard disk from a set of floppy disks, from a CD-ROM disc, or from a network location. The Setup program prompts you for the information it needs. Before you launch Setup, disable your virus detection utility (if you are running one) and close any Windows-based applications that you might have open. If you are upgrading from a previous version of Office, you do not need to remove the existing version before you install the new one—but you do need to close it.

Insert disk 1 if you are installing from floppy disks. To start Setup, choose the Run command from the File menu in Program Manager, type a:setup in the

text box, and press Enter. (If you're running Setup from a location other than drive A, substitute that location in the command.)

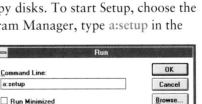

From that point on, you make choices as directed by Setup. You choose the type of setup you want—Minimum, Typical, or Custom/Complete—and the locations for applications. You can choose a Help button or press the F1 key for an explanation of your options at any stage. If you're installing Office

WHEN IN ROM

If you install Office from a CD-ROM disc, you're presented with the option of installing the program so that it runs from the disc. With the CD-ROM, Setup installs online versions of the user documentation, which you navigate in a Help-like interface. Installation from a CD-ROM is convenient, but if you run the programs from the disc, don't expect them to load as swiftly as they do from your local hard drive.

LIMITED FREEDOM

In some organizations, the network administrator creates a customized installation script to eliminate some of the variability in Office setups. For example, you might not be able to choose the Custom/Complete setup to select only the Office components you want on your workstation.

from floppy disks, your biggest job is to swap disks when you get your cue on screen.

Even though you install the major Office applications to the directories suggested by Setup, some Office components will crop up in other directories. For example, Setup copies shared applications, such as Microsoft WordArt

and Microsoft Graph, to your Windows directory in a subdirectory called MSAPPS. Copying such applications to a common location saves disk space by offsetting the chance that you'll wind up with multiple copies of them.

When Setup concludes, it creates a program group in Program Manager called the Microsoft Office group (by default). In this group, you'll find icons for the major Office applications.

The Office icon itself shows up by default in the Startup program group. If you leave it there, Windows will launch Office as part of its startup routine.

Modifying Your Office Installation

NO MAINTENANCE

With a Minimum installation (normally for laptop computers) or with a Workstation installation (a special variety for certain network configurations), you cannot use the Office Setup and Uninstall command on the Office menu. These configurations do not include (or they prevent access to) the Setup maintenance program. In many cases, the solution is to run the original Setup program to make the modifications you want.

The Microsoft Office program group includes a program icon for Office Setup, a maintenance version of the initial Setup program that helps you modify your Office installation. And when you meet MOM, in the next section, you'll see that a command for starting this Setup program is available from the Office menu. One way or the other, you might use this program more than you expect. In part, you'll find that the extent and complexity of the suite lead you to make certain refinements to make better use of your disk space or to add items, such as drivers, as you reach farther and wider for information. You might also have occasion to update an application between revisions of the suite. Finally, you might discover that trouble finds you if you make changes outside of Setup.

Double-click the Office Setup icon (or choose the Office Setup and Uninstall command from the Office menu) to start the program. You might see an initial dialog box from which you can choose the Setup program you want to start. If you installed one of the Office components using its own Setup program (rather than Office Setup), highlight the application's Setup program when you want to add or remove components. If you don't see the specific program you want to modify, highlight the Office installation. After you make your choice, click OK.

On the Setup Maintenance screen, there are three major maintenance options: Add/Remove, Reinstall, and Remove All. We'll look carefully at the Add/Remove option. Reinstall and Remove All either restore your previous installation (should a file be corrupted or deleted accidentally) or reverse the installation process (not completely, but as far as possible). Note that you do not need to use Remove All if you're simply upgrading your version of Microsoft Office. Setup will overwrite the files it needs to replace.

Adding and Removing Office Components

When you choose Add/Remove, Setup displays a Maintenance Installation dialog box in which you indicate the components you want to add or remove. Click a check box to change its status: If you select a check box, Setup installs the component; if you deselect it, Setup removes the component. Notice as you

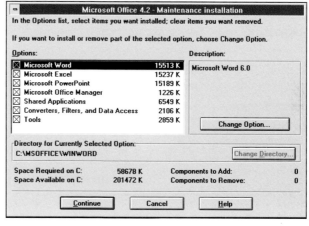

select different options that you can "drill down" in many of them by clicking Change Option to make choices among the subcomponents. For each item you highlight, Setup gives a description of the role that the item plays in Office and lists the disk space (in KB) the item occupies.

If you change options to add or remove components, Setup tallies your changes at the bottom of the window. A grayed-out item is unavailable for selection because it was previously installed by another application; you cannot reinstall or remove it using Office Setup—go back to the Setup program for the application itself. When you finish making choices, click Continue to proceed with the changes. If you are installing files from floppy disks, Setup prompts you to insert the disks it needs.

Installing a New Version of an Office Application

Between upgrades of the Office suite, you might obtain a newer version of one of the component applications. To install it, you do not need to remove the existing version of the application. The Setup program for the new version will overwrite files as necessary, assuming that you are installing the new version in the directory that the existing program occupies.

REMOVING ACCESS?

If you need to remove Access version 1.1 or earlier, you can't do it with the Setup maintenance program. You can use File Manager to delete the files and directories from your disk.

SETUP STRATEGIES

You shouldn't run Setup while other programs are running. Fortunately, you can open your Windows Task List (Ctrl+Esc) while you are using the installation program—a handy way to close applications without exiting Setup. If you originally installed Office from a network location, Setup will look to the earlier connection to locate additional files or replacements. If you failed to note the drive letter or path you used for the previous connection, you might find that information in the Setup error message.

Meet MOM

In lots of ways, MOM—the Microsoft Office Manager program—is the manager you've always wanted:

- It stays out of the way unless you really need it.

- It helps you get the resources you need to do your work.

- It's adaptable to your work style in a lot of attractive ways.

In fact, the hardest thing about using MOM initially might be finding its toolbar on the screen. You already know how to start the program—you double-click the Microsoft Office icon, if it wasn't launched automatically from your Startup program group.

Unless you've changed its appearance deliberately, the MOM toolbar—also known as the Office Manager toolbar—is a row of small buttons along the top right edge of the screen. The toolbar is typically parked in the title bar of your top (maximized) application. And that's where it remains. As you switch applications or rearrange other windows, the toolbar stays put and remains visible. This can be inconvenient in some situations—you don't want MOM to hide the name of the document, for example—so there is, as you will see, an easy way to make the toolbar disappear. (See "Getting the Toolbar Out of the Way," later in this chapter.)

The buttons on the Office toolbar represent the major Office applications—they are simplified versions of the program icons you would see in Program Manager. There are a couple of important exceptions, however: the Find File button and the Microsoft Office button. Find File is a utility that locates a file based on directory information, summary text, or text from within the file. It's the Office equivalent of the Find File command on each application's File menu.

The other exception, the Microsoft Office button, is even more important. It's the gateway to the full range of MOM's capabilities. Click

Microsoft Office
Find File
Microsoft Mail
Microsoft Access
Microsoft PowerPoint
Microsoft Excel
Microsoft Word

Program Manager
File   Options   Window   Help

the button, and you get the Office Manager menu. It displays a set of commands for launching other applications, getting help, customizing, and the like. It's also your ticket to exiting MOM. Choosing the Exit command eliminates the toolbar. If you have Office applications open, they are unaffected; only MOM and its features are discharged.

You can display the toolbar in three sizes, your first view being the most compact. The larger versions are easier on the eyes, although all are reinforced by the ToolTips feature—small identification labels that pop up when you let the mouse pointer hover over a button for a second. The regular and large toolbars are more likely to be in your way, blocking other application buttons and such, but you can move them and park them wherever you please, unlike the small toolbar. Details about changing the size and location of the toolbar are on the next page, under "The Office Manager Toolbar: Made to Order."

The three faces of MOM. The small version of the toolbar always appears in the top right area of your screen.

Power Launching

MOM has a clear and limited job description. Its primary duty is to start or switch to an application. Click a button, and you launch the application it represents. If the application is already running, Windows switches to that application. It's that simple.

What you don't find on the Office Manager toolbar might be on the Office Manager menu. Here's what the menu looks like fresh from the box.

As you'll see in the next section, you can modify both the toolbar and the menu as you wish: you can remove items, add items—yes, non-Office applications, even non–Windows-based applications—and change their order.

MOM really joins the circus when you click a toolbar button while you're holding down one of the control keys—

Ctrl, Shift, or Alt. Clicking a button to launch an application while holding down the Ctrl key opens a *new* session of the application. For example, if you are working in Microsoft Word and you already have a Microsoft Excel document open in the background, pressing Ctrl and clicking the Microsoft Excel button launches Excel a second time rather than switching to the current document. But take heed: Launching multiple instances in this way fills your computer's memory in a hurry, so have a good reason for doing so. If you merely want to open a different document in Excel, that's no reason to launch the application again. You can simply choose Excel's File New command or File Open command to move the current document into the background.

Like the Ctrl key, Shift and Alt produce variations in MOM's behavior. Hold down Shift while you click a button, and MOM starts the application (or switches to it) but tiles the new window horizontally with the current window. Tiling two windows, whether they contain different Office applications or two instances of the same application, is useful if you want to drag and drop information from one to the other. Hold down Alt and click the toolbar button to close the corresponding application.

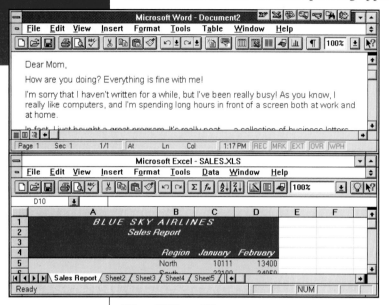

You might want to experiment with the various control keys, especially if all of your work is comfortably saved. You can use Ctrl, Shift, and Alt in combination with commands on the Office menu to get the same effects that you get with the toolbar buttons. Of course, the key combinations are intended for use with Windows-based applications; they don't necessarily have the advertised effect with commands such as Find File and MS-DOS Prompt.

In Word, you can hold down the Shift key and click the Microsoft Excel button to launch (or switch to) Excel tiled with Word.

The Office Manager Toolbar: Made to Order

How can you adapt the Office Manager toolbar? Time to count the ways. You can change the size, shape, and location of the toolbar (or hide it altogether), you can add and remove toolbar buttons and Office Manager menu commands, you can reorder buttons or commands, and you can modify buttons or commands with parameters. None of these is the least bit hard to do.

Sizing Up the Toolbar The Office Manager toolbar comes in three sizes: small, regular, and large. To change the size, with MOM running, click anywhere on the toolbar with the right mouse

Variations with MOM

Click a button on the Office Manager toolbar, or choose a program from the menu—the result is the same: Windows launches the application that corresponds to the button or menu item. If the application has been launched already, you simply switch to the session that is already running.

Double-click a button—Same effect as clicking, but harder to do.

Ctrl+click a button—Launches a new session of the application.

Shift+click a button—Launches the application (or switches to an existing session) tiled horizontally with the current application.

Alt+click a button—Closes the application.

Ctrl+Shift+click a button—Launches a new instance of an application and tiles it with the current application.

button, and choose one of the three sizes from the shortcut menu. If you'd like to have a little practice, choose Large Buttons to see how large is large. Go ahead.

Unlike the small toolbar, the regular and large versions look like miniwindows and can be reshaped and relocated. You can grab the "window" by the title bar and drag it with the mouse pointer. You can leave it somewhere out in midscreen (try it), and you can grab the boundary to change its shape. At the screen edge, it flattens itself against the perimeter, with the buttons arranged like players in a dugout. Double-click the title bar, and the toolbar toggles between its most recent midscreen and sidelined shapes.

Changing the Lineup The procedures for changing the lineup on the toolbar or on the Office Manager menu are nearly identical. Choose the Customize command from the full Office Manager menu or from the shortcut menu, and select either the Toolbar tab or the Menu tab. (If you haven't used one of these tabbed dialog boxes before, you'll probably figure out how to use it right away: Just visualize a series of folders and click the upper, labeled part of the one you want to see.)

On the Toolbar tab, shown here, you find a scrolling list of not only the current toolbar items but also many potential items: key Windows components (such as File Manager), other Windows-based applications (whether they're installed on your disk or not), key Windows accessories (such as Calculator), even the MS-DOS prompt. Check boxes denote the items that can show up as toolbar buttons. Only the Microsoft Office button (not in the list) is a permanent resident. You determine the others by clicking the check boxes to select or deselect them.

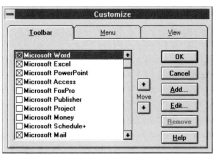

The same items in the toolbar list, plus a few new ones, appear in the list on the Menu tab. By default (in a new installation), the toolbar and the menu contain different items. That makes sense: You probably don't need access to the same item both ways. But where you choose to put them is up to you. If you want a toolbar button for File Manager, you can select it in the list on the Toolbar tab; you can then deselect the check box for File Manager on the Menu tab (but it's entirely up to you).

The order of the buttons and menu items is also up to you. To change the order, highlight an item in either list. (Be careful not to click in the box itself if you don't want to change its status.) Then click one of the Move arrows,

SAVE THAT SCREEN

If you use a screen saver program, consider adding a button to launch the screen saver from the Office Manager toolbar. The screen saver must already be registered with Windows—through the Desktop dialog box in Control Panel. Adding the button is easy enough: As you follow the procedure for adding a toolbar item, select the box opposite Screen Saver in the list.

ONCE IS ENOUGH

As you're adjusting the lineups for the toolbar and the Office Manager menu, avoid duplication. No need to have an item appear in both places.

as shown in the figure on the preceding page, to move the item above or below its neighbors. When the toolbar is horizontal, the top items from the customizing list will appear on the left.

Of course, there's nothing terribly exclusive about the Office Manager toolbar. You want it to have a button to launch Lotus 1-2-3? To start a game of Solitaire? To log your work hours in a specific Excel file? Simply choose Customize from the Office shortcut menu, and then click Add on the Toolbar tab. Supply the requested information, as shown here. To specify the command line, either type the complete command line from memory or use the Browse button. Browsing is easy and reliable: You maneuver through drives and directories to the file that launches the program (or the data file you want to open), and Office gathers the pathname as you navigate.

POWER PLAY

Hello, Dalí

When you add (or edit) a new item on the Office Manager toolbar, you'll find several button images to choose from in the drop-down list: CLUB.BMP, HEART.BMP, and so on. The button bitmaps in the list are located in the MS-BTTNS directory of MSOFFICE (your Office directory). But these images might not suit you. To create your own bitmaps for the toolbar, open one of the BMP files such as SMILEY.BMP —in Paintbrush. Then zoom in on the image and modify it pixel by pixel as much as you like. The upper image is for the small buttons; the lower (larger) one is for the other

two sizes of buttons. You can create completely new images if you like, but use the existing bitmap as your sizing guideline and avoid changing the background color.

When you finish editing, zoom out and save the edited file with a different filename (in the same directory). The next time you add a program item to the Office Manager toolbar, you can select your own button image in the drop-down list.

Getting the Toolbar Out of the Way   To get the Office Manager toolbar out of the way, you don't have to exit Office. If you don't want the toolbar to be visible, choose the Minimize command from the shortcut menu if you have small buttons, or click the Minimize button on the toolbar if you have regular or large buttons. To restore the toolbar, click the minimized icon or press Ctrl+Esc to display Task List and then double-click Microsoft Office.

You can also have Windows minimize the toolbar whenever another window is active. To do so, choose Customize from the Office menu (or the shortcut menu). On the View tab, deselect the check box labeled Toolbar Is Always Visible, and click OK. Thereafter, the toolbar stays out of sight unless you restore it or return to the View tab and click the box you deselected earlier.

More to MOM Than You Thought

You might have discovered already that there's more to MOM than meets the eye. In the next chapter, we'll highlight a number of additional features throughout the Office suite that help you get results in a hurry. But first, in the section below, we'll explore the Find File feature, which is available on the Office Manager toolbar as well as through individual applications.

If you get stuck while using MOM and trying to explore its full range of options, remember that you can always resort to online Help. The next chapter discusses the various Help resources in more detail.

Finding Files (and More)

Find File is MOM's file clerk. It is virtually identical to the Find File command that's available on the File menu of each of the core Office applications. The differences are minor—a few changes to the drop-down lists that are tailored to the applications and default filename extensions in the Office suite. But it functions in largely the same manner as the Find File command in Word or Excel or any of the other Office applications.

Even if you aren't very familiar with the Find File command in those other applications, you'll find it straightforward to use. Click the Find File button on the MOM toolbar to open the Find File dialog box. Then click the Search button and, in the Search dialog box, specify what to search for and where to conduct the search. All the files matching your search criteria are then found and displayed in a sorted list. Find File can also do more than conduct a simple search for files. The Advanced Search options provide powerful controls to conduct very selective searches, while the file management commands give you full control of your files.

Using Advanced Search

The Advanced Search options are spread out across a three-tab dialog box. (To get to it, choose the Advanced Search button at the bottom of the Search dialog box.) On the Location tab, you can limit the search to a drive and a directory—or a whole list of them. Add the locations from right to left;

highlight directories by navigating among the drives and directories boxes on the right and add them to the search list on the left by clicking the Add button. If you need to expand your search to remote locations, you can make a network connection by clicking the Network button. The Include Subdirectories check box applies to the entire search and cannot have a different setting from one directory to the next.

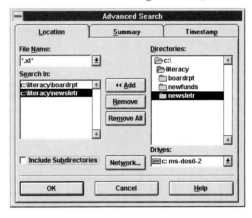

SUMMARY INFORMATION

The Summary Info command for viewing and editing summary information is on the File menu in Word, Excel, and PowerPoint.

The Summary tab goes a step further than it advertises. Yes, it lets you narrow a search based on the Summary information, that (optional) boxful of details that you can attach to your files with a title, the author's name, a description of the subject, and so forth. That's useful in itself (if you can get into the habit of supplying the information when you save your files), but the kicker is that you can specify file contents as part of the search. Type a word or a brief phrase, and Find File sifts through your files and lists only the ones that contain the text you specify.

SUPER SEARCH

You can extend the content-searching capability yet another step by selecting the Use Pattern Matching on the Summary tab of the Advanced Search dialog box check box. This enables you to complicate your search strings with a set of possible expressions and operators. With enough motivation, you can certainly benefit from these, but few of them apply to casual searches. See online Help for details.

The Timestamp tab allows you to narrow a search to a range of dates that bracket the creation date of the file or the date on which it was last saved. Here's how you might use it to search for a file created in October or November of 1993. If you don't want to limit the search in one direction or the other, be sure the corresponding text box is left blank.

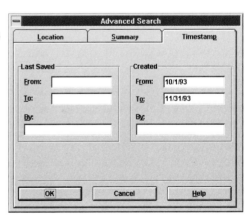

Managing Files

How often have you wanted the convenience of deleting or copying files without leaving an application? Even though Office makes it awfully easy to open File Manager, you'll probably appreciate the commands that Find File provides.

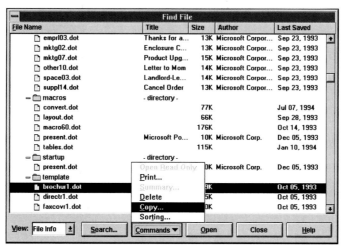

Before you use a command, conduct a search to find the files you want and then highlight the file or files you want the command to act on. In fact, the Commands button is not active unless some files are listed, so you need to define the search before you start bumping and flipping your files about. You can delete, copy, or print a group of files at one time—use Shift+click to select a block of files, or use Ctrl+click to select a set of files that are not in sequence. (Selecting files is not relevant to the Sort command; the command affects all the files in the list, regardless of what you select.)

Using the commands in combination with Search can open up some useful possibilities. For example, you can search for all the files on your hard disk that have the BAK extension, and then consider which of them you can afford to delete. Or you might search for files that were last saved prior to a certain date, sort them by their dates, and then move down the list, backing up files you no longer need (or deleting them entirely).

2 The Office Fast Track

Chapter 3

Learning on the Job

Tackling the Curve

One of the benefits of the Microsoft Office suite is the ease with which you can get up to speed quickly, hit the ground running, learn on the fly, and all the rest of those inspiring phrases. But even so, there's still a learning curve. You need to master terms and concepts and explore the available tools so that you can eventually come to visualize your tasks using the model that the program is based on. There's never a perfect meshing of your expectations with the interface; you can always expect to do some groping.

Luckily, the developers of Office have stressed consistency in designing the interfaces for the component applications. The result is a payoff whenever you attempt a task that's familiar in one Office application and find that it's done in the same way or in a predictably similar way in another application. The online Help system also provides an easy way to find explanations of interface elements and procedures. In fact, Microsoft Office Manager has online Help of its own, in addition to the online Help that accompanies each application. And as you'll see in this chapter, online Help is often more context sensitive and more richly interlinked than the printed documentation.

This chapter will help you take advantage of the consistencies within Office so that you'll find yourself guessing right a lot of the time. And it will help you develop a strategy for using online Help. After all, most people's strategy goes no further than "When you run out of guesses, click the Help menu." But before tackling that subject, let's explore some of the program features and behavior that defy many people's best guesses, for one reason or another.

Words to the Wise

With every program you learn, you come to a few hard-won realizations that have you grumbling, "Well, why didn't they just say that!" Unfortunately, these discoveries seem to be different for everyone. So much depends on which applications you've used previously, because they tend to shape your assumptions about the new ones. But there just might be a set of discoveries that are common enough to be worth mentioning. And because most Office users will approach one or more of the components as a novice, let's venture a few predictions as to where the rough spots might lie.

What follows, then, is a rundown of the slings and arrows you're likely to encounter when you try to learn one of the major Office applications. These "discoveries" might, in fact, be stated clearly for you in the documentation or elsewhere, but perhaps you didn't read them (deadlines, deadlines), or perhaps you read them but didn't grasp their significance at the time.

Incidentally, these observations have been gleaned from the experiences of live training professionals. If this advice catches you at the right moment, it might alert you to hazards you can happily avoid. But if you're bent on learning only what will drag you over the immediate hurdle, skip ahead to the section titled "Online Help, with a Strategy," later in this chapter.

Word Hurdles

Paragraph Formatting vs. Character Formatting Logical as it may seem once you've grown used to it, Microsoft Word's division of formatting actions into two groups is initially puzzling. Some actions, such as font changes, affect characters only; others, such as tabs and indents, apply to whole paragraphs.

Drag and Drop This feature is simple but smart: Point to a selection and drag it to a new location. The biggest trick is learning how it thinks—and learning not to use it when it gets cumbersome (when you have to do a lot of scrolling, for example).

AutoText For some, the first hurdle is realizing that this feature replaces Glossary, that misnamed feature from earlier versions of Word. Essentially, the AutoText feature inserts previously stored text or graphics when you tell it to. Another snag for some: You should select text only when you want to create an AutoText entry; otherwise, just type the entry name and then click the Insert AutoText toolbar button or press F3. Avoid introducing AutoText fields (and thereby adding a whole new level of complexity) unless you really need them.

Inserting Clip Art and Other Objects   Inserting objects in Word (using the Insert Object command) seems a bit like voodoo, but it's often the layout problems they create that can frustrate you the most. Using Page Layout view can help, but it might slow down your computer.

Drawing Layers   Whether you use Draw objects in Word or in other applications, shifting the layers can teach you patience. The concept can be tough to work with because you have to start visualizing parts of your drawing on separate sheets that are arranged in a stack. And then you have to bear in mind that Word treats the text as yet another layer that sits behind or in front of the whole drawing.

Section Breaks and Page Breaks   They're not hard to insert using the Insert Break command, but these manually inserted divisions override Word's automatic divisions and can cause confusion when you start to consider printing and formatting, especially with variable headers and footers.

Tables   Word gives you the option of using Word tables or tables from other applications, such as Excel. Word tables are easy to use once you understand that they are composed of cells and that the editing techniques are more similar to those in Excel than to those in Word. Tables are among the most commonly linked or embedded objects, so prepare to master their complexity if you want to take advantage of tables within Word documents and without.

Styles   Each component of a document—text, headings, notes, and so on—can have a standard format that's applied automatically as its style. You can explore these in depth if you choose, but learn the basics at least: They're powerful and they underlie other features, such as outlining.

Templates   Templates are used as the basis for different types of documents. You might want to avoid learning about templates until your interest in styles or macros draws you in. Be aware that template files have a DOT extension, not the DOC extension that Word gives to ordinary documents.

Fields   Fields are essentially programming codes that you insert directly into a Word document. Because they're treated differently from ordinary text, fields defy some of the normal text-editing techniques. Word has come to depend on fields for certain other features—such as headers, cross-references, and forms —so you wind up inserting them without realizing that you are. If nothing else, remember that when you see something cryptic in {curly brackets}, pressing Alt+F9 will toggle between showing field codes and displaying field results throughout the document.

Mail Merge and Printing Envelopes   Despite the introduction of wizards for both mail merge (form letters) and envelope printing, these tasks are tough initially. For one thing, they lead you into the complex world of fields. (Some offices keep a typewriter just for addressing envelopes.)

Macros   With a macro, you can define a series of actions in Word that you initiate by choosing a command, clicking a button, or using a key combination. You can "record" macros or learn a variety of Basic (called WordBasic) to create more complex macros with loops, conditionals, and file-handling power. You *don't* need macros simply to insert routine text and graphics; AutoCorrect and AutoText can handle most of those cases.

Excel Hurdles

Entering Data   Not difficult, but you need to make an adjustment: You have to press Enter, or otherwise leave a cell, to enter the data (and to use a number of commands that don't work if you're in the midst of data entry).

Functions as Parts of Formulas   You might struggle with the mechanics of using a function as part of a formula. Your best bet is to study a few examples—and don't underestimate the importance of parentheses. The Function Wizard can be a big help here.

Auto Commands, Such as AutoFill and AutoSum   These are too good to pass up, but you have to adjust to their logic. With AutoFill, the data format is critical, and remember that the Fill command on the Edit menu gives you more control than dragging on screen does. AutoSum guesses which cells are to be summed, so you might need to select different cells, especially if you are summing discontinuous cells.

Charts   With the ChartWizard, you can create some basic charts by making a series of choices. Still, you have to begin by selecting the correct cells, and you have to develop a feel for the type of chart that best represents your data.

Split and Freeze Panes   These commands are important as you begin working with larger worksheets. You can use them to compare rows and columns that are far apart and to keep headings visible as you page through a large worksheet.

Custom AutoFilter   If you use Microsoft Excel for data management, Custom AutoFilter is an important way to extend your control of which data is displayed. Like database queries, however, filters require that you learn a few syntax rules.

Macros and Excel Visual Basic for Applications (VBA)   A macro represents a series of Excel actions that you can initiate with a button, a command, or a key combination. You can either record macros, in which case Excel records your actions, or you can write your own macros using the VBA language.

PowerPoint Hurdles

Startup Dialog Box   To help you get started, especially as a new Microsoft PowerPoint user, the program displays a dialog box whenever you start the program and whenever you start a new slide. You can turn either or both of these off (using the Options command), and you can change the default presentation.

Templates, Masters, and Color Schemes   Develop an understanding early of how these relate: A template represents a set of masters and color schemes for the various presentation components, including such items as slides, speaker's notes, and audience handouts. Templates have multiple versions, depending on the medium—35-mm slides, overheads, and so forth.

Views   What's impressive to most new users is how different the views in PowerPoint are. In Slide view you might see a single, colorful, attention-grabbing slide; Slide Sorter view shows all the slides in the presentation; Outline view presents a sequence of text elements from all the slides at once; Notes Pages view is back to single slides but has room to include additional text unique to that slide; and so forth.

Grouping and Ungrouping Slides   Because the program works with your slides as sets of objects, you should learn to see them that way, grouping and un-grouping them as you alter the formats and colors of different components.

Access Hurdles

Database Design   If you hope to get your queries and forms to work well and be truly beneficial, design your database structure before you start. The database should contain nonduplicated, related information in the tables, with appropriate keys, and developed relationships between tables, indexes, and fields.

Tables and Forms   Microsoft Access has diverse tools for viewing your information; be clear about the role of each. Tables function as storage places. Forms provide a way to show and collect data in polished ways—a more public face for gathering and exhibiting records.

Queries   A query is a powerful tool for examining your data, especially when you want to relate items from different tables. Be aware that you can create queries of different kinds for a variety of purposes (selecting data, deleting records, and so on). With queries, you must learn to use the criteria that translate your information needs into terms that Access can apply.

Reports   The challenge with reports lies in convincing Access to print exactly what you want to see. This entails understanding how reports relate to queries and learning how to work in Design view.

Data Types and Properties You need to be aware of how these affect the appearance of your information and the way Access manipulates it.

Security Adventurous use of the Security menu can get you into a heap of trouble. You might be tempted to experiment with limiting access to individual tables and queries, but proceed cautiously. Because of the interrelation of tables and queries, you can create problems that are difficult to untangle.

The Benefits of Consistency

When do you benefit from design consistency (but perhaps take it for granted)? The first time you attempt to format text in an unfamiliar Office application and you find a Format menu in the expected place and familiar buttons on the toolbar for italic and boldface, text alignment, and so on. More examples can be cited. Consistency makes for easy learning, and often it makes for unbroken productivity because the only thing you need to learn is that you already know how to do the task. If you know how to use even one of the Office applications, here are some of the tasks you can accomplish easily in the others:

- Opening, saving, and printing files using the commands on the File menu

- Cutting, copying, and pasting selected text using keyboard shortcuts (Ctrl+X, Ctrl+C, Ctrl+V)

- Using menus and recognizing menu "shorthand": Ellipses indicate dialog boxes, grayed-out commands are unavailable, dots and check marks signify active options, and so on

- Setting options in dialog boxes, including the tabbed dialog boxes that Office applications employ

- Summoning online Help and navigating through the linked topics

- Employing the Clipboard within or between applications to paste information (once or many times)

- Displaying shortcut menus to use the most frequently needed commands in a given situation

Online Help, with a Strategy

If you bought Microsoft Office in the box, you probably still remember your trip from the counter to the car. Or maybe you brought a pickup. The box should probably come with wheels, like luggage. And yet, for all its size and weight, the printed documentation for each application is not overwhelming.

REVERSING YOURSELF

You can try new features more confidently with the knowledge that an application has an Undo command to back you out of a mistake. Word has a super Undo feature that backs you out of a whole series of missteps. Beware of two assumptions, however. Don't assume that you can back out of every action. Saving a file, for instance, is not reversible. And don't assume that all Office applications have the multiple Undo capacity of Word. Most can take you back only a single step. For peace of mind, save your file before you risk some action that might not be reversible.

Industrywide, the move has been toward online documentation, with the assumption that you'd rather pay in hard disk space for the added convenience. There are, of course, convenience gains and losses with either approach, but the choice is being made to reduce the printed matter, and you'd do well to learn how you can get the most from online resources.

How much online help do you get with Office? With Word alone, you can count up to 3.2 MB in a typical installation without even trying. (Clearly, when you go to a minimum installation, this is one of the areas that gets trimmed.) Add similar amounts for the other applications, plus the online help that's unique to Microsoft Office Manager, and the total amount of information is mind-boggling. Online help comes in several flavors. Some of the help is built into the application, while other help is contained in individual programs. The good news is that the applications make it easy for you to get the right kind of help.

Many of the programs have their own help features, and some of these features are common among the Office applications. ToolTips is one of the most useful help features built into the Office applications.

To see a ToolTip, simply let your mouse pointer hover over a button on a toolbar. Because ToolTips are context sensitive, a moment later you see a small box displayed below the button that identifies its function in a word or two. In most cases, ToolTips are accompanied by messages in the status bar

that explain the function in more detail or supply an important fact.

Another type of help is Cue Cards. These cards provide information on how to accomplish specific tasks while providing an overview of the tasks. You can view the cards while you try out the procedures. To see the cue cards for Office Manager, choose Cue Cards from the Office Manager menu.

The third type of help is the Help program itself. Most Microsoft Windows-based applications have this type of help, and you find information in much the same way. The difference between the individual Help programs in Office is that each one contains the information about the specific application. To see the Help program for an application, choose the Contents command from the application's Help menu.

What's in the Help program? A variety of information, including overviews and demonstrations of product features, step-by-step procedures, definitions of terms, explanations of options, and descriptions of commands, functions, error messages, and the like.

You could not easily navigate through all of this information were it not for a few important factors. In combination, they give online Help an edge over the printed documentation:

- **Context sensitivity.** In the best cases, Help has been "prenavigated": The information that matches the currently highlighted command or dialog box is displayed immediately when you press the Help key (F1).

- **Searching.** The Search facility and Index feature let you try different words or phrases to track down the Help topics that answer your questions.

- **Hyperlinks.** Once you've caught the trail of your information quarry, you can use links in the Help text to jump to related topics, expanding or refining your search.

- **On Top capability.** Once you've displayed the Help topic you need, you can keep it on your screen as you return to your work in the application. This is handy if the Help topic supplies instructions for a lengthy step-by-step process.

- **Customizing tools.** You can copy, paste, and print entries; add your own notes; and set bookmarks to wring the greatest value from the information in the Help system.

Leave the Driving to Help

The easiest way to find information in online Help is to let Help find it for you. The key to this feat is what's called context sensitivity: The Help system recognizes the context on the screen and makes a concrete (and usually appropriate) assumption about the elements for which you want information.

But the real trigger for context-sensitive help is the F1 key. When you press F1, Help checks the onscreen context for a highlighted menu command or an active dialog box, and displays the Help topic that's appropriate for that command or dialog box. For example, open the File menu in Word, press the Down arrow key until the highlight reaches the Save command, and press F1. Help displays a window that describes the Save command, as shown on the facing page.

In a similar way, you can display a dialog box and then press F1 to see information about the dialog box and the options it makes available. In such a case, pressing F1 is equivalent to choosing the Help command button in the dialog box.

INDEPENDENT HELP

Because Help is a separate program, you can minimize, maximize, move, and size the Help window. Use the familiar Windows techniques (Alt+Tab or Ctrl+Esc) to switch between the Help program and your application. You can even add the application's Help file to the Office Manager toolbar (Help files have the HLP file extension) for easy reference and quick switching.

EXCEPTIONS, EXCEPTIONS

Online Help is not among the most consistent features of the Office suite. For example, some of the applications use Cue Cards; some use How To screens; some use both. PowerPoint does not respond to F1 when you highlight a command on a menu— you have to use the Help button. And so on.

But what if you can't highlight the screen element for which you want to get help—a toolbar button, for example? Or what if you

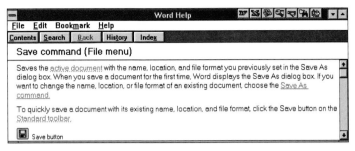

simply prefer using the mouse to get help? The Help toolbar button to the rescue. Clicking the Help button on the Standard toolbar (or pressing Shift+F1) changes the standard mouse pointer to a Help arrow. Clicking a screen element with this mouse pointer displays online help about the screen element.

Help button

If Help does not recognize a specific context on the screen, it displays the Contents screen—a general starting point (like the table of contents for a book) that leads you to progressively more specific information. You'll find details about the Contents screen in the sections that follow.

POWER PLAY

Revealing Formats

In Word, you can use the Help toolbar button to display a pop-up window with formatting information for any character in the work area: Click the Help button, point to a character with the Help arrow, and click either mouse button. The pop-up window reveals in detail the character and paragraph formatting that apply. You can continue clicking different characters to see their formatting. This can be a great resource if you're inheriting files in a group work

context because it lets you check indents and other measurements and it shows whether a formatting attribute has been assigned directly or as part of a paragraph or character style. Press Esc or click the Help button again to cancel the format-revealing feature.

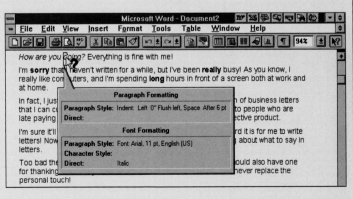

HELP FOR DISABLED COMMANDS

If a menu command is "grayed-out" (unavailable), you can't display its online help using the Help toolbar button. Press the F1 key, or choose the Search For Help On command from the Help menu instead.

PREVIEW FORMATS

In Word, you can also use the Help button to reveal formats in Print Preview.

Use the Search Tools

If you can't get Help to respond to F1 or to the Help button with the specific information you need, try a search of your own, beginning with the Help menu. Some of the commands on the Help menu differ from one application to another, but most of the differences are minor. The Help menu in Word is fairly typical. The first three commands—Contents, Search For Help On, and Index—represent different paths to the same body of information: the collection of topics that pertain to the application. As you can see in the figure on the facing page, the various paths, in this case, lead to "Changing column width in a table."

Experiment with the various ways to find information in Help, and choose the one that best suits you or your situation. All of the Office applications have a Contents command, and all of them have a Search dialog box (accessible from the Contents screen if not from the Help menu). Almost all of them have an Index command too, Access being the exception.

The Search facility and the Index command are very similar. Index is geared for somewhat more open browsing of the topic list, whereas Search assumes that you are a bit more confident in identifying the topic you are seeking. But ultimately the topic lists are nearly identical, with Index offering the advantage of direct links to any examples and demos that Help might provide.

Just as using Index is like perusing the index of a book, using the Contents screen is like burrowing into an expanding table of contents. If you like to find information in books by looking through the table of contents, this might be the path for you. For many people, this approach works best when you want to get an overview or when you don't know the names of the specific features or procedures you're looking for. From one application to another, however, you have to be flexible as you browse; the organization of topics below the top level of Contents varies significantly among the Office components.

Hyperlinks: Here, There, or In Between?

As you begin to range freely across the Help terrain, you might easily forget which path got you to the current topic—especially when you've been leaping around by means of hyperlinks, those onscreen hot spots (usually underlined green text) that take you, with a single click, directly to another topic. So let's take stock of the navigation options and predictable features so that you don't find yourself zagging when you thought you'd be zigging.

One of the happy points of consistency on the online Help circuit is that green text indicates a link to some other information. Further, if the text has a solid underline, it jumps to another topic, and if the text has a dotted underline, it opens a pop-up window in the current window with additional information—

HELP HIGHWAY

If you choose Help from the Office menu, you see a Contents screen from which you can jump not merely to topics related to MOM or information sharing but also to the Contents screen for each of the Office applications. Often this is a faster way to investigate online help for an application than first launching the program and then going to its Help menu.

QUICK SEARCH

Double-click the Help button to start Help and display the Search dialog box.

HYPERLINK

A *hyperlink* is part of a web of connections within a body of electronic information and lets you move nonsequentially to associated terms and topics.

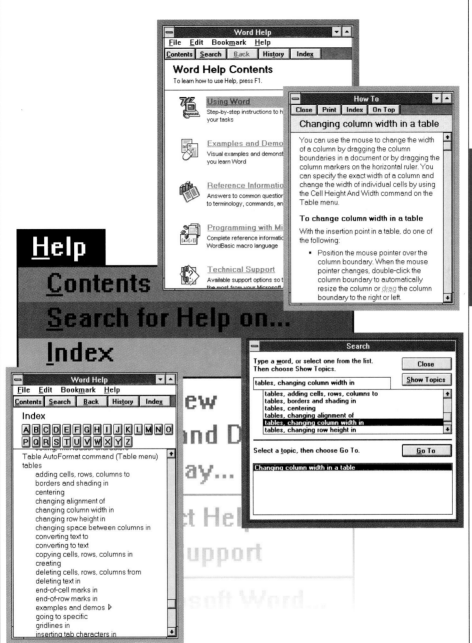

The Help menu is a gateway to the different ways of finding useful information.

a definition or a set of other links to choose from. Ordinary text can also be designated as hot spots, as in the Index listing; and hot spots might also be signaled by colored dots or arrowheads. The surest sign of a hyperlink is the change you see in the mouse pointer: It changes from an arrow to a hand with an upward-pointing finger when it moves over a link.

Other reassuring features are the History and Back buttons. You can probably see why they are valuable. First,

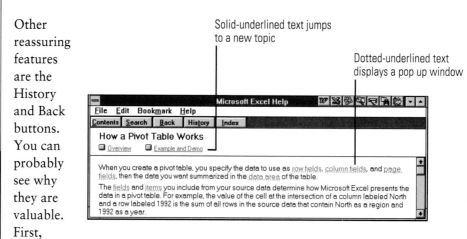

Solid-underlined text jumps to a new topic

Dotted-underlined text displays a pop up window

History: At some point, you might be eager to retrace your better Help steps and gather some of the information gems you left strewn along the way—to reread them or print them or whatever. As for the Back button: You might see a topic that looks promising, jump to it, gasp, and want to retrace your steps at once. The History and Back buttons are almost always available, as long as you don't close the Help window. You might have to close some window that you've landed in—a How To window or a demonstration—but you can usually get back to a Help window that's equipped with these buttons.

Keeping Help on Top

One of the handiest ways to use Help, once you've located the topic you need, is to keep the information window on top (and off to one side) while you return to the task that stumped you in the first place. You can do this with most Help windows, although some were designed to stay out of your way. The prime example is Cue Cards, which present information in a series of narrow windows that stay on top as you work your way through the corresponding task. PowerPoint, Access, and MOM itself use Cue Cards to present common procedures. In Word and Excel, How To windows can function in a similar way, but they do not stay on top by default; you have to choose the On Top button if you want them to remain visible.

For sharing information among Office applications, the Cue Cards on the Office menu are especially valuable. They offer step-by-step instructions for many common situations, such as inserting charts and spreadsheet data from Excel into Word documents or PowerPoint presentations. (An example of a Cue Card window is shown at the top of the facing page.) As they lead you through your options for a given information-sharing scenario, the Cue Cards explain them in fairly easy-to-follow terms. You can resize the cards and move them around on your screen to keep more of your work visible.

ALWAYS ON TOP

Almost any Help window will stay on top when you move back to the application, if you give it the right encouragement. If the button bar across the top of the window does not have an On Top button, check the Help menu (in the Help window) for an Always on Top command. Choose the command to activate it.

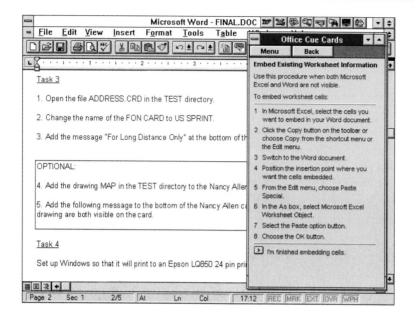

Customizing: Help Yourself

Let's turn now to ways that you can tailor the Help system to suit your own purposes. You can add annotations to Help topics to clarify a point, to indicate how the information relates to your work, or to point out sources of related information. And if you refer repeatedly to certain Help topics, you can add them to your Bookmark menu for faster access.

Adding Annotations   Let's say you're using Excel's online Help and you finally determine which functions you'll use in your analyses. Instead of going through the whole process of determining the most appropriate functions in the future, you want to annotate the Help entry. Fortunately, the Help system for Excel and other Office applications has a provision for making notes and attaching them to the Help topic.

You can add one annotation per Help topic. You do so by typing your text in the Annotate dialog box, as shown on the next page. When you click Save, the dialog box closes and a green paper clip appears in the Help topic. Your annotation text should be specific—the paper clip for your annotation always appears at the top of the Help topic, so it might not be associated as closely as you'd like with the Help text to which it refers. To see the annotation text, simply click the paper clip and the Annotate dialog box appears, displaying the annotation text.

> **Adding an Annotation**
>
> Adding an annotation is a simple matter. With the topic you want to annotate displayed:
>
> 1. Choose Annotate from the Edit menu. The Annotate dialog box appears.
> 2. In the dialog box, type the text of your annotation.
> 3. Choose the Save button to close the Annotate dialog box and attach the annotation to the Help topic.

To edit or delete the annotation, return to the Help topic and either click the paper clip or choose Annotate from the Edit menu. In the Annotate dialog box, choose Save to record your changes; choose

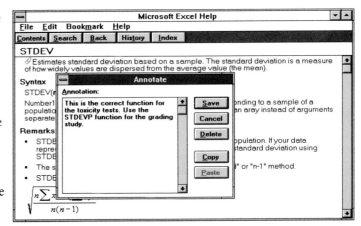

Delete to remove the note. Oh, and one minor work-saver: If you choose the Copy button without first selecting text, the entire annotation is copied to the Clipboard.

Placing Bookmarks in Help   Suppose you keep showing up at the same location in Help (on purpose). Perhaps it's an overview of Excel error codes or a table of keyboard shortcuts in PowerPoint. To find that topic more quickly and easily the next time you need it, you can do what's called "placing a bookmark" in that location. You place a bookmark by defining a name for the topic. The topic name is then placed on the Bookmark menu, and choosing the name from the menu takes you directly to the topic you want to see.

Choose the Define command on the Bookmark menu whenever you want to create or delete a bookmark. If you create more than nine bookmarks, a More command will appear on the menu to let you display and scroll through the complete list.

NOT HOW TO

Unfortunately, the Bookmark menu is not available in some of the most useful Help windows—the How To windows. The best you can do is to insert a bookmark for the Contents window, from which you can jump to the topic you really want. As a cue to yourself, you might give the bookmark the name of the topic to which you need to jump.

MARKED MESSAGE

A powerful way to personalize your Help system is to use an annotation and a bookmark for the same Help topic. Use the Bookmark command to jump to the topic, and then view the annotation to see your notes about the topic.

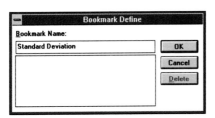

Placing a Bookmark

To place a bookmark at your current Help location:

1. Choose Define from the Bookmark menu.
2. In the Bookmark Define dialog box, either accept the suggested name for the bookmark (the title of the Help topic) or type a name of your own.
3. After you click OK, the new item appears on the Bookmark menu.

Copying and Printing Help   For the most part, you won't need to copy or print online Help information. Having it accessible on line is generally as much convenience as you need. And the printed documentation already duplicates much of the information from the online resource. Still, you might encounter situations in which you want to copy Help information to another document or print a topic for ready reference. Both are easy to do.

You'll figure out how to copy the first time you try. The only trick is that, if you are in the Help window, you choose the Copy command from the File menu *before* you select text. Help then displays a Copy window in which you select the text block you want to copy. Click the Copy button to place the information on the Clipboard. Don't expect the pasted text to retain formatting from the Help window.

To print the entire Help topic, you simply choose the Print Topic command from the File menu, or click the Print button in a How To window. If you've added an annotation to a topic, it is not printed with the topic. If you need to print an annotation with the topic, copy it to the Clipboard and paste it into a document containing the pasted Help topic text. You cannot copy or print the text that appears in a pop-up window. To change printers, choose Printer Setup from the File menu; the change applies to the Print button in the How To window as well as to the Print Topic command on the File menu.

When Help's No Help

If online Help lets you down, don't despair. Try another avenue. For some, the next avenue is the printed documentation. (Although its content overlaps with online Help, try it.) Use the index to steer you toward the right information; Microsoft documentation is typically well-indexed. If that does not solve your problem, try the following alternatives:

- Look at the README Help file. You can display it by clicking the appropriate Readme Help icon in the Office program group of Program Manager. The information in this file was not available when the documentation was printed, so it might address your problem.

- Check out "Answers to Common Questions About..." in the application's Help file. You'll find these topics listed under the Technical Support heading in the Contents window. Your question might turn out to be a common one, and thus restore your sense of normalcy.

- If the problem concerns the interaction of Office applications, be sure that you have looked at the "Getting Started" booklet that accompanies the Office suite and at the Cue Cards available through the Office menu. Of

GETTING SUPPORT

Some hardware dealers preinstall Microsoft Office on the hard disks of computers they sell. In those cases, information about how to contact the Microsoft Support Network might not be included in the Technical Support section of your online Help. Refer to the documentation that you received with your hardware or contact your dealer for technical assistance.

course, use this book's index and pay particular attention to Chapter 15, "Real Questions, Real Answers." The advice in that chapter was written by product support engineers, people who swim daily in the sea of user comments and concerns.

Use the Microsoft Support Network after you've run out of other options. The Technical Support section of your Help Contents screen provides detailed information about the different types of support available. The section also tells you how to prepare for your call, what information to have ready, and that sort of thing.

Chapter 4

Results in a Hurry

Ready to Serve

Microsoft Office is stocked with a powerful assortment of shortcuts for getting a finished-looking product in a hurry. Most of them are easy to use; they're supposed to be. They should remind you of making brownies from a mix: You add water and an egg, you stir, you bake, you serve. Oh, and you decide at some point whether you want them cakelike or chewy. In this chapter, we'll survey some of these cake-mix features—wizards and templates, AutoFormat, and others—that get you from point A to point G posthaste. We'll also look at some of the popular shortcuts by stepping through a few examples—creating a newsletter using Microsoft Word's Newsletter Wizard, inserting a Microsoft Excel function in a formula using the Function Wizard, and using the Expression Builder in Microsoft Access.

Sounds marvelous: finished-looking newsletters, résumés, presentations, and data forms. All the trappings without the pain. So what's the downside? As with baking, the difficulties arise when you want to bake something for which there is no mix: You're back to sifting and measuring, and you never learned how to separate an egg. Or you want to modify a mix, but you don't really understand what's in it or how it works. Clearly, we can't fill in all the gaps in a single chapter. But with some guidance, you'll at least be happy with the result and much closer to completing your work. And you'll be better equipped to figure out what else you need to do.

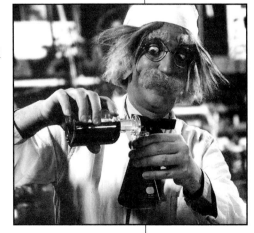

Let's start at a fundamental level—choosing the right application. If you're getting started on a significant task, you need to begin with the tool that's best suited to the task. This can be an important choice: The efficiency of many subsequent tasks depends on it.

Which Office Application for the Job?

You might have piles of information about your clients or your products that you want to maintain using Microsoft Office, but should you enter it in Word as a table, create an Excel worksheet, or set up a database in Access? Or is there yet another option that you haven't thought of? Having a suite of applications at your disposal can make your choices more complicated. And Office provides not only a range of resources, but also a number of options for combining resources (courtesy of OLE) to produce compound documents. Compound documents, compound choices.

Let's save the OLE considerations for the next chapter. Here, we'll simply move through some common issues that arise when you need to match a set of information or a task to an application. The primary questions are, of course, what kind of information do you have and what do you want to do with it?

Lists in General

If you need to create and maintain a list, you might consider Word, Excel, or Access for their various strengths. All offer basic sorting and formatting capabilities. And all have macro languages, derivatives of Basic, that can help you automate routine operations.

- Choose Word if the list is part of a larger document or if you want the convenience of adding bullets or numerals automatically.

- Choose Excel if you want quick entry, sorting, and look-up capabilities—especially for a long list. Excel has useful features for lists of numbers, such as formatting options and functions for analyzing and summarizing the contents.

- Consider Access if you want to assemble elements from different sources or if you need to share the list with other people routinely—especially if the list is related to the information flow of your entire organization.

Names and Addresses

Where should you keep and store a list of names and addresses? Lots of choices here. If the names and addresses exist in a database somewhere, you should look for a way to use them from their current location—especially if the list is already well maintained. Word can merge data from a number of file types—including Excel and Access. And using ODBC drivers, you can also set criteria and select records from a range of larger, more remote data sources. ODBC drivers are shared by the applications that use them, such as Word, Excel, and Access, and are installed during the Office setup or from the ODBC

ODBC

ODBC is the Open Database Connectivity protocol that facilitates the transfer of information between database management systems. You need an ODBC driver that is designed specifically for each database system you want to access.

section of Windows Control Panel. Office comes with ODBC drivers for dBASE, Microsoft FoxPro, Access, Paradox, and SQL Server.

If you're planning to maintain a list primarily to merge names and addresses into form letters, Word might be your first choice. To support mail merge operations, Word provides a mechanism for setting up a data-source document that functions as a database. You can create and maintain the database directly, or you can work through the options in the Mail Merge Helper. As you'll see in Chapter 11, "Mastering Mergers," the mail merge features are fairly well-rounded, enabling you to query, sort, obtain error reports, and view your main document with the data from the records in place.

Word reaches its practical limit somewhere beyond 300 records, depending on the size of the records and the configuration of your computer. Beyond that point, Excel is a good choice: It gives you ready access to its fast sorting capabilities and easy table manipulation features. Choose Access if you want the capabilities of a full relational database; you can range across a vast amount of information in multiple tables, and you can create and save complex queries.

Drawings

Where you should turn to create a drawing depends on a few different factors, which we'll explore in more detail in Chapter 12, "Graphics and Other Gizmos." For now, be aware that you have the Paintbrush program available to you from the Accessories program group in Microsoft Windows, in addition to the drawing features of each application and Word Picture. In many ways, the drawing features have a more limited range than Paintbrush does, but they are integrated into your current document smoothly. Choose Paintbrush if you want to create or edit a graphic with a somewhat wider variety of tools (but still have no need for great sophistication). For more complex art, you can use one of the powerful stand-alone drawing programs. Don't forget that you can insert clip art from the Microsoft ClipArt Gallery. Consider also that you can edit many clip art files to better fit your needs, within the limits of the application's drawing features or Paintbrush or whatever other drawing programs you have available.

Tables

Both Word and Excel have excellent capabilities for organizing and presenting information in a table. If you're already using either of these applications, there's little reason to look elsewhere for resources. Both can resize, add, and remove columns, as well as format text flexibly.

If you're constructing a PowerPoint presentation, you can insert a table from Word or a block of cells from an Excel worksheet with equal ease. For

DATA FORMAT

If you maintain a Word data-source document directly, be aware that you need to follow a few important procedures. The file holds your records as a set of rows in a table or as a series of paragraphs—with appropriate separators (delimiters) between items. The first row or paragraph holds your field names, unless you create a special header file just for these names. You might do well to use the Mail Merge Helper the first time. Later, you can open the document it created to see what a workable format looks like.

IMPORTING ART

As you'll see in Chapter 12, "Graphics and Other Gizmos," Word Picture uses the graphic filters that accompany Windows and Office, and it can import pictures from a wide range of sources. With Word Picture, you can sometimes import and edit files that Paintbrush can't open.

complex formatting—indents, kerning, greater spacing control between lines, and the like—choose Word. If you want the table to contain calculations, Excel is the more natural choice, although you can find sums and produce other simple calculations within Word as well.

Forms

You can create electronic or printed business forms in Word, Excel, or Access to collect and present information. To choose an application, first consider what you want to do with the information you gather. If you plan to add the information to an existing Access database, you should probably create the form in Access: You can coordinate the information-gathering with the structure of the database and use electronic controls when the information is gathered or entered on line. If the database is only a gleam in someone's eye, weigh the time and effort required to develop the database. Even using wizards, you'll need plenty of patience to create the database and generate the appropriate form.

Word and Excel also have tools for creating electronic forms that contain check boxes, drop-down lists, and other online controls. You can protect parts of the form that users are not supposed to alter, and you can use macros or file-saving options to collect the users' entries as individual records. As you collect responses, you can store them in your database, regardless of whether they'll eventually reside in a Word data source, an Excel worksheet, or an Access file.

You should probably choose Excel if you plan to keep the information in Excel for storage, analysis, charting, and the like. Excel can create a simple form for you so that you can enter or edit the data in an existing list or database. You can also create custom forms on an Excel worksheet by using the Forms toolbar. Excel forms can contain numerous types of controls, but formatting of the form is limited by the underlying grid structure of the worksheet.

Word is a good choice if you want to use a flexible layout—or if you're planning to export the document to a desktop publishing program for final refinements and have the form printed professionally. Also, if you're using an electronic form to collect a limited number of names and addresses that will reside in a Word data source (for mail merging), you might prefer to create the form in Word.

If you need simply to create a form and distribute printed copies, Word is an ideal choice because of the formatting flexibility it offers. But when you need a uniform layout, with blanks to be filled in or columns of boxes to be darkened, Excel's basic grid can give you a head start.

Charts and Graphs

You can create charts in all of the major Office applications. Word and PowerPoint have a button on the Standard toolbar for inserting a Microsoft Graph object (in Word it's the Chart button, in PowerPoint it's the Graph button), and Access has a wizard to help you create a Graph object. If you are graphing a simple set of numbers, such as summary statistics, and you don't mind entering the data in a Graph worksheet, Graph is a useful tool. In Word, you can also use data in a Word table to generate the graph, and in Access you can use the data in a table or a query to create the graph.

Graph does have its limitations. You cannot do any number crunching in the graph worksheet and you must be willing to accept Graph's limited formatting choices. If the data is complex, and especially if you need to manipulate it, you should create the chart in Excel. You can leave the chart in Excel for printing or for presenting in another form, or you can insert it into Word, PowerPoint, or Access. Excel charts also give you more control of chart formatting than Graph does, so you can create a customized presentation of the data.

POWER CHARTING

If you want complete control of the way your graph looks in PowerPoint, you can paste an Excel chart as a picture into PowerPoint, double-click the chart to convert it to a PowerPoint object, and then use PowerPoint's drawing tools to modify the chart.

Wizards

Wizards have found their way into all of the major Office applications, and they are earning their keep. Their purpose, in every case, is to help you get results in a hurry. They do nothing that you could not do otherwise (more slowly) by using the commands and options available in the application interface, but they transport you down the road in a great leap by offering you fewer choices. You make a couple of key decisions, and presto, you have a cover sheet for your fax or a design for your presentation or an inventory form. Generally, you'll want to make further modifications, but the sizable head start is valuable.

WIZARD

A *wizard* is a tool that telescopes a potentially complex process into a series of friendly windows that present only the essential choices. You trade your control of the details for speed and some good professional judgments on what works for most people most of the time.

Wizards and templates are closely related, as you'll see in this section and in the next one. In fact, one way that wizards cut corners is to rely on templates, most notably in PowerPoint and Access. If a template can be modified—and most of them can be—the wizard is altered in the process.

Word Wizards

You can select any of the Word wizards in the New dialog box. By default, they all create a document using the Normal document template but define the styles to reflect the choices you make as you progress through the wizard windows. Notice, however, that in the New dialog box you can specify that the wizard result be either a normal document file or a template file.

Wizard	Description
Agenda	Creates a meeting agenda and a form for taking notes on accomplishments and decisions; a range of formats from modern to traditional.
Award	Creates an award or a certificate with a title and other information you supply; a range of styles in either landscape or portrait orientation.
Calendar	Creates monthly calendars for the months and years you specify; a range of styles in either landscape or portrait orientation. Also gives you the option of inserting a picture for each month.
Fax	Creates a fax cover sheet that you can customize with your name, address, and phone numbers; a range of styles in either landscape or portrait orientation.
Letter	Creates a letter—business or personal—using the name and address information you supply for yourself and for the recipient; a range of styles for letterhead or plain paper. Also provides prewritten business letters for many common situations, such as requests for credit reports or notifications of price increases.
Memo	Helps you design a customized memo with a list of recipients in the heading or on a separate cover sheet; a variety of styles and headings.
Newsletter	Creates an attractive single-column or multicolumn layout for a newsletter; a range of standard elements in classic or modern style.
Pleading	Creates a legal pleading; fine-tuning options include line numbers and spacing, vertical lines on the left and right sides of the page, and various box styles for plaintiff/defendant identification.
Resume	Creates a résumé tailored to your experience and objectives; a variety of headings and styles. Includes the option (at conclusion of wizard) to launch the Letter Wizard to create a résumé cover letter.
Table	Creates a professional-looking table with a variety of layouts and an assortment of typical column headings; a range of format options (using AutoFormat).

An Example Using the Newsletter Wizard   The Newsletter Wizard is typical of the wizards in Word. To select it, choose File New and highlight *Newslttr Wizard* in the Template list, as shown here. (More on templates in the next section.)

Click OK in the New dialog box to move to the first step of the Newsletter Wizard. You can create a newsletter format that has a Classic look or a Modern look. To compare the two, click the option button that is currently deselected. The preview box changes to show you the alternate look. Click Next after you've indicated which one you prefer.

In the next step, shown at the top of the facing page, you decide how many text columns you want across the page. In Word, you can make the columns different widths, but that's typically too refined for a wizard. Here, the three columns are of equal width. You make the basic choices in the wizard; refinements can come later. Remember that you can try selecting each option to see how the preview changes. Click Next after you've made your choice. Notice that you can also go back to the previous steps by clicking the Back button.

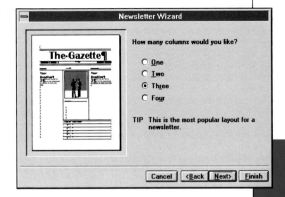

In the remaining steps, you make choices about the name of the newsletter, its probable length, and the items you want to include. In the last window, click Finish to have Word create a new document that has the characteristics you chose. The document is not yet saved. Examine the layout, make changes if you like, and then save the file.

If you want to use the file as a template for subsequent editions of your newsletter instead of rerunning the wizard every time, be sure to save the file as a template (instead of as a Word document) in the Save As dialog box.

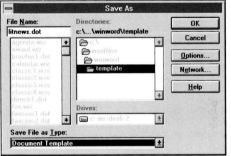

You can save the result of the wizard as a document or as a template. Here, it is saved as a template.

When you want to create a new document for your first edition, select your new newsletter template in the Template list in the New dialog box.

Excel Wizards

In Excel, wizards focus on simplifying common but complicated tasks within a workbook, such as charting or creating pivot tables. Most of the wizards start automatically when you choose the corresponding menu commands; you can also initiate them by clicking the corresponding toolbar buttons.

Wizard	Description
Chart	Leads you through the process of creating a chart.
Function	Helps you use a function correctly by displaying the syntax and prompting you for the arguments; gives you direct access to online Help for the chosen function.
PivotTable	Guides you through the steps for creating and modifying a pivot table.
Tip	Provides tips about using commands and buttons, and suggests efficient ways of executing the most recently used procedures.

PIVOTAL BUTTON

The toolbar button for the PivotTable Wizard is located on the Query and Pivot toolbar. If you use the wizard frequently, you can place the button on the Standard toolbar or create a custom toolbar especially for your stable of hot commands (and styles and macros and whatever else). To modify a toolbar, choose Toolbars from the View menu and click the Customize button. The PivotTable Wizard is in the Data category. Select Data, and then drag the button from the dialog box to the spot on the toolbar you want it to occupy.

Among the Excel wizards listed on the preceding page, the TipWizard is unique because it doesn't lead you through a task; instead, it comments on actions you perform to suggest a more direct or efficient way to accomplish the task. For example, if you regularly type a series of dates as column headings, the TipWizard might suggest that you use AutoFill next time. The Tip-Wizard gives you a particular tip only once during an Excel session. During subsequent sessions, it gives you the same tip only if you perform the associated action three times.

An Example Using the Function Wizard If you've been unadventurous in experimenting with Excel functions, the Function Wizard is a valuable way to expand your range. You can use it to find the right function for a certain task; it walks you through the process of supplying arguments, with online Help near at hand. Consider a situation in which you want to create a payment schedule for a four-year car loan.

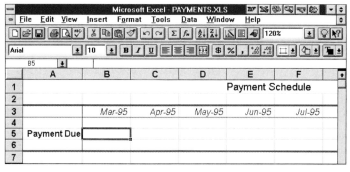

You know there must be a function for this purpose, but you don't know off the top of your head what it is. Highlight the cell that will contain the formula, as shown above. (You can copy it across the row later.) Click the Function Wizard button, and in the first step of the Function Wizard, select the Financial category to look for the function you need. As you click the different functions in the Function Name list, the wizard gives a brief description of the highlighted function. *PMT* looks like the one you're looking for.

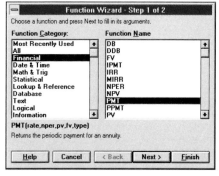

Click Next to move to the second step, which shows the arguments, neatly stacked in the order in which you must supply them. As you move down the list, the wizard cues you with a

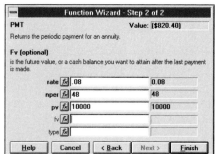

description of the current argument and tells you whether the argument is required or optional. After you provide the required amounts, you see the value of the function in the upper right box: $820.40! Seems too high for a monthly payment on $10,000 at 8 percent, doesn't it?

FUNCTION HELP

A quick way to get online Help for a function that is already in a cell is to select the cell and then click the Function Wizard button. The Function Wizard starts in editing mode for the function. Click the Help button to get the information you need.

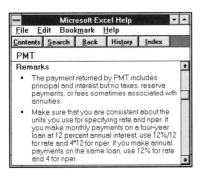

Click the Help button. Help, endearingly context sensitive, displays the reference entry for the PMT function. You read about the optional arguments, but they don't apply. Aha—a telling comment in the Remarks section: "Make sure that you are consistent about the units you use for specifying rate and nper." Just so. You've supplied the rate of interest annually and the number of periods in months.

Close Help, fix the rate argument in step 2 (.08/12), and check the new result: $244.13. That's more like it. Click Finish to conclude the wizard. If the cell!

was properly formatted beforehand, you're looking at the correct result. You can use AutoFill to copy the cell value across the row, as shown here.

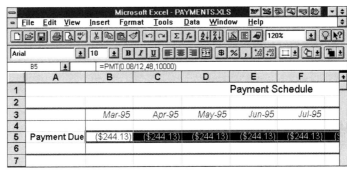

PowerPoint Wizards

PowerPoint has two prominent wizards: the AutoContent Wizard and the Pick a Look Wizard. Both are neatly integrated into the program and are available when you start PowerPoint. Each can also be launched using a menu command.

Wizard	Description
AutoContent	Creates a generic outline for a presentation, based on the presentation objective you specify.
Pick a Look	Helps you choose a template for your presentation and identify its major components.

To jump-start a presentation, you can't do much better than the AutoContent Wizard. It's available in the PowerPoint dialog box when you first start PowerPoint, and also in the New Presentation dialog box, which you can display using the File New command. The wizard itself is brief: It directs you

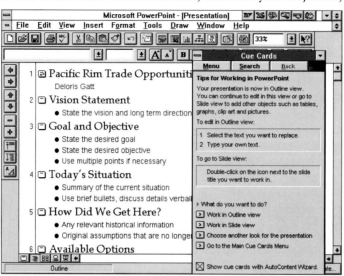

The AutoContent Wizard provides a generic outline that you can use as a starting point for your presentation.

to one of six basic content schemes, based on your objective, and it launches you (with Cue Cards at your side) into a generic presentation in Outline view. You decide what you want to do from there, relying on the Cue Cards for as long as you want them.

Start the Pick a Look Wizard from the Format menu to work on an existing presentation, or select it in the PowerPoint dialog box or the New Presentation dialog box if you want to begin working on a presentation by shopping for a look. Like the AutoContent Wizard, the Pick a Look Wizard asks a few basic questions about the medium and components of the presentation and lets you browse (and preview) a full range of corresponding template styles. (See the illustration on the facing page.)

Access Wizards

For a relatively new database product, Access has enjoyed rapid and wide distribution. Aimed at a broad category of users, it has provided many people with their first experience of using a full-featured relational database management system. Perhaps in response to legions of new users, Access includes a long list of new task-simplifying features: wizards, builders, and add-ins. Of these, wizards tend to be the most accessible and self-explanatory. Builders, in general, address more technical needs than wizards do—the Expression Builder, as you'll see later, helps you assemble an expression (much as you would put together an Excel formula) with minimal assistance. Add-ins guide you through activities that extend Access in some fashion—to import tables from outside the current database, for example.

As you can see from the partial list of Access wizards, which appears later in this section, the wizards help you create basic database objects quickly by raising crucial design issues and simplifying your choices. As you work with the wizards, look out for the Hint button, which often reveals useful supplementary information.

The Pick a Look Wizard recommends one of four standard visual styles and gives you access to the full catalog of templates, if you prefer to browse.

Wizard	Description
Control	Guides you in adding controls, such as list boxes and combo boxes, to a form or a report (in Design view). A wizard does not exist for every control. Adding a graph summons a wizard of its own.
Form	Creates a form based on the fields in a table or a query; there are different Form Wizards for different types of forms—Single-Column, Tabular, Graph, and so on. When you finish, you can view and add data immediately, or you can tweak the controls in Design view.
Input Mask	Creates an input mask (as a field property) when you are working on a form in Design view. Use the Builder button to start the wizard (strange but true).
Query	Creates a query. You choose a query type—Crosstab, Find Duplicates, Find Unmatched, or Archive—to start one of the four wizards.
Report	Creates reports of different types. There are, in fact, many Report Wizards—one for Single-Column reports, another for Mailing Labels, and so on. One wizard is provided expressly for mail merging with a Word document.
Table	Creates a table by letting you choose predefined fields from an assortment of sample tables (either business or personal). When you finish, you can add data to the table or have the Form Wizard create a form for you to use to enter the data.

As you work with Access, look for the Builder button. Unlike Access wizards, which slice through complex design processes, builders help you complete a task, such as putting together an expression or inserting a field into an existing table. Typically, they don't simplify the choices so much as they march you through them in a structured way. You can launch the Expression Builder, for example, from a location in which an expression is appropriate. In some cases—beside certain properties, for instance—you'll find a Builder button to launch it. In other cases, such as the Field cell or Criteria cell in a query, you choose Build from the shortcut menu.

Two ways to start the Expression Builder.

In the Expression Builder window, you see at the start any expression that already exists in the box. The builder helps you create or add to an expression by browsing field names (thereby identifying them accurately) or by selecting constants, functions, and operators in lists (or by clicking quick-access buttons). You benefit from the accuracy that comes from browsing (in place of your own recall) and from the chance to explore new functions and operators, backed up by online Help.

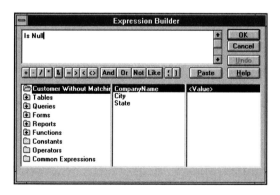

Most of the other builders are useful for developing AccessBasic routines—coding projects that are beyond the scope of this book. At their best, however, the builders help to make those jobs less formidable, so look for them as you expand your skills and ambitions.

Among the add-ins, be sure to notice the Attachment Manager command and the Import Database command. They're particularly useful if you want Access to interact with tables or databases outside the current file. As you can see in the Power Play below ("Customizing an Access Wizard"), Add-in Manager is also useful if you want to customize a wizard.

POWER PLAY

Customizing an Access Wizard

Access wizards reside in special databases, called library databases, which are loaded when you start the program. Although you can't open a library database in the same way that you can a regular database, you can customize several of the wizards contained in these libraries. For example, you can change the table names, field names, and properties of the sample tables listed in the Table Wizard. You can also make changes to some of the Form Wizards and Report Wizards and to the Input Mask Wizard.

To customize a wizard, follow these steps:

1. Open any database.

2. From the File menu, choose Add-ins, and then choose Add-in Manager from the submenu.

3. In the Add-in Manager dialog box, select the library containing the wizard you want to customize, and then click the Customize button. (The button is unavailable if the library isn't customizable.) For example, select Table Wizard to edit one of the sample tables or to add a table of your own. Or select Control and Property Wizards to customize a default input mask—to change the mask for phone extensions from five characters to four, for instance.

4. Choose a specific item or action —Customize Tables, for example, or Customize Input Mask.

5. Make your changes in the dialog box or form that appears. If you're working in a form, notice that you can select a different record or a blank record using the controls at the bottom of the window. When you finish, click OK or Close, or double-click the Control-menu box.

Templates

Templates play a role in the Office suite, but they are not equally conspicuous in every application. Wherever they appear, they represent models, or patterns, for documents or components of documents. You use a copy of the template as a starting point for your own document.

Often, as you've already seen, templates are closely related to wizards and even interact with them. In PowerPoint, for example, the Pick a Look Wizard can spin you off into the Presentation Template dialog box if you want to browse through all of the available looks.

Without trying to cover all of the templates that figure in the Office suite, let's go through the applications again and highlight strategic ways that you can use or modify templates.

Word Templates

Typically, a Word template reflects a set of preparations you might make if you want to optimize your Word settings to produce a certain kind of document, such as a letter or a brochure. You might create styles for the predictable text elements, define a certain header or footer, set up margins and tabs, customize the toolbars, establish a set of AutoText entries, and perhaps develop macros for toolbar buttons. You might even enter certain text elements if you regularly insert them in documents of a certain type. All of these components might belong to a given template.

To protect your template files, Word assigns them a DOT extension and routinely saves them in the TEMPLATE subdirectory of your primary Word directory. As a result, you are less likely to open templates directly and change them accidentally, although they are completely editable if you want to alter them. When you want to use a template, you select it in the New dialog box (just as you would select a wizard). Word then creates a new document that uses the template as a model (for all the settings we just noted); it does not open the template directly. If you don't specify a template, Word uses one anyway: the Normal template (NORMAL.DOT), which, you can edit like any of the others. (See the Power Play on the facing page.)

Exploring Word Templates   When you create a new document with a given template, you might not—at first glance—notice anything special about it. Sometimes the margins or the tab settings are different from the Normal template, but most of the customizations are not floating about at the surface and are not obvious. The Style command and the Style Gallery command on the Format menu are good tools for visualizing the look of a template. Each command has a preview box that shows the various elements with their

STYLE SAMPLES

Among the AutoText entries for most Word templates (but not for the Normal template) you'll find Gallery Example and Gallery Style Samples. Try inserting the Gallery Example entry (preferably in a blank Word document) to study a sample document in detail. In many cases, you'll get a better idea of the appearance by switching to Layout view or printing the sample.

assigned formatting. The Style Gallery is especially useful because it can show your current document, a specially created example, or a set of style samples. The reduced text in the preview box is not always clear enough to be conclusive, however.

When a Template Is Really a Form Word offers a toolbar for creating electronic forms that contain drop-down lists, check boxes, and other information-gathering controls. When you create a form, you begin by opening a new document template—this makes any AutoText entries and macros available to users of the form. Then you enter text and insert the form fields to build the form itself. You can specify formatting for the text in certain fields or assign data types or default values to the fields.

At the end of the process, you use the Protect Document command on the Tools menu to protect the content of the form; this command allows users to fill in the fields only.

SAMPLE FORM

To see a sample form, create a new Word document with either the Invoice template or the Purchord (purchase order) template.

POWER PLAY

Who's to Say What's Normal, Anyway?

In Word, the Normal template, NORMAL.DOT, is the default template for new documents you create. If you click the New button on the Standard toolbar, you don't even pass the New dialog box on the way: You simply find yourself looking at a blank document created with the Normal template.

NORMAL.DOT is not an elaborate template—it's pretty bland, really: The styles are minimal and the other settings are geared for the most common circumstances of editing and printing. What if you want to shake up this situation—add some styles you invariably need or substitute different template, say Manual1, for the default?

If you want to change the properties of the Normal template, you can do so easily. But be careful: Changing NORMAL.DOT has global consequences; the changes affect the working environment for all documents. To

retain the original template, create a copy named EXNORMAL.DOT or copy the original to another directory. Having a copy might be valuable when you want to create a new template because Word will, by default, base it on your soon-to-be-customized NORMAL.DOT.

To make changes, use the File Open command to open NORMAL.DOT—not a document modeled after it, but the file itself—and alter it directly. You can add or modify styles, revise toolbars and menus, create macros, define AutoText entries, and so on. Use the Organizer (from the File Templates command or the Format Styles command) to borrow elements from other templates. If you simply want to replace NORMAL.DOT with another template, rename the replacement or copy it to NORMAL.DOT (after you've made a backup).

DOT TO DOT

AutoCorrect entries are saved as part of your NORMAL.DOT file. To transfer your entries to another machine, copy NORMAL.DOT to the second machine (in the TEMPLATE subdirectory of your Word program directory).

Excel Templates

Like Word, Excel uses templates as document patterns. You first create a template—say, to provide a refinancing analysis for a home mortgage—and then you create a workbook from the template each time you want to help a customer weigh the benefits of a prospective deal. When you save a workbook as a template, Excel gives it an XLT extension. To use the template, you open it as you would open any Excel workbook—Excel creates a new file patterned after the template and keeps the original intact.

PowerPoint Templates

As you've seen, PowerPoint provides a rich set of templates as a central feature of the product. The templates are almost always at hand. In most PowerPoint views, you can click the Template button at the bottom right of the screen to choose among the presentation templates. You'll find, as you explore the TEMPLATE directory, that PowerPoint provides a different version of each template for electronic slides, color overheads (transparencies), and black-and-white overheads.

When you start a new presentation, PowerPoint uses the template for the default presentation, DEFAULT.PPT, which is located in your main Power-Point directory (not in TEMPLATE). You can change the default template by opening DEFAULT.PPT and attaching a different template to it, presumably a template from one of the TEMPLATE subdirectories. You can also make any of your own presentations the default file by copying it to DEFAULT.PPT. In any case, note that PowerPoint will use only the template from the default presentation, not its contents (if it holds any).

Access Templates

Although templates might not seem to be prominent features of Access, much of the application's ease of use depends on templates. The various wizards, as they prompt you through the creation of objects such as tables, forms, and reports, present samples you can choose and modify to produce your own objects. These samples function, in fact, as templates. They serve as patterns for the objects you create. (Even fields have templates of a sort that define the properties they possess by default.) And as you saw in the Power Play a few pages back ("Customizing an Access Wizard"), you can include additional samples (templates) or modify the existing ones using Add-in Manager.

Use Add-in Manager to add, remove, or modify templates in Access.

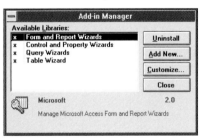

AutoFormat

One of the least complicated ways to get results in a hurry in Word and Excel is to use the AutoFormat command. AutoFormat runs through your document or the selected block, analyzes its content, and then formats the elements it detects. The result is generally a significant advance—especially if you are starting with largely unformatted text.

Word's AutoFormat command has applied heading, text, and list styles; used smart quotes; and even replaced two hyphens with an em dash.

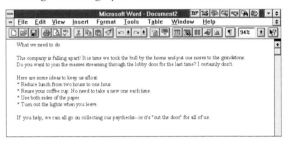

AutoFormat: Word Documents

To get an idea of the formatting changes you can effect with Word's AutoFormat command, choose AutoFormat from the Format menu. In the AutoFormat dialog box, click Options to display the AutoFormat tab of the Options dialog box and review the many ways you can customize the command's behavior. To start, you can prevent AutoFormat from changing styles that you have already applied. Then you can decide which elements in the text you want Word to apply styles to—such as headings, lists, and other paragraphs (body text or a letter salutation, for example). AutoFormat also follows a set of rules to adjust spacing and to replace symbol characters and plain punctuation with more polished-looking symbols and marks. The important thing to note is that you can control each item so that AutoFormat does a lot or a little—whichever makes it truly useful to you or your organization.

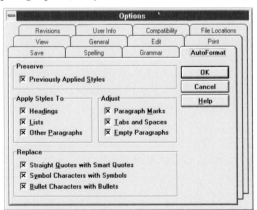

AutoFormat gives you the option of reviewing each formatting change it suggests and either accepting or rejecting the change. You should routinely review the changes—and work with selections rather than entire documents—while you learn how AutoFormat analyzes the styles that a document needs. Even so, you might be grateful that Undo can reverse automatic formatting in one clean sweep.

SET IT ON AUTO

AutoFormat is only one of several Auto commands. These commands range from AutoSave in Word and Excel, which automatically saves documents at preset intervals, to AutoDialer in Access, which dials the number in the current field. Search for *auto* in online Help for any application to see what effort-saving features you can discover. Most of them are easy to use.

AutoFormat: Word and Excel Tables

Word has a cousin of AutoFormat, designed especially for tables, which closely resembles the AutoFormat feature in Excel. In Word, you can't use Table AutoFormat unless the insertion point lies within a table or you're using the Insert Table command (on the Table menu) to create a table. In Excel, AutoFormat is not available unless you first select a block of cells for it to act on or select a non-blank cell. If you select a single cell that contains some data, Excel assumes that the table to be formatted is composed of contiguously filled cells, and it automatically selects and formats a block bounded by blank cells.

When you choose the AutoFormat command (from the Table menu in Word, from the Format menu in Excel), you see a dialog box that previews each of a long list of table formats. For tables and spreadsheets, as for Word documents, you can set options to limit the changes that the command makes automatically. The AutoFormat options in Excel, shown here, are similar to

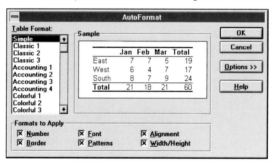

the options for table formatting in Word. (Click Options to display the set of options at the bottom of the dialog box.) The check boxes let you limit the command's formatting changes to any combination of six categories.

Chapter 5

Office Connections

Data Is for Sharing

This chapter gets to the heart of the Microsoft Office integration features: techniques that blur the boundaries between one application and another. The veterans of information sharing are Cut, Copy, and Paste. In Office, as throughout Microsoft Windows, these commands let you transfer selected information from one file to another using the Windows Clipboard. With drag and drop, you can even bypass the Clipboard by dragging a selection within a document or from one document to another. At the new location, you simply drop the selected information (or a copy of the information) to paste it.

Information sharing takes on new meaning with OLE. This chapter sorts out the special kinds of pasting that enable you to move information as an *object* so that it remains editable in its original format. We'll look at linking and embedding, and you'll learn exactly what those terms mean (likewise a handful of other OLE terms they run with). Along the way, you'll get some practical insight into the attractions of OLE.

OLE involves pain as well as gain, but linking and embedding are worth the trouble. In fact, the overview in this chapter will prepare you for the scenarios coming up in Part 3 of this book, "Where's the Meeting?" Invest some time now, and you'll benefit later from the convenience and the time savings that OLE can provide.

The picture of information sharing is incomplete without a discussion of importing and exporting, techniques by which entire files move from one application to another. In the best of circumstances, the move is flawless: All of the information in the file survives the crossing, and you can use the tools of the destination application to edit the information as if it had originated there.

Moving and Copying Information

There's still a role for Cut, Copy, and Paste. Sure, OLE offers new techniques for transferring information, but they aren't meant to replace the simplicity and convenience of ordinary cutting, copying, and pasting. At least not in most cases. Later in this chapter, we'll compare pasting with linking and embedding, but for now, let's run through the highlights of the basic Cut, Copy, and Paste procedures.

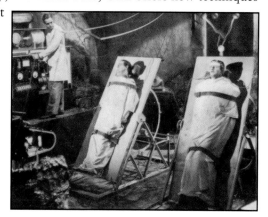

Pull down the Edit menu in any Office application, and you'll probably see some grayed-out (unavailable) commands. The Paste command is not available until you've used Cut or Copy to place information on the Clipboard, and neither Cut nor Copy is available until you've defined a selection. So let's begin with selecting.

Selecting

You're probably familiar with selecting text—in Microsoft Word or elsewhere. You drag over the area you want to select, which then appears highlighted. Alternatively, you can hold down the Shift key and then move the insertion point—with the keyboard or the mouse—to select a block.

The same techniques work in other Office applications, and the various programs have additional shortcuts of

Cut (or Copy) and Paste

Cutting or copying information to the Clipboard and then pasting it to a new location is easy to do.

1. Select the block to be cut or copied. Starting at the top left or bottom right of the block, drag with the mouse (or hold down the Shift key and press the arrow keys). The selected area is highlighted.
2. Choose the Cut or Copy command from the Edit menu or click the Cut or Copy button on the Standard toolbar. You can also use the shortcut keys Ctrl+X to cut or Ctrl+C to copy. The information is placed on the Clipboard.
3. Move to the location where you want to insert the Clipboard contents or highlight the text or cells you want the inserted information to replace.
4. Choose the Paste command from the Edit menu or click the Paste button on the Standard toolbar. You can also use the shortcut keys Ctrl+V to paste. The Clipboard contents appear at the new location and replace any text or cells you highlighted. You can reuse the Clipboard contents until you quit your Windows session or replace the Clipboard contents with another selection.

their own. As you explore the range of editing situations, you'll run into certain variations and complications.

If you're editing tabular information, you can select within a cell or you can select multiple cells, but not both. For a fairly restrictive example of this behavior, experiment with a Microsoft Excel worksheet. You'll find two distinct levels of selecting. When you double-click a cell to edit the text, you can select one or more characters within the cell. While you are in this editing mode, you cannot select multiple cells—you have to finish editing the contents of the cell first. When you are not actively editing the contents of a cell, you can drag to select a block of cells, but you cannot select part of a cell.

You can also select objects, such as graphics, embedded tables, and linked charts. You cannot select part of an object—the entire object is selected when you click it. Different applications have different rules for selecting when both text and objects are involved. In Excel, for example, you can select text or you can select an object, but you cannot select both. In Word, however, you can include both text and objects in a selection by dragging over all the items you want included in the selection. And even in the same application, some of the rules differ for text and objects.

In Word, if you double-click anywhere in a word, the word is selected. But if you double-click an object, something entirely different happens: The source application for the object (or another application that has been designated as the editor for the object) might start, or some other feature specific to the object, such as a sound recording, might be triggered.

Cutting or Copying

After you create a selection, you indicate the action you want to take. To cut or copy the selection, you basically have three choices: using drag and drop, using the Edit menu commands, or using keyboard shortcuts. You can choose whichever you prefer, but some techniques fit certain situations better than others.

Using Drag and Drop   Drag and drop works best when you want to move or copy a small block of text to a new location that is already visible on the screen. (It's riskier if you have to scroll to a more distant location—it's easy to drop information accidentally.) The technique is wonderfully simple: Within the highlighted selection, the mouse pointer changes to an arrow; you move the selection by dragging it to a new location. You hold down the Ctrl key while you drag if you want to copy rather than move the selection.

Don't forget that you can juxtapose widely separated parts of a document by using commands on the Window menu. In Word, you can split the window horizontally by using the Split command—or by simply dragging the split bar

SELECTING WITH F8

In Word and Excel, you can simply press F8, rather than hold down the Shift key, to make a selection using the keyboard. Press Esc to get out of the selection mode.

GET A GRIP

In Excel, the mouse pointer changes to an arrow (for dragging the selected cells) when you move the mouse pointer to the border of the selection.

(the black rectangle above the vertical scroll bar). In Word and Microsoft PowerPoint, you can collapse a document or a presentation to its headings in Outline view and then drag and drop whole sections to reshuffle the headings.

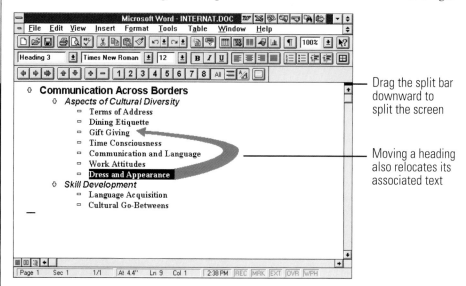

Drag the split bar downward to split the screen

Moving a heading also relocates its associated text

In Excel, you can split a worksheet horizontally or vertically; if you want to drag and drop selected cells across the divider, you must also use the Freeze Panes command. Freeze Panes, also on the Window menu, prevents scrolling of the rows and columns above and to the left of a specified cell (whichever cell is highlighted when you choose the command).

You can also use drag and drop between two documents, whether they were created with the same Office application or with different ones. When you use drag and drop within a single application, it moves or copies in the normal way. Tiling two windows (using Arrange or Arrange All from the Window menu) often makes the procedure more practical; even so, the Clipboard method is usually more convenient.

Using drag and drop between Office applications is not always what you'd expect. It's not possible in all circumstances, and when it is possible, it's not always a matter of simple cut and paste. Instead, it can involve a special variation of the Paste command, which is described later in this chapter, in the section titled "How to Embed."

Using the Clipboard   Apart from the abundance of ways to move information to and from the Clipboard, there's little to say about the process itself. The Clipboard has been a part of Windows from very early on. In addition to choosing the Cut and Copy commands from the Edit menu, you can click the

Cut or Copy button on the Standard toolbar. From the keyboard, Ctrl+X and Ctrl+C have become standard shortcuts in the Office applications for cutting and copying information to the Clipboard.

In Word, notice that Cut and Paste have special, optional properties that make for rapid text editing. The program calls these properties "Smart Cut and Paste" because Word anticipates the spacing between words and next to punctuation marks and automatically corrects many of the annoyingly common errors that are introduced during editing. Note that the smart behavior applies to drag and drop as well as to the Cut, Copy, and Paste commands.

Suppose you select a word or a phrase in a sentence, cut or copy it, and then paste it to a new location. Prior to Smart Cut and Paste, it was easy to foul up the spacing when you pasted the word or the phrase—you'd end up with no space preceding it and two spaces after it, or something like that. Or perhaps you'd cut a word at the end of a sentence and end up with an extra space in front of the period. Smart Cut and Paste helps you avoid these situations.

SMART IS OPTIONAL

If you are editing a Word document for which the usual rules for selecting and pasting do not apply, you can cancel Smart Cut and Paste by choosing the Options command from the Tools menu and deselecting the appropriate check box on the Edit tab of the Options dialog box. On the same tab, notice the Automatic Word Selection option, which selects the entire word if you drag across part of it. In the right circumstances, this can save you a lot of time, but if it cramps your work style, leave it turned off.

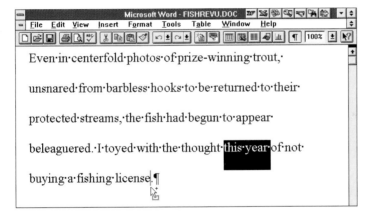

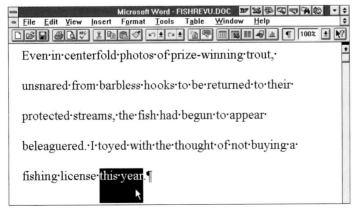

In Word, Smart Cut and Paste adjusts the spacing between words when you drop text at a new location.

POWER PLAY

Preserving the Clipboard Contents

The information on the Clipboard is usually invisible to you. You see it when you paste the information somewhere, or you can see it by opening the Clipboard Viewer—available from Program Manager in the Main program group. If you copy information to the Clipboard that you want to preserve, you should learn which actions do and don't affect it. Basically, you can take most actions safely—except exiting Windows or using the Cut or Copy command with a new selection.

Drag and drop sidesteps the Clipboard. This is easy to demonstrate. First, copy some text to the Clipboard (select the text and press Ctrl+C). Then drag and drop a different selection. Next, paste the selection from the Clipboard to somewhere nearby. The Clipboard is not affected by the drag-and-drop action; it still produces the text you copied to it originally.

Deleting information—with the Del key, the Backspace key, or the Clear command—does not involve the Clipboard either. Unlike the Cut command, deleting simply erases the information, with no effect on the Clipboard.

In addition, Word has a command called Spike that strings together a series of text blocks that you cut from a document. (Picture one of those spikes next to a cash register, on which your restaurant bill is impaled.) When you use the Clipboard, any information that you cut or copy replaces whatever was there already. The Spike collects the information you cut to it (the Spike command always cuts; it doesn't copy) in a sequence of paragraphs. To circumvent the Clipboard's one-entry limitation, the Spike uses Word's AutoText feature instead of the Clipboard.

To move text or graphics to the Spike, select the first block and then press Ctrl+F3. Continue adding selections from one or more Word documents. When you are ready to retrieve the contents of the Spike, press Shift+Ctrl+F3. This command also clears the contents of the Spike. To paste the information that the Spike contains without clearing it, type spike and choose the AutoText command. Remember that the Spike is a Word feature: Its contents are available only to Word documents.

Linking and Embedding: An Object Lesson

Beyond simple cutting, copying, and pasting, you come to OLE territory. You might think of linking and embedding as *dynamic* forms of cutting, copying, and pasting. How so? Well, these OLE techniques let you create *compound documents:* Inside the destination document, the inserted information takes the form of an object that is dynamic—you can still edit it in its original application.

If you paste the contents of an Excel worksheet into a Word document in the normal manner, for example, the values become relatively static—editable as table entries in Word, but no longer chartable or recalculable, as they are in Excel. But if you paste the same contents into a Word document as an Excel object, it retains its identity as Excel information. It emigrates, but it doesn't change its citizenship: The worksheet information is still Excel data that responds to Excel commands.

All the major Office applications can function as destination applications. That is, their documents can contain objects inserted from other applications. However, only Word, Excel, and PowerPoint can create objects that you can insert in a destination document. Microsoft Access is the key exception: You cannot place an Access object in another Office document. You can transfer information from Access to other applications in a number of ways, but not as an Access object that is editable with Access in its new location.

Beyond the major applications, you might wonder about the lesser Office applications: the shared applications. Their situation is opposite to that of Access: They can create and edit objects, but they can't usually function as destinations for objects. Accordingly, you can insert a WordArt object in a document, but the WordArt object can't serve as a container for objects from other applications.

So where do linking and embedding fit into this picture of dynamic cutting and pasting? Linking and embedding are different ways in which a pasted object remains dynamic. They differ simply in the location of the information. Linked information is represented in but remains separate from the compound document; embedded information is actually located in the compound document. Although they are often mentioned together, linking and embedding are quite different. An object is either linked or it's embedded, not both and not something in between. Some objects can only be linked, other objects can only be embedded, and still other objects can be either linked or embedded, depending on your needs. Let's take a look at linking and embedding one at a time.

Linking establishes a connection by which information in a source file can be displayed at another location, a destination document. The chief advantage to linking is that you can update a single document and OLE sees to it that the linked locations—one or many—reflect your changes.

Embedding is a special way of pasting that inserts information in a destination document as if it were a separate minidocument. The embedded object might

OBJECT

An *object* is a self-contained entity that combines information with behavior. A Microsoft WordArt object, for example, conveys information as text characters, but the characters also know how to stretch and twist in ways that in most other applications they cannot. Even stricter senses of the word "object" exist, as in "object-oriented programming," but we can afford to let those sleeping dogs lie.

be a transplanted copy from another document, or it might be created expressly to reside within its destination document. When activated, the embedded object is dynamic—you can work with it as a full-blown data file from its source application.

For both linked and embedded objects, the source application must be available when you edit the object, but when you edit a linked object, you are actually opening a file that is distinct from the compound document.

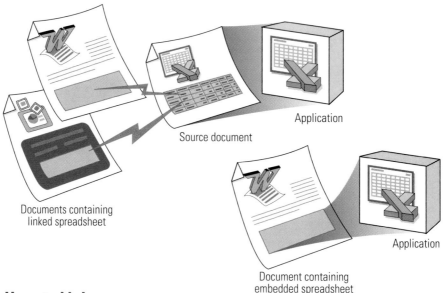

Documents containing
linked spreadsheet

Source document

Application

Document containing
embedded spreadsheet

Application

How to Link

Linking and embedding are not difficult to accomplish. The basic techniques do not vary significantly from one situation to another, but the details do—and the details often matter. In this chapter, we'll stay focused on the basic techniques. Part 3 of this book—"Where's the Meeting?"—goes into the details for each major Office application and suggests some information-sharing possibilities that you might not have considered.

Let's start with linking, which is in some ways the more straightforward process. Remember that you create a link between two files: an information source and a destination document. You can represent the linked document as an icon, or you can define the specific information in the source document that becomes visible as an object in the destination document.

You usually initiate the link from the source document. Open the document and select the information that you want visible in the destination document. The selection might simply be text, or it might be a graphic, or it might include both. The selection might even include another object—it could be a Word document that contains a chart or a WordArt object.

Copy the selection to the Clipboard by pressing Ctrl+C. (Don't use the Cut command: Eliminating the information from the source that you are attempting to present by means of the link is completely counterproductive—like withdrawing the funds from your checking account and then writing a check.)

Switch to the destination document and move the insertion point or the pointer to where you want the linked object to appear. From the Edit menu, choose Paste Special to display its dialog box. The exact contents of the box varies with the current application and the object on the Clipboard.

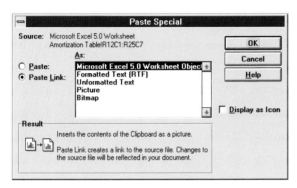

Select the Paste Link option button. (Paste is usually the default.) Then highlight the object type you want in the As list box. The Result section, below the list box, gives a brief description to help you verify that the transfer will have the characteristics you want. Pay attention to these object types—the default choice is not always the one you want. The type of object you select influences the format in which the information is presented. As long as the link exists, you'll be able to edit the information (in the source file) in its native format—with the changes reflected in your destination document.

PASTE AND PASTE LINK

If the Paste Link option button is not available in the Paste Special dialog box, the object you copied cannot be linked to your destination document. But you can still include the object in the document by selecting the Paste button and embedding the object.

CHANGING ICONS

Some applications provide a small selection of icons that you can choose from—generally, these are bound right into the program. If you do not see an appropriate icon in the Change Icon dialog box, click the Browse button, select a Windows executable file, such as CLIPBRD.EXE, and click OK. Generally, you'll find one or more icons you can borrow.

Linking an Object

Linking usually begins with the source application. Start by displaying on your screen the information you want to link.

1. Select the information that will appear at the linked location in the destination document.
2. Copy the selection to the Clipboard.
3. Open the destination document and choose Paste Special from the Edit menu. The destination application displays the Paste Special dialog box.
4. In the dialog box, select the Paste Link option button, select an object type in the list, and select the Display as Icon check box if you want the compound document to show the linked information as an icon only. Click OK to establish the link.

Next, select the Display as Icon check box if you want the linked file to be represented as an icon in the destination document. If you do not select this option, the object will appear as it did in the source document. When this option is selected, the dialog box displays another button, Change Icon, which lets you specify a different icon and description to represent the link.

Finally, click OK to create the link. If you do nothing to break the link, whenever you open the destination document the application will look for this linked file.

QUICKER UPDATES

In Word and Power-Point, you can update a manual link quickly by selecting the object and choosing Update Links from the shortcut menu.

CAN'T BUY AN UPDATE

If you've made changes to a source document but those changes aren't reflected at a linked destination, check the Links dialog box. If the link is manual, click the Update Now button or change the link to automatic to force the information to be updated.

The Ins and Outs of Links

When you create a link, the destination application usually sets it up by default to update automatically. This means that the linked information in a destination file is updated whenever information is added or changed in the source document. If the destination file is closed, the update occurs the next time you open it. You can change this default and modify the link in other ways using the Links command on the Edit menu. The Links command is unavailable (grayed-out) unless the current file contains a link.

Modifying a Link   Take a look at the Links dialog box from Excel, shown here. Manual updating is available if you want the information to be updated only when you expressly request an update—by clicking the Update Now button in this dialog box. (If you have multiple links in a file, be sure to select the link or links you want to edit before you start making changes.)

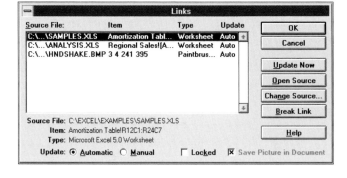

To eliminate a link, select it in the list and click the Break Link button. The link disappears from the list. Meanwhile, back in the destination document, the linked information persists in whatever form it *represented* the linked information—often as a picture. But the information is now independent of the source file, and the link cannot be restored. You can insert the information again and create a new link, of course, but you can't simply relink the existing information.

You've probably wondered what happens when a source file is moved or renamed. Does the operating system keep track of the change for you?

No, it doesn't. To maintain the link, you need the Change Source button (also in the Links dialog box). The button opens the Change Source dialog box, in which you can type or select the new filename or location.

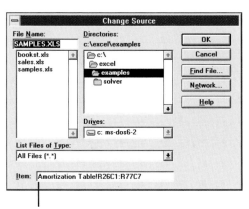

In Excel, changing the source might require you to define a different cell range

Editing a Linked Object To edit a linked object, you need to load the source document. To do that, first click the object to select it. Then either double-click the object or open the Edit menu, choose the command that refers to the linked object at the bottom of the menu, and choose Edit from the submenu that appears. Momentarily (more than momentarily, if your system resources are heavily taxed), the screen changes as the source file opens in its original application.

When you finish editing, save the document. Then exit the source application, or if you need to keep it open, close the file and click the appropriate Office Manager toolbar button to return to your destination document.

How to Embed

You can embed information from a wide variety of applications—more, in fact, than you can link from. To peek at the possibilities, choose Object from the Insert menu, and on the Create New tab of the Object dialog box, scroll through the Object Type list box. Some of the entries are from the major Office applications, which may generate more than one type of object—Microsoft Excel 5.0 Chart and Microsoft Excel 5.0 Worksheet, for instance. You'll recognize many of the others as shared applications in Office, such as Microsoft Equation 2.0 and Microsoft WordArt 2.0 (introduced in Chapter 1, "Small Step, Giant Leap").

To embed a new object, select the object type in the list and click OK. Creating new objects is not a consideration with linking: The whole point of linking is that the object already exists independently, and updates at the source are reflected at the linked locations. But embedding does not rely on an independently existing object. Often, you embed a new object first and then supply its content.

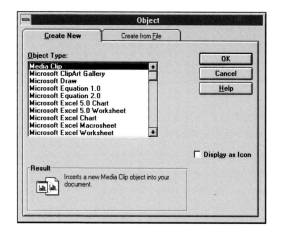

PAST LIVES

If you have used previous versions of the Office applications, you probably have multiple versions of many embedded applications, such as Equation Editor 1.0 and Equation Editor 2.0. Their objects are distinct, so you wind up with different entries, even if you don't have multiple versions of the application still on your disk.

As with linking, you can and often will embed existing information. In such cases, you start by opening both the destination file and the file with the existing information, exactly as you do when you link. Then you select the information in the server application, copy it to the Clipboard, and switch to the destination document.

POWER PLAY

Adding a Toolbar Button to Embed Objects

As you explore Office, you'll find buttons on a number of toolbars for embedding specific, commonly needed types of objects. Word's Standard toolbar, for example, has buttons for embedding an Excel worksheet, a drawing, and a chart. PowerPoint's Standard toolbar has buttons for inserting a Word table, an Excel worksheet, an organization chart, clip art, and a graph.

If you find such toolbar buttons handy, you can try adding buttons to embed other objects that you insert frequently. From the View menu, choose Toolbars, and then click the Customize button. Browse the categories of buttons; most of what you need will be in the Insert category. Click any button to see

how its result is currently defined. (In PowerPoint, simply point to the button and the ToolTip will tell you its purpose.) If you find the button you need—to insert an equation in Word, for instance—drag it to a toolbar location and release it. When you finish adding and re-arranging buttons (using drag and drop), click OK.

If you don't find a button that inserts the object you're after, you can record the process of embedding a new object with the application's macro recorder and then assign the macro to a button on whichever toolbar you prefer. (PowerPoint does not have macro-recording capabili-ties, but it provides buttons for inserting most objects.)

SERVER

The application that creates and edits an embedded object is generally called its *server.* Perhaps you've just gotten used to calling it the *source applica-tion,* as in the case of linked objects. Of course, you're right. The distinction is not entirely neces-sary. But it rein-forces the defining difference between linking and embed-ding: The linked object remains out-side the destination document (close to its source), while the embedded object resides in the destination document.

Position the insertion point or the pointer where you want the embedded object to appear. Choose Paste Special from the Edit menu. To embed, be sure that the Paste option button is selected, rather than Paste Link; then select the item in the As list box that ends in "Object," as in MS PowerPoint 4.0 Slide Object. Click OK, and there's your embedded object.

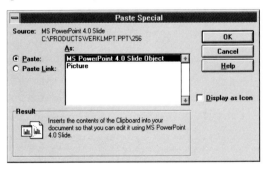

Editing an Embedded Object   Before you edit an embedded object, remember that the image you see in the destination document is just that—an image. "Behind" that image is the information that lets you reopen the server appli-cation and edit the data. The first step in editing is therefore to "activate" the object, which makes the resources of the server application available.

For many objects, such as a chart or a worksheet embedded in a Word document, you initiate editing simply by double-clicking the object. When double-clicking has some other effect, such as playing back an embedded PowerPoint presentation, you can activate the object for editing by opening the Edit menu, choosing the command at the bottom of the menu that refers to the object, and choosing the Edit command from the submenu that appears. Better yet, you can point to the object and display the shortcut menu (by clicking the right mouse button), on which you'll find a command for editing the object. The commands on the shortcut menu vary, depending on the application and the object type—sometimes you have to look for the Edit command on a submenu of the shortcut menu.

What happens when you activate an object depends on the object type. When you edit embedded clip art from the Microsoft ClipArt Gallery, for example, a separate window opens with the special resources that the ClipArt Gallery provides. If the window has menus, you can choose Update from the File menu to see an updated version of the object in your destination document without closing the server application. If the server application's window does not have menus, you must exit the application to update an object in the destination document. After you finish editing, exit the server application. Generally, you can do this by choosing the Exit command or by double-clicking the Control-menu box in the upper left corner of the server application's window.

EDIT OR OPEN

In some cases, you'll find both an Edit command and an Open command associated with an object. When that's the case, the Edit command lets you edit the object in place, while Open launches the server independently. Choose Edit unless you have a partic- ular reason to prefer Open.

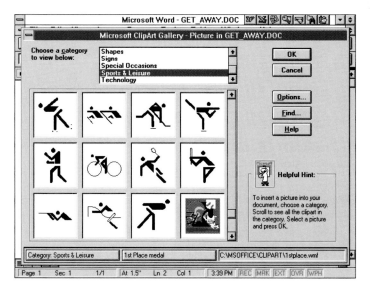

Activating an embedded Microsoft ClipArt Gallery object opens a separate window; you can then choose a different picture and change the content of the object in your document.

NO OBJECT

To delete an em- bedded object, select it (click it) but don't activate it; then press Del. You can't delete the object while it is active.

At other times, such as when you activate an embedded Excel worksheet in Word or PowerPoint, you see a change in the interface of the destination application. Excel's menus and toolbar buttons temporarily replace those of

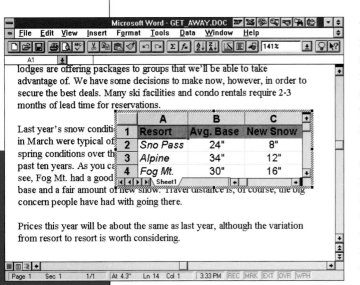

the destination application (except for the File menu and the Window menu). The embedded Excel object is activated, yet the destination document remains visible while you edit the object. This condition is known as editing "in place," or "in situ." It lets you see how your editing and formatting changes mesh with the surrounding document. To return to the destination application and update the embedded information, click somewhere in the document outside the embedded object.

The Excel chart above is being edited in place as an embedded object in a Word document. Notice the Excel menus and toolbar.

Paste, Link, or Embed—Which One to Use?

Once you grasp the differences between pasting, linking, and embedding, the advantages of using one over the other to transfer information between applications can be simply stated. You'll notice, however, that you don't always have all three options. In some circumstances, one or more of the techniques is impossible.

Pasting is appropriate when you have information in a document created with one application and you want to introduce that information in a document created with a different application. To take a common example, you might have an Excel worksheet with a block of cells that summarizes investment returns. To include the summary in a letter to a client, you can paste the block of cells in a Word document. The pasted information becomes a Word table. You can edit the cell contents in Word—to tweak the format, perhaps. You'll no longer be able to edit the pasted information in Excel, but that's okay—you're through what-if-ing and recalculating, and you don't plan to update or reuse this letter. Pasting, in short, is ideal.

For some transfers, pasting is not an option. If the destination application cannot edit the Clipboard contents, it embeds the information instead. Failing that, it pastes the information as a static picture, a form that is not editable. For example, let's say you copy a series of PowerPoint slides to the Clipboard, switch to a new Excel worksheet, and choose Paste from the Edit menu. Excel, which is unable to paste

Embedding a New Object

Often, you'll embed a new object rather than start with an existing one. In such cases, you work from the destination document.

1. Position the insertion point or pointer where you want to embed the object.
2. Choose Object from the Insert menu and select the object type that you want to insert.
3. Click OK and begin editing the object, using the tools that the server application provides.
4. Close the server application. If it's in a different window than the destination application, exit the server application; otherwise, click outside the new object.

POWER PLAY

How Much Disk Space?

One factor to weigh when you are deciding among pasting, linking, and embedding is the effect that each method has on file size. Consider the following experiment: From a typical Excel worksheet, a block of cells—52 rows by 7 columns—is copied to the Clipboard and then transferred to a Word document in three different ways, each time to a blank document. First, the information on the Clipboard is pasted, then it's linked (as an Excel worksheet object), and finally it's embedded (also as an Excel worksheet object). After each transfer, the file is saved and a new file is created.

PASTED.DOC weighs in at about 22 KB. The worksheet has been converted to a Word table, and the Excel formatting is essentially retained.

LINKED.DOC comes in at 51 KB. With the same data as PASTED.DOC, plus linking information, it has an additional 29 KB. (The printed file is identical to the hard copy of EMBEDDED.DOC, but it lacks a border.)

EMBEDDED.DOC lumbers in at about 193 KB. The object does not show all of its formatting until you activate it (by double-clicking). Once activated, the object can be edited using any of the Excel interface controls. When you print it in Word, the formatting shows up fine, along with a box that borders the entire worksheet.

This experiment reveals the typical relative file sizes using these three techniques. Pasting consumes less disk space than linking, which consumes far less than embedding. The ratio will vary somewhat, of course. In addition, inserting the objects as icons makes a great deal of difference: In the above scenario, LINKED.DOC becomes smaller than PASTED.DOC, at 9 KB, and EMBEDDED.DOC shrinks to about 150 KB.

the slides into the worksheet in a form that it can edit, embeds the series of slides as a PowerPoint slide object. From Excel, you can initiate a slide show to display the series you embedded, or you can open the slides in PowerPoint to edit them.

When you transfer your slides to Excel, you might think that you don't need to edit the slides further, but if you do want to edit them for some reason, Excel's resources will be of little value compared to those of PowerPoint, which were used to create the slides in the first place. To summarize, embedding is useful when you want to transfer information to a document in a different application but be able to edit the information in its original application. And when you distribute the file to other people, they can view and print the document, even if their computers lack the application that you used to embed the object (the server). They cannot edit the embedded object, of course, without access to the server application.

So when does linking become valuable? Suppose you want to represent the same information in a number of different documents. And suppose further that the information—the return-on-investment summary you pasted earlier, for example—is subject to change or revision over the months. By linking to the block of worksheet cells, you can make revisions in Excel, modifying figures and formulas and recalculating as necessary. And having changed the source information, you can update all of the linked documents automatically to reflect the changes.

Linking can save storage space and time by updating the same information in many different locations. Linked information is far less bulky than the same information embedded in a document. And many of the objects that you might want to insert in a document, such as sound and video clips, can be huge. The link, as you'll recall, is merely a representation of the information—with ties to the source document.

For people working in a group, linking requires that all of the users have access to the linked source file if they are going to benefit from updates to the source. They can view and print the linked object without the benefit of its source application, but to open or edit the linked object, a member of the group must have the source application installed locally or be able to use it across a network.

Importing and Exporting Files

To accommodate the transfer of entire files between applications or between versions of a single application, Office provides a number of importing and exporting resources. In most situations, the process is nearly invisible: Conversion is built into the process of opening or saving the file.

Suppose, for example, that you choose the File Open command, specify a file that isn't native to the application, and click OK. The application frequently does the rest: It identifies the foreign file format—often from information in the (normally undisplayed) file header; then, assuming that the application is equipped with the appropriate conversion utility, it simply announces that it is converting the file as it loads and displays the contents in a normal application window. Exporting to a file format other than the default format is often similarly uncomplicated.

File transfer is possible between many pairs of Office applications. Sometimes you have to export the file to accomplish the transfer—by saving it in the format of the destination application. More often, you can simply open (import) the original file in the destination application directly. Even when they work well, file conversions can have limitations. Certain fonts or other format features might simply not be available in the destination application. For a description of some of the more complicated conversions, including customizing and batch processing, see Chapter 14, "Importing and Exporting."

Simple Importing

To use a converter when you import a file, you typically click the Open button on the application's toolbar or choose the File Open command. In the Open dialog box (shown below), you type the filename with its current extension or select it by navigating through the drive, directory, and file lists. Don't forget that the files in the list are usually limited by the pattern in the File Name text box. To change the pattern and display files of different types, select a different entry in the List Files of Type drop-down list. Often, the list will include an entry for the type of document you want to convert.

When you click OK, the application loads the file and converts it. If it does not recognize the format, the application displays a Convert File dialog box in which you can indicate the converter to be used. Note that the conversion does not change the original file.

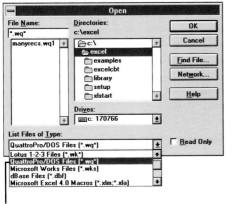

Selecting this entry changes the File Name pattern to list files with typical Quattro Pro extensions

When you finish working with the converted file, choose Save As to save it (with a different filename or extension) in the converted format without overwriting the original. If you choose Save, the application lets you determine which format you want the resaved file to have.

Common importing situations within the Office suite include opening a document created with an earlier version of an application and opening a Word document in PowerPoint to import the text headings as a presentation outline. To understand the importing options among Office applications, see the tables on the next two pages.

Simple Exporting

As with importing, the simplest file exporting is almost automatic. It occurs as part of the file-saving process, which you can control by means of the Save As dialog box. Choose Save As from the File menu. The converters that the application provides are listed in the Save File as Type drop-down list;

BACK TO SETUP?

If you did not perform a complete installation of Office, your setup might lack some of the converters or graphic filters you need. For a full listing of the file formats that each application can import or export, see the documentation for the application or use the Setup Maintenance program from Office Manager.

STRANGE CHARACTERS

If the converted file does not appear as you expected—say, it contains strange characters or symbols or bizarre formatting—try a different converter. (If the conversion occurred automatically in Word, select the Confirm Conversions check box in the Open dialog box.) Sometimes, if the problem is occurring in Word, you can change the font substitutions on the Compatibility tab of the Options dialog box.

that is, if you choose to save an Excel worksheet to DBF 3 (dBASE III) format, Excel has a converter that makes the changes and substitutions. Scroll through the list to see whether the format you need is listed.

When you export a file to a different file format, the new file frequently has a different filename extension, which the Save As command supplies for you. If the extension is identical, as it is when you save to the format for a different version of the same application, the program asks whether you want to overwrite the existing file. Normally, you should alter the filename or use a different directory to avoid overwriting the original.

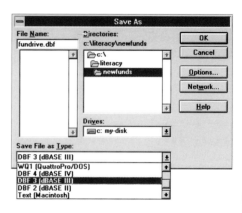

Office Overview

The following tables summarize the standard importing and exporting activities between major applications in the Office suite. As you've already seen, many of these activities are incorporated into the interface—the Report It toolbar button in PowerPoint, for example. Others require that you take a few additional steps. Chapter 14, "Importing and Exporting," further explores the powerful tools for controlling the flow of information between applications.

Exporting from Word	
Importing To	**Methods**
Word	Word has converters that let you open files from other versions of Word, including Macintosh, MS-DOS, and Windows. You can also use the converters when you save a Word document so that the document is stored in the format of the importing version of Word.
Excel	Choose the File Open command in Excel to open a Word file saved as text only. Excel has a Text Import Wizard that walks you through the conversion options.
PowerPoint	Choose the File Open command in PowerPoint and select Outlines in the List Files of Type list box. PowerPoint imports the Word headings as a presentation outline. From within Word, you can use the PresentIt (global) macro to launch PowerPoint and export the outline.
Access	Choose the File Import command to import a Word data source as an Access table. Convert the Word table to save Word data as text with delimiters (such as tabs or commas) between columns and paragraph returns between rows, and save the file as text only. The first row can become field names.

Exporting from Excel

Importing To	Methods
Word	You can open an Excel worksheet or a part of a worksheet directly as a Word table. Word prompts you for the worksheet you want to open and the range of the worksheet you want to use. Graphics can only be transferred using the Clipboard.
Excel	You can open Excel files from previous versions of the application. You can also import Excel files that have been saved in the format of the importing version of Excel, including workbooks and worksheets from earlier versions. And you can import Excel files that have been saved as text files.
PowerPoint	You can open a workbook, worksheet, or part of a worksheet directly in PowerPoint to import rows as outline text. (In the List Files of Type list box, select Outlines.)
Access	You can import the information in an Excel worksheet (or from a specific range) directly. Access can extract field names from the first row in the worksheet or range.

Exporting from PowerPoint

Importing To	Methods
Word	Use the Report It feature in PowerPoint to export the outline of your presentation as a Word document. The less direct route is to use PowerPoint's Save As command to save the presentation as the Outline (RTF) type, which you can open in Word. (Word cannot simply open a PowerPoint document.)
Excel	In Excel, you can insert a slide or a series of slides exported from PowerPoint as a Windows metafile (WMF). You can import text that's been exported in outline (RTF) form, especially if it's been subsequently resaved as text only.
PowerPoint	You can import files from earlier versions of PowerPoint for Windows and from some versions of PowerPoint for the Macintosh. You can export to some earlier versions of PowerPoint for Windows.
Access	As with Excel, you can insert slides that have been exported as a Windows metafile.

Exporting from Access

Importing To	Methods
Word	Don't look for Save As on the File menu. Most of the time it isn't there. Use the Output To command to save a table, query, or form with formatting (RTF) or as text only (TXT). Then open the document in Word. Note that graphics are not included. You can also use the Export command, but you'll lose formatting.
Excel	Use the Output To command to export a table, query, or form with formatting as an Excel worksheet (XLS). Then open the document in Excel. Graphics are not exported in the process. With the Export command, you can also export any of these as worksheets, but you'll lose formatting.
PowerPoint	Use Output To to export a query or a report as a formatted text (RTF) file to be imported as an outline. The query or the report must be carefully designed to produce a useful PowerPoint presentation.
Access	You can open databases created with previous versions of Access, but you can't save changes to object designs within those files.

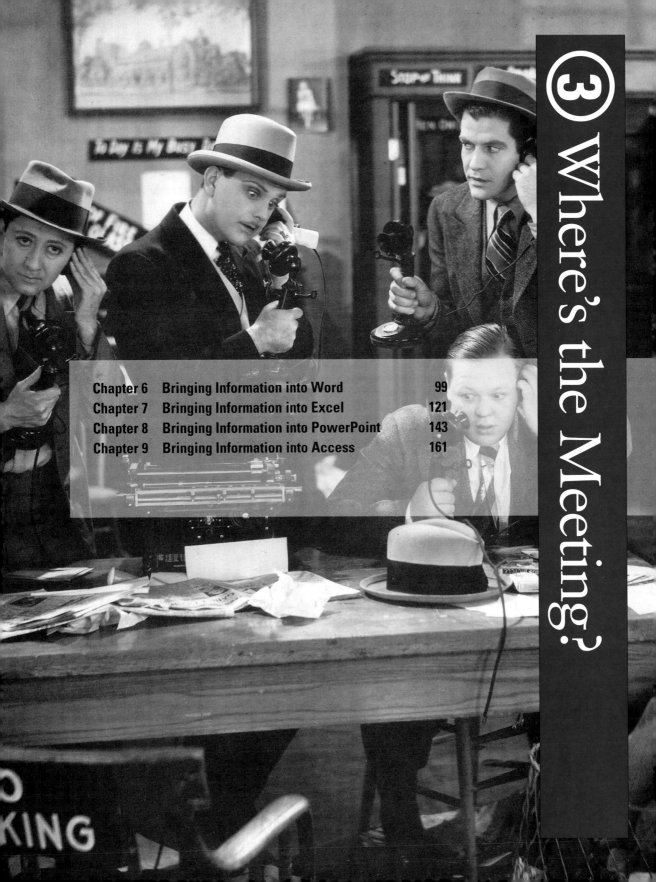

③ Where's the Meeting?

Chapter 6

Bringing Information into Word

Meeting Your Host

In its purest form, the docu-centric model described in Chapter 1 would result in compound documents that are essentially generic. The documents would collect objects from sundry applications but would not belong to any one more than another. But Microsoft Office takes a slightly different approach. In Office, someone's got to host the meeting—there are no conference rooms in the Office suite. And Microsoft Word documents are most often the hosts.

In a typical scenario, a person creates a document with Word for printed or online distribution. If components of the document rely on numeric information presented in tabular form or as charts of some sort, chances are that the information already exists (or can best be manipulated) in Microsoft Excel or Microsoft Access. The document might be a proposal or a report, such as a market analysis or a sales update.

The more often the document needs updating, the greater the chance that linking or embedding will prove worthwhile. Likewise, the more unstable the numeric information, the greater the chance that the figures or charts will have to be updated by the time the rest of the document is finished. Keep the information in a dynamic form—linked or embedded—if there is value in doing so. But remember that pasting can be the simplest and most economical choice if you don't need the benefits of OLE.

POWER PLAY

Pumping Up Word

Beyond the performance enhancements for Microsoft Windows suggested in Chapter 1, "Small Step, Giant Leap," there are a couple of ways that you can tweak your Word setup to improve sluggish responses. You can increase the speed at which Word redraws bitmapped images in a document and you can increase the scrolling speed, by earmarking blocks of memory for those activities. To do so, add the following two settings to your WINWORD6.INI file, located in your Windows directory. To edit the file, load it in Notepad by double-clicking the filename in File Manager. Both settings belong in the Microsoft Word section of the file—that is, in the block of instructions that falls between the bracketed Microsoft Word label and the next bracketed label in the file.

- The BitmapMemory setting reserves a certain amount of memory (in kilobytes) as cache memory for bitmaps. Increasing this number increases the size of the bitmap cache that Word uses to redraw pictures quickly. A setting of 1024 should provide enhanced performance in Word (256 is the default setting). The BitmapMemory setting should not exceed the amount of available random access memory (RAM). Insert the command anywhere in the Microsoft Word section using the following syntax:

    `BitmapMemory=xxxx`

- The CacheSize setting reserves a certain amount of memory (in kilobytes) as cache memory for Word documents. The default value for the CacheSize setting is 64. Increasing this setting (in multiples of 64) speeds up a number of Word actions: scrolling, searching and replacing, the Go To command, and document loading and saving. If your system has plenty of memory (12 MB or more of RAM) and you work with many large documents, consider setting the CacheSize value to 256 or 512. Insert the command anywhere in the Microsoft Word section using the following syntax:

    `CacheSize=xxx`

A proposal or report might also originate as a Microsoft PowerPoint presentation. Word can build on the outline of the presentation to develop an expanded proposal or report, and the Word document can include slides that present information as text or graphics. A document that is distributed on line can even include an entire PowerPoint presentation that recipients can view.

This chapter focuses on typical information-sharing opportunities that arise when you use the Office applications—primarily, linking and embedding scenarios between Excel and Word and between PowerPoint and Word. Access cannot participate in linking or embedding, but you can share information from Access by outputting formatted text that you can open in Word. The chapter concludes with a description of this outputting feature.

Absent from this chapter is a description of Word's Mail Merge feature, which draws on information saved by other applications. Look to Chapter 11, "Mastering Mergers," for that scenario. See Chapter 12, "Graphics and Other Gizmos," for coverage of the numerous shared applications that are frequently called upon to embed objects in Word documents.

How Word Stores an Object

In a Word document, the objects you link or embed are stored as *fields*. Now, you might feel uneasy at the mere mention of fields. If so, don't worry. You can link and embed all day long with Word documents and never know that you are using fields. Nevertheless, there are circumstances in which you might encounter field codes where you expected to see a chart or a spreadsheet. So a little knowledge is helpful, if only so you can switch the view back and hide those disturbing codes. The following is a brief overview of fields; if you don't need it, skip to the next section, "Working with Linked and Embedded Objects."

Broadly speaking, fields help you update information automatically, whether by inserting the correct date in the heading of a letter or renumbering figures in a technical article. For OLE information, fields can give you an automatic

POWER PLAY

Word's Linking Fields

Word uses three different fields to link information: A LINK field, an INCLUDEPICTURE field, and an INCLUDETEXT field. The LINK field is used when you choose the Edit Paste Link command to paste text or graphics that you copied from a running application. The field code gives you substantial control over how the link is established and managed.

The INCLUDEPICTURE field is used when you insert a graphic using the Insert Picture command and select the Link to File check box. Word uses a graphic filter (if available) to convert the graphic into a format it can use.

The INCLUDETEXT field is used when you insert text or a mix of text and graphics by choosing the Insert File command and selecting the Link to File check box. Word uses a text converter (if available) to convert the text, or text and graphics, into a format it can use.

FIELD

A *field* is a code that Word recognizes as instructions within your document. Word has more than 70 types of fields. Some fields are used to mark a location or to generate a certain action; most often, a field produces some automatic, visible result in a document.

SKIPPING THE SOURCE

The INCLUDEPICTURE and INCLUDETEXT fields can be useful tools if you have information stored in another file and you do not want to, or cannot, start the application to create the link. If you do not have the correct graphic filters and text converters, run the Office Manager Maintenance Setup program to install the needed files.

way to open an application and edit a given set of data or a file. Word inserts a LINK, INCLUDEPICTURE, or INCLUDETEXT field when you create a link, depending on what you are linking and how you created the link. Word inserts an EMBED field when you embed information.

Typically, a field is visible in either of two forms: as a code or as its result. You can switch between them easily—by pressing Alt+F9—to display either field codes or field results throughout your document. If you see an EMBED field where you expected to see an object, you can press Alt+F9 to make the object visible. To switch back and forth between a single field code and its result, click the field code or its result and press Shift+F9.

By default, a field result looks like any other text or graphic in your document—until you move the insertion point to the result or include the result

POWER PLAY

Anatomy of a Field

If you look closely at a field code—let's use the code for a LINK field as an example—you'll find a few consistent components:

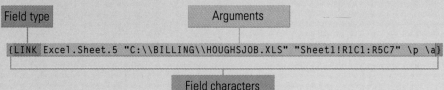

Field type Arguments

`{LINK Excel.Sheet.5 "C:\\BILLING\\HOUGHSJOB.XLS" "Sheet1!R1C1:R5C7" \p \a}`

Field characters

Each field code is set off by a pair of special characters at either end of the code. They appear as boldface curly brackets, but they are more than that. Word inserts them when you insert a field; typing curly brackets does not produce the same result.

Following the first curly bracket comes the field type. As you've seen, OLE uses LINK and EMBED field types. Other common field types in Word are DATE, TIME, and MERGEREC. The field type is generally followed by one or more arguments that guide or modify the field result in some way. Some arguments appear between quotation marks; others don't. One species of argument, called a *switch,* begins with a backslash character. Switches generally influence the way the field behaves or the way it formats the field result.

In the LINK field code example, the arguments identify the application (Excel, specifically an Excel worksheet), the linked pathname and filename, and the part of the file that is linked (here, a range of cells). The switches, \p and \a in our example, indicate that the linked object is displayed as a graphic and that it is updated automatically.

TWO VIEWS OF A FIELD

Sometimes you'll find it handy to view a field code and its result at the same time. You can accomplish this by splitting the document window and setting different options for each pane (on the View tab of the Options dialog box).

POWER PLAY

Changing LINK and EMBED Fields Directly

This is something of an *un*-Power Play, because modifying an OLE field by editing its code is sometimes unwise—or even impossible. It's better in most cases to use the Links dialog box for such alterations as switching between manual and automatic updating or redefining the source location. Do not, for example, change the application identifier directly in the field code. You can change the source file location for a link accurately by using the Change Source button in the Links dialog box: You can browse for the new location rather than type a pathname and filename from memory. (And you don't have to remember to type the pathname using double backslashes.)

But some defaults cannot be changed conveniently (or at all) without editing the field code. Suppose, for example, that you've embedded a new worksheet object that reveals five columns and you decide to add a row of subtotals in a sixth column. By default, when you grab a sizing handle on the embedded object to increase its size, the five currently displayed columns grow to fill the box rather than revealing more worksheet cells. But if you edit the EMBED field code to add an \s switch, you can show the sixth column of cells because the original cells won't grow to fit when you expand the object's border. Here's how the edited field code might look:

```
{ EMBED Excel.Sheet.5 \s }
```

as part of a selection. Then, if the field result contains some text, the entire result becomes shaded, indicating the extent of the result. Field results that are graphics only do not become shaded when selected. Field code, regardless of the type of field result, becomes shaded when the insertion point is placed just to the left of or inside the field code. Any field result that can become shaded, and all field codes, take on darker shading when the entire field is selected.

The usual way to insert a field directly is to use the Insert Field command, select the field name, and complete the field instructions in the Field dialog box—sometimes with help from its Options button to figure out the arguments. Some of the most commonly used fields have their own keyboard shortcuts (Alt+Shift+D for a DATE field, for instance). Others are introduced by menu commands without your necessarily being aware that you're using them. The EMBED field is one of these.

Ordinarily, you don't manually introduce EMBED fields—or LINK fields—into a document. Instead, you insert EMBED fields by choosing the Insert Object command or by using Paste Special. Similarly, Word inserts a LINK

FIELD SHADING

You can change the way fields are shaded. Choose the Tools Options command, and on the View tab of the Options dialog box, select a different setting from the Field Shading drop-down list. When Selected is the default, but you can eliminate all shading by selecting Never or you can have all of the fields shaded all of the time by selecting Always from the list.

LINK Field

A LINK field uses OLE to establish a link with content in a file that was created in another application. The field code uses the following syntax:

{ LINK **ClassName Filename [PlaceReference] [Switches]** }

See Word's online Help for more information on the LINK arguments. You can add the following switches to customize the LINK field:

\a updates the LINK field automatically (delete the \a switch for manual updating).

\b inserts the linked object as a bitmap.

\d prevents graphic data from being stored with the document, thus reducing the file size.

\p inserts the linked object as a graphic.

\r inserts the linked object in Rich Text Format (RTF).

\t inserts the linked object in text-only format.

EMBED Field

An EMBED field inserts an object created in another application. The field code has the following syntax:

{ EMBED **ClassName [Switches]** }

The EMBED field is not available in the Field dialog box, and you cannot insert it manually. You can, however, directly modify the switches (described below) in an existing EMBED field. See Word's online Help for more information on the EMBED arguments.

\s returns an embedded object to its original size when the field is updated. To keep the sizing or cropping you've applied to the object, delete this switch, if it is present, from the field.

* mergeformat applies the sizing and cropping of the previous result to the new result. To preserve previously applied sizing and cropping when you update the field, do not delete this switch from the field.

field when you use the Paste Link option with the Paste Special command. You can specify the switches and other arguments indirectly, as you make selections in documents and select options in dialog boxes.

Working with Linked and Embedded Objects

Although it isn't essential that you recognize OLE objects in Word as specific field types, you gain some advantages when you work with the objects. Specifically, you can draw on your knowledge of fields to understand how objects behave and to modify their behavior in helpful ways. For example, you can tell immediately whether an object is linked or embedded: Simply press Alt+F9 to show the field codes and check the field name—LINK, INCLUDEPICTURE, and INCLUDETEXT are linking fields; EMBED is an embedding field.

WORD TO WORD

It might occur to you that you can use a LINK field or an EMBED field to insert a Word object in another Word document. You can try it and it will work, but it's rarely an efficient way to go. An INCLUDETEXT field is usually a better choice.

Editing an Object It's easy to initiate editing of objects inserted in Word with LINK or EMBED fields: In most cases, you simply point to the object and double-click. If the field code is displayed, rather than the object, you need to switch the view back to the result (object) before you double-click. In either view, you can also edit the object by selecting it, opening the Edit menu, choosing the command at the bottom of the menu that relates to the selected object, and choosing Edit from the submenu that pops up to the right of the object name. The menu command is essential if the object is one that responds to double-clicking in some special way—by playing back a sound clip, for instance.

Edit	
<u>U</u>ndo Typing	Ctrl+Z
<u>R</u>epeat Typing	Ctrl+Y
Cu<u>t</u>	Ctrl+X
<u>C</u>opy	Ctrl+C
<u>P</u>aste	Ctrl+V
Paste <u>S</u>pecial...	
Clea<u>r</u>	Delete
Select A<u>l</u>l	Ctrl+A
<u>F</u>ind...	Ctrl+F
R<u>e</u>place...	Ctrl+H
<u>G</u>o To...	Ctrl+G
AutoTe<u>x</u>t...	
<u>B</u>ookmark...	
Lin<u>k</u>s...	
Linked Worksheet <u>O</u>bject	<u>E</u>dit / <u>O</u>pen / Con<u>v</u>ert...

Depending on the type of embedded object, initiating an edit either changes the menu commands and toolbar to offer the tools of a different application or it opens a separate, "nested" menu or toolbar with resources that are specifically suited to editing an object of the type in your document. The way you complete the edit depends on the application: Close the window if it is nested within Word; click outside the object if the server's commands and toolbars have replaced those of Word.

Editing a linked object switches you to the source application with the linked file opened. After completing the edit, you must save the file to incorporate the changes into the Word document. To return to Word, save the changed file, close the file if you have completed all of your editing, and, if you no longer need it, exit the source application. The editing changes may or may not immediately appear in your Word document, depending on the type of link; some links must be updated before the changes are passed to Word. For details, see the section titled "Updating a Link," on the next page.

Deleting an object is easier than you might think. Like any field result, an object cannot be erased using the Backspace key. The trick is to select the object first so that (in the case of a picture) the sizing handles are displayed. Don't double-click to select the object—that's right, double-clicking generally loads the linked source file or invokes the server application. If the linked object is not a picture, be sure to select the entire object. Then press Del to delete the selection.

To copy or move an object within a document, select it and use the Cut, Copy, and Paste commands as you would normally. Word relocates a linked or embedded object just as easily as it does any other field.

Locking and Unlocking a Link You can lock or unlock a link to control whether changes made to the source file are reflected at the linked location.

EDITING CONVERTED LINKS
You cannot edit objects placed in Word with INCLUDEPICTURE and INCLUDETEXT fields directly from Word. Because these fields use graphic filters and text converters to modify the file's contents, you must load the file into its source application, edit it, and save it. If you double-click a linked graphic in Word to edit it, the graphic is converted to an embedded Word Picture object and the link to the file is broken. You can then edit the graphic as a Word Picture.

If the same information is linked to several locations, each link is unique and can be locked and unlocked separately. To lock or unlock a link, choose the Edit Links command to display the Links dialog box, select or deselect the Locked check box, and click OK.

If you're familiar with Word's keyboard shortcuts for locking and unlocking fields, you might guess that they would have the same effect on a LINK field—they would lock or unlock the link. You'd be right. Click a linked object (either the field code or its result) and press Ctrl+F11 to lock the link, or Ctrl+Shift+F11 to unlock it.

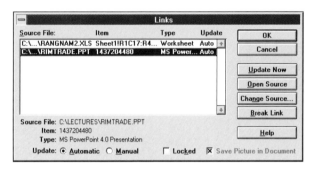

As an experiment, you might try the keyboard shortcut for locking or unlocking an object and then open the Links dialog box to verify that the Locked check box reflects the change.

Updating a Link   A LINK field, when created, is set for automatic updating. With automatic updates, any change to the source file is immediately displayed in the Word document. You can change the link to manual updating by choosing the Edit Links command and selecting the Manual option button in the Links dialog box or by directly editing the field code.

To update a manual link, you can choose the Edit Links command and click the Update Now button in the Links dialog box. The Update Now button is grayed-out if the link is locked, which is apparent in the Links dialog box if the Locked check box is selected.

Because the link exists in Word as a LINK field, you can also click the object or its field code and press F9 to update the field—and thus update the linked information. You can also have Word automatically update all of the links before you print the document. To do so, choose the Tools Options command, and on the Print tab of the Options dialog box, select the Update Fields check box.

Breaking a Link   Breaking a link severs the connection between the inserted information and its source file. All that remains is a representation of the information—Word data or a picture of the once-linked information, depending on the type of link. Remember that the break is permanent.

Here again, you can use the Edit Links command or you can unlink the field as you would any other Word field. To use the first method, choose the Edit

ON THE BUTTON

Word provides a button for manually updating all selected fields, which you can use in place of F9 to update the current link. Choose the Tools Customize command, and on the Toolbars tab of the Customize dialog box, locate the Update Fields button.

In the lower right section of the dialog box, choose the template for which you want the change to apply (Normal is global). Then drag the button from the dialog box to the toolbar on which you want it to reside. If you want the change to apply to future sessions, be sure to save your changes to the template when you close the document.

Links command to display the Links dialog box, select the link, click the Break Link button, and click Close. To break the link to the source file by unlinking the field, select the linked object and press Ctrl+Shift+F9.

Changing the Source Document for a Link Using the Edit Links command is probably the safest way to change the source file for a link. Choose the command to display the Links dialog box, and then click the Change Source button. (The Change Source dialog box appears, as shown below.) To be sure that you specify the pathname and filename accurately, navigate to the source document using the lists in the dialog box.

You can even make network connections using the Network button. That way, you don't have to worry about mistyping a filename.

Now, suppose you've created a link to an Excel worksheet and you want to change the range of cells that you originally specified for the link. You can make this change in the Change Source dialog box. Noticing that the cell references do not match Excel's default notation, you enter the new range in

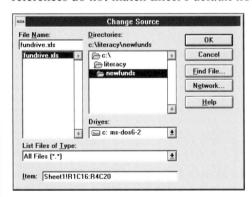

the Item text box using the same RC (row number, column number) notation. (You can't simply use Excel's normal A1 notation and expect Change Source to translate it for you—you'll get nothing for your efforts.)

A more direct method exists for changing the source for the link. You can display the field code for the linked object in the Word document (by pressing Alt+F9) and edit the link reference as it's represented there. The only hitch is that you have to be careful with the syntax. The field code requires that you double the backslashes in a pathname and leave the quotation marks as you find them. For linked worksheets, RC cell references are required in the field code instead of the customary Excel notation.

HIDING IS OKAY

If you don't want to show linked information, you need not delete the linked object. You can hide a linked or embedded object, just as you can hide any text, graphic, or field in a document. To hide the object, click it and press Ctrl+Shift+H to format it as hidden text. To be sure that the hidden text is not included when you print, choose the Tools Option command and select the Print tab of the Options dialog box. The Hidden Text check box should be deselected.

EASY ADDRESS

If you have difficulty figuring out the appropriate row and column number, Excel can help. In Excel, choose the Tools Options command and, on the General tab of the Options dialog box, select the R1C1 option button and click OK. The column letters change to numbers on the worksheet.

Transferring Information from Excel

Excel and Word manage information in different ways. Yet the information you maintain in Excel frequently complements that in a Word document. So the potential for transferring information between the two applications is high. And given that Excel is sufficiently powerful to account for much of your day-to-day, month-to-month numerical analysis, you'll probably find many opportunities to link and embed information that you report or exhibit routinely.

Linking and embedding are not the only ways to transfer the information in a worksheet or a chart; you can insert files and databases directly into a Word document, and you can import Excel files. But in this chapter, we'll focus on linking and embedding, as well as on moving and copying; look for more details on importing and exporting (including inserting) Excel files in Chapter 14, "Importing and Exporting."

Linking a Worksheet or Chart

Linking a word document to an Excel file—to present a chart or a block of worksheet cells—is a common way to take advantage of OLE. It can save you a lot of effort if you have key information that you:

- maintain in Excel to track your business

- store at a stable location

- incorporate in Word documents that need to reflect the original information accurately

Before you establish the link, consider these factors. In particular, be sure to save the Excel information at a location that is unlikely to change. The Excel file does not have to be accessible to all who view the Word document—Word inserts a picture of the information for those who need only to look. It must, however, be accessible to all who need to open the Excel document or otherwise take advantage of the automatic updating. The link will not yield any fresh information if the source file moves or is inaccessible from the current location. A location that is shared across a network is sometimes just the ticket. (In that case, of course, the link is only as reliable as the network.)

To link a Word document to an Excel source file, open both documents and switch to the source file. Select the object or range that you want Word to display at its end of the link. Copy the selection to the Clipboard and switch to the Word document.

As usual, the insertion point in Word determines where the upper left corner of the worksheet or chart is inserted, so position it before you choose the Paste

Special command. Then, in the Paste Special dialog box, select Paste Link and select one of the information formats in the As list box. Selecting Paste Link is crucial. Without it, no link.

The choices in the As list box depend on whether you are linking a worksheet or a chart. Generally, you have more choices for a worksheet than for a chart: The information in a worksheet is editable as text, so you can choose to insert it as either formatted or unformatted text.

Because you are establishing a link to the Excel file, the object, regardless of its type, can be updated to conform to the source file. In fact, the object is updated automatically (by default) as long as you maintain the link. If you anticipate using the link often to open and edit the source file, Microsoft Excel 5.0 Worksheet Object is the best format to select in the Paste Special dialog box. You can open the source file to edit it simply by double-clicking the object in the Word document. To edit the source file when the information has been inserted using one of the text formats, select the entire object (so that the field is highlighted, not merely shaded) and then choose Edit from the submenu for Linked Worksheet Object, at the bottom of the Edit menu.

The various object types give you different formatting and printing options, but as long as you maintain the link, you should edit the contents at the source. You can edit the formatted (tabular) text representation of a linked worksheet simply by making changes in Word, but the changes will be overwritten to match the source the next time you open the document, as long as updating is automatic. Refer to the quick reference card for the LINK field earlier in this chapter to see what effect the switches have on sizing and formatting changes you make in Excel.

> **Linking a Worksheet or Chart**
>
> Open both the destination Word document and the source file—the Excel document that contains the range of worksheet cells or the chart you want to insert. Switch to the Excel document.
>
> 1. Select the range of cells or the chart you want to link to.
> 2. Copy the selected range or chart to the Clipboard.
> 3. Switch to the Word document and place the insertion point where you want the upper left corner of the worksheet or chart to appear.
> 4. Choose Paste Special from the Edit menu.
> 5. In the Paste Special dialog box, select the Paste Link option button. In the As list box, select Microsoft Excel 5.0 Worksheet Object (to link a range of cells) or Microsoft Excel 5.0 Picture Object (to link a chart).
> 6. Click OK.

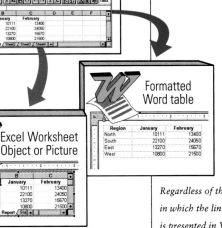

Regardless of the format in which the linked info is presented in Word, editing the source document results in an update to the object in Word.

POWER PLAY

Name That Range

Remember that a LINK field uses row and column numbers to identify the block of cells to which you are linking. For example, a LINK field might contain the following code to designate a link to the region from row 10, column 1 to row 16, column 7:

```
{ LINK Excel.Sheet.5
  "C:\\BIDS\\ESTCOST.XLS"
  "Sheet2!R10C1:R16C7" \a \p }
```

Not only does the row and column notation not employ the cell-naming conventions that Excel normally uses (which would identify the above range as A10:G16), but it also lacks the flexibility that comes from assigning range names. Within a named range, you can insert or delete rows and columns but still have a reliable way of referring to the portion of the worksheet you intended. Fortunately, links can also recognize range names.

The best way to introduce the range name into the LINK code is to assign the name before you establish the link. In that case, the field code picks up the name automatically. If you've

already linked to the cell range, you can name the range subsequently and then edit the field code.

Naming a range in Excel is a simple matter of selecting the cells in the range and then typing the name in the box at the left end of the formula bar. You have to click in the name box initially to activate it, and press Enter after you type the name.

To edit the field code, switch to Word and display the worksheet cells that are linked to the Excel source file. Press Alt+F9 to display the field code and replace the cell notation with the range name. In our sample LINK field, suppose that the cells in the range itemize expected labor costs. If you name the range in Excel and then edit the field code to use the name, you get a result such as the following:

```
{ LINK Excel.Sheet.5
  "C:\\BIDS\\ESTCOST.XLS"
  "Sheet1!LaborCosts" \a \p }
```

Embedding a Worksheet

You can embed a range of cells from an existing worksheet or you can embed a new worksheet and then enter formulas and data in it. Let's first consider the case in which the information you want to insert is in an existing worksheet. Here, too, you have a few choices. You can drag and drop the selected block of cells from one application to the other, or you can use the Clipboard and the Paste Special command to effect the transfer.

Using Drag and Drop   Once you get used to the idea that drag and drop can produce an embedded object (rather than a normal cut-and-paste "change of address"), this method becomes very appealing. You'll probably like it even more if you have a large, high-resolution monitor.

The mechanics of the process are exactly like those for dragging and dropping within a document. That means, of course, that you have to hold down the Ctrl key while you click and drag if you want to copy rather than move the cells.

Using the Clipboard Begin by opening the Excel document that contains the information to be embedded, as well as the Word destination document. In Excel, select the block of cells that you want to embed and copy it to the Clipboard. For convenience, use the Copy button on the Standard toolbar or choose Copy from the shortcut menu. Sure, you can use Cut, but it's less likely to be the appropriate choice, and it will be harder to undo the embedding process if you need to retry for some reason.

After you copy your selection, switch to the Word document. (The Microsoft Office Manager toolbar provides a handy way to do this.) Place the insertion point where you want the upper left cell in the range to appear, and choose Paste Special from the Edit menu.

Drag and Drop: Excel to Word

Drag and drop provides a simple and straight-forward way to embed (rather than move or copy) a range of cells or a chart in a Word document.

1. Tile your Excel and Word windows.
2. Select the cells or the chart in the Excel document.
3. Point to the outer border of the cells or inside the chart area; hold down the Ctrl key and drag the object from Excel to the place where you want to insert it in the Word document.
4. Release the mouse button (and the Ctrl key) to drop the object. Word embeds the information as an Excel object, either a worksheet or a chart, and lets you edit the object in Excel when you double-click it.

DROP A COPY

You can undo a drag and drop action in Word, but if you move (cut) cells from an Excel document, they do not automatically re-turn. Dragging them back from Word to Excel does work, but to be safe, drag and drop a copy.

Embedding an Existing Worksheet

To embed an existing Excel worksheet, open both the Excel worksheet and the Word destination file, and switch to the Excel document.

1. Select the range of cells you want to embed.
2. Copy the selected range to the Clipboard. You'll see the marquis border around the selected cells.
3. Switch to the Word document, and place the insertion point at the location for the upper left cell in the range.
4. Choose Paste Special from the Edit menu.
5. In the Paste Special dialog box, select the Paste option button and select Microsoft Excel 5.0 Worksheet Object in the As list box.
6. Click OK.

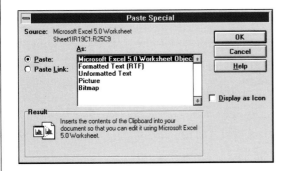

In the Paste Special dialog box, be sure that the Paste option button is selected rather than Paste Link. To embed the worksheet, select Microsoft Excel 5.0 Work-sheet Object in the As list box—the full range of options is summarized below. Pasting the Clipboard contents as any of the other types does not embed an object that you can edit in Excel as a worksheet. Note that you have the choice of displaying the block of cells as an icon—a good choice if you are motivated to minimize the size of the compound document. Click OK to complete the process.

Paste As	Result
Microsoft Excel 5.0 Worksheet Object	The information is arranged and presented as it is in Excel. You can modify the object as Excel information—changing formulas, recalculating, etc.
Formatted Text (RTF)	The text is arranged in a Word table whose rows and columns correspond to those in the worksheet range.
Unformatted Text	The text has no character or table formatting. Keep this in mind if you want to copy Excel information as regular text rather than as a table.
Picture	The information is represented as a composite of drawing objects (lines, circles, text boxes, etc.). Use this object type if you don't need to revise the information in Word or Excel or if you want to modify the drawing objects.
Bitmap	The information is represented as a pattern of pixels. You can revise the content by changing the individual pixels (you can do this by using a paint program such as Paintbrush). The printed quality is not as good as a Picture object, and the information takes up more room in the document file than a Picture object would.

Using Insert Object The Insert Object command is used principally to create new embedded objects. But the command also provides a way to create an object from an existing file, so you can use it to embed an existing worksheet in your document. The drawback of this method is that it embeds the entire contents of the file and displays the complete worksheet. If it is a large worksheet, the sizing is likely to need significant modification to fit in your Word document.

If you want to embed an entire worksheet (perhaps as an icon), choose Object from the Insert menu and then select the Create From File tab of the Object dialog box. Specify the pathname and filename, and select the Display as Icon check box if you want the icon rather than the worksheet to appear in your document. Because you are embedding the file as an object (rather than linking it), do not select the Link to File check box. Click OK to embed the file.

Embedding a Chart

A chart is as changeable as the data on which it is based, so embedding can be the best way to include a chart when the data or the formatting is not frozen. To embed a chart, you follow much the same procedure as you do for embedding a worksheet range, but your options are extremely simple. Word can embed the chart in a form that Excel can edit—as an Excel

POWER PLAY

Using Frames to Lay Out a Page with Objects

In Word, you can isolate an object, such as a chart or a worksheet range, so that it holds its position on the page. Word inserts a frame, which enables you to place two charts side by side, for example, or to flow text alongside a block of worksheet cells. It also lets you anchor an object to a particular paragraph or group an object with its caption.

To insert a frame, you can start by switching to Layout view. You have to be in Layout view to see, size, or move the frame anyway. Select the object to frame—let's say it's an Excel chart—and choose Frame from the Insert menu. (There's also a Frame command on the Format menu, but it has a different purpose, which you'll see shortly.) The frame shows up on the page as a hatched border when the chart is selected, but it is invisible when not selected and during printing.

A frame is always anchored to the nearest paragraph. In Layout view, an anchor symbol appears next to the first line of the associated paragraph. (Click the Show/Hide ¶ button if no anchor is visible.) By

dragging the frame, you can relocate the chart anywhere on the page. The paragraph to which it's anchored changes as you move the frame, unless you lock the anchor. To do so, drag the anchor to the paragraph at which you want to lock it; then double-click the anchor symbol and select the Lock Anchor check box in the Vertical section of the Frame dialog box.

Note that the Frame dialog box also lets you remove the frame, specify the size and location of the frame, and control whether text flows around it. You can display the Frame dialog box at any time by selecting a frame and choosing the Frame command from the Format menu.

Chart Object—or it can paste a picture of the chart that you can modify using Word Picture, but you cannot edit the data to modify the chart. These are your only choices.

In fact, the procedure for embedding a chart is identical to the one for pasting; you don't even need the Paste Special command. Simply open both documents, copy the chart to the Clipboard, switch to the Word document, and paste the chart at the desired location. Because Word can't paste a text

MODIFYING CHARTS
Resizing a chart is best accomplished by activating it in Excel. Of course, you must activate it (by double-clicking) to make other modifications, such as changing the chart type or editing the legend.

equivalent of the chart (as it can for a worksheet), the Paste command simply does the embedding. If you were to use the Paste Special command, in the Paste Special dialog box you would select the Paste option button and then select Microsoft Excel 5.0 Chart Object to embed the chart—equivalent, in this case, to using the Paste command.

Embedding New Objects

Because the information in an embedded object (unlike the information in a linked object) is independent of files outside the current document, you can embed an object without copying information from an existing file. This is obvious with objects that you create with WordArt and similar shared applications—they cannot exist independent of the document in which they're embedded. But Excel worksheets and charts can also be embedded as new objects in a Word document; in fact, Word makes it especially easy to embed a new worksheet.

Embedding a New Worksheet With the Insert Microsoft Excel Worksheet button (on the Standard toolbar), embedding a worksheet is a simple click-and-drag procedure: Click the toolbar button to drop down a grid on which you define a blank Excel worksheet. Drag within the drop-down box to highlight the dimensions. Word inserts the corresponding worksheet when you release the mouse button; the Excel menus and toolbars also appear to let you start editing the worksheet right away. In the worksheet, you can scroll outside the area you initially defined, and you can modify the dimensions of the window while you are editing in Excel.

2 x 4 Spreadsheet

You can also embed a new Excel worksheet using the Insert Object command: From the available object types, select Microsoft Excel 5.0 Worksheet Object. The Object dialog box, unlike the toolbar button, gives you the option of embedding the object as an icon. Word embeds a blank worksheet to which you can add information—both data and formulas. You can resize the window to change the number of cells displayed before you close it, and Word will display the object in the new size with the new number of cells.

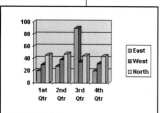

Embedding a New Chart To embed a new chart, select Microsoft Excel 5.0 Chart in the Object dialog box. Word embeds a workbook with two sheets. The first holds a sample column chart; the second contains the spreadsheet information on which the chart is based. You can modify the chart or create your own chart by editing the information in the worksheet. To include data from additional rows or columns, use the Insert Data command. To create a new chart on a separate sheet, use the Insert Chart command.

Another method of embedding a chart is to use Microsoft Graph rather than Excel. Graph provides some of the same basic charting options, but it lacks Excel's rich features for editing and manipulating the spreadsheet information.

To insert the chart, simply click the Insert Chart button on the Standard toolbar. Like the new Excel chart described on the facing page, the Graph object is displayed with sample data in its datasheet and a corresponding column chart. You can switch back and forth between the views to edit and format them.

Enter or import your own data and re-create the chart to suit yourself. You can insert a chart based on information in an existing Word table if you select the table or the portion of the table you want to chart before you click the Insert Chart button.

Transferring Information from PowerPoint

Moving information between Word and PowerPoint is easy. You can develop a presentation based on a written report or a proposal and then move the information from the Word document into PowerPoint. Or you can move an outline or notes or slides from PowerPoint into Word so that you can elaborate on a presentation in a printed document. We'll explore the second case in the sections that follow, with emphasis on linking and embedding. We'll also take a quick look at exporting a PowerPoint presentation outline to Word.

Linking to a Slide or Presentation

Presentations have a way of evolving, based on changing information and audience reaction. Linking to PowerPoint slides from a Word document offers the advantage of automatic revision to the document as the presentation evolves. You can paste PowerPoint slides into your Word document and create a link to the source presentation so that the slides in the Word document always match the source slides in PowerPoint.

To select a slide that you want to link to, switch to PowerPoint's Slide Sorter view. In that view, you can select a single slide (by clicking it) or multiple slides (by using Shift+click or by choosing Select All from the Edit menu). Selected slides have a thick black border. Choose the Copy command to copy the slide or slides to the Clipboard.

Switch to Word, place the insertion point where you want the upper left corner of the first selected slide to appear, and choose the Paste Special command. In the Paste Special dialog box, select Paste Link. In the As list box, select MS PowerPoint 4.0 Slide Object (or MS PowerPoint 4.0 Presentation Object, if the object includes multiple files). Click OK to create the link.

NO SAVE, NO LINK
Although saving the source file before linking is always prudent, it's essential that your Power-Point source file be saved before you attempt to link to it. If the presentation has never been saved, the Paste Link option button (in the Paste Special dialog box) will be unavailable.

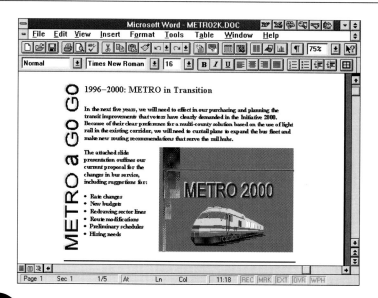

Linking to a Slide or Slides

First, be sure that you have saved the Power-Point presentation. Then take the following steps to link to one or more slides:

1. In PowerPoint, switch to Slide Sorter view and select the slide or slides you want to insert in your Word destination document.
2. Copy the selection to the Clipboard.
3. Switch to the Word document and position the insertion point where you want the slide (or the first slide of the series) to appear.
4. Choose Paste Special from the Edit menu.
5. In the Paste Special dialog box, select the Paste Link option button, and select the MS PowerPoint 4.0 Slide Object or Presentation Object in the As list box.
6. Click OK.

The object you see pasted in the Word document is always a single slide. As with embedding, you might have selected multiple slides, but Word displays only the first slide in the selected series. So why did you bother to select more than one slide? The payoff comes when you use the link to view a full-screen slide show. To start the show, double-click the object (or open the Edit menu and choose Show from the submenu alongside Linked PowerPoint 4.0 Presentation Object). Note that if the Word object is linked to a single slide rather than to a series of slides, double-clicking doesn't launch a slide show; instead, it opens the file in PowerPoint and displays the linked slide for editing.

Embedding a Slide

You can embed a PowerPoint slide, a series of slides, or a whole presentation in a Word document. The slides might enhance or summarize the points discussed in the Word document, or the document might serve as a commentary on the PowerPoint presentation.

In any case, embedding existing slides is easy. In PowerPoint, switch to Slide Sorter view to select the slide or slides. You can select multiple slides by holding down the Shift key as you click individual slides. Use the Select All command on the Edit menu to select the entire presentation. Then you simply copy the selection to the Clipboard and paste it into the Word document. By default, Word pastes a slide or a group of slides from the Clipboard as an embedded PowerPoint object.

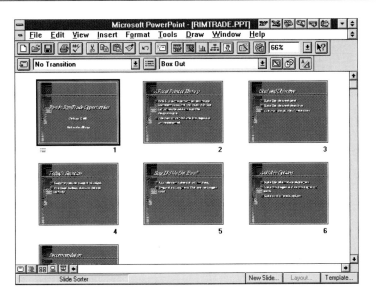

Use PowerPoint's Slide Sorter view to select the slide or slides to be copied and embedded.

If you paste multiple slides at once into a Word document, they are embedded as a PowerPoint Presentation Object. Only the first of the selected slides is visible in the document. To see the other slides, double-click the embedded object for a full-screen show (or open the Edit menu and choose Show from the submenu alongside MS PowerPoint 4.0 Presentation Object). Click with your mouse or press Enter to step through the slide show.

You can use Paste Special (instead of the Paste command) to embed the slide or slides that you've copied to the Clipboard. The Paste Special dialog box offers you a few choices that you don't have with the Paste command. Simply pasting slides embeds an MS PowerPoint 4.0 Presentation (or Slide) Object, which you can edit with PowerPoint. That object type should be selected in the As list box—unless you want to edit the slide image in Word as a picture, in which case you should select Picture in the As list box. The following table summarizes your choices:

REVEALING CODES
Don't forget that you can press Alt+F9 in Word to switch between the field result and the field code. Viewing the code lets you determine whether an object is a single slide (PowerPoint.Slide) or a presentation (PowerPoint.Show).

Embed As	Result
MS PowerPoint 4.0 Slide Object	The object is a single slide that you can double-click to edit with PowerPoint resources.
MS PowerPoint 4.0 Presentation Object	The object is a set of slides (a few or an entire presentation) that you can double-click to view in sequence.
Picture	Double-clicking lets you edit the image as a Word Picture object.

Exporting an Outline

Exporting a presentation outline as a Word document is probably the most straightforward way to transfer information from PowerPoint to Word. It's also the most useful. You're likely to have information that you've structured—in skeletal form—to present publicly that you'll later want to elaborate on in written form.

What makes the exchange smooth is the use of formatting styles. In Power-Point, the styles are applied unobtrusively as you develop the slide series and list major points, perhaps using the AutoContent Wizard to lend some shape to the presentation in its initial stages. Each time you add a slide or promote an item in your outline, PowerPoint applies a style to that item. When you export the presentation to Word, the hierarchy of the PowerPoint outline survives in the heading levels that you see in the Word document.

The exported file uses Rich Text Format (RTF), which preserves many of the font characteristics between applications. Font sizes are adjusted downward, however, for printed output. For example, a top-level heading in a PowerPoint presentation might have a size of 44 points; in a Word file, the same heading would measure something like 14 points. The Word document will not, of course, contain any of the graphical elements that the PowerPoint presentation includes.

PowerPoint automatically assigns the exported file the filename of the presentation, with the RTF extension. With the Save As command, you can save the file in Word format, with a DOC extension, if you prefer.

> **Exporting a PowerPoint Outline**
>
> Use the following steps to create a Word outline from a PowerPoint presentation:
> 1. Open the presentation in PowerPoint. You don't have to launch Word.
> 2. On the Standard toolbar, click the Report It button.
> 3. The command launches Word and opens your presentation in Word as a document in Rich Text Format (RTF).

You can export slides from a presentation by saving them individually in a picture format. To do so, display the slide you want to export or select it in Slide Sorter view. Then choose Save As from the File menu, select Windows Metafile as the file type, and click OK. To import the file into a Word docu-ment, use the Insert Picture command.

Transferring Information from Access

Choose the Insert Object command and scroll through the list of object types you can embed. No Microsoft Access objects to insert. Access is not a server application, at least not in the same way that Excel and PowerPoint are OLE servers. You can extract information from an Access table to fill mail merge fields in a Word document, but you can't link to Access objects from another application or embed them in a destination document.

We'll look at Word's mail merge feature—and the ways in which it can involve Access—in Chapter 11, "Mastering Mergers." In the section below, we'll explore the other standout information-sharing feature in Access: the Output To command.

Outputting to a Word Document

With the Output To command, you can save information that you've created in Access as a Word document. The information might consist of a table or a query (or a selection from either), or it might comprise data in a form, report, or module. And you might output the information for a variety of reasons: so that you can edit it with Word's editing and formatting resources, for example, or so that you can share the information with another person—say, someone who uses Word but not Access. The Output To command preserves most of the formatting in the Access object.

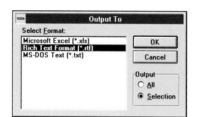

To use the Output To command with an Access table or query, load the database and open the item you want to save. Then select the (adjacent) rows or columns you want to save—or make no selection if you want to save the entire table or query. Choose Output To from the File menu to display the Output To dialog box.

If you plan to load the file into Word, you probably want to retain as much formatting as possible, including the tabular arrangement, shading, and font formatting, so select Rich Text Format as the destination file type. If you indicated a selection of information, the Output option panel is active: You can decide to output either the selected information or the entire table or query. Click OK after you finish.

The next Output To dialog box is basically a Save As dialog box: Assign a name and location to the output file. When you click OK, Access saves the file. The new document, opened in Word, closely resembles Datasheet view in Access. If the saved information includes a memo field, some of the data might be truncated. The Output To command saves no more than 255 characters in a single memo field (whereas Access allows 64,000).

If you want to work on the table or the query immediately in Word, select the AutoStart check box in the Output To dialog box before clicking OK. Then, when you click OK, Word is launched and the new file is loaded directly into Word. The figures on the next page show the before and after screens.

NO DIRECT ACCESS

Access cannot save in a Word format the contents of OLE fields—pictures or charts or other objects that are linked to or embedded from other applications. When they're essential, you can usually copy and paste these items separately.

SELECTIVE WAYS

You can use the Show Columns command to show and hide columns if you want to select (and output) fields that are not otherwise adjacent.

QUICK OUTPUT

To quickly output an Access report to Word, open the report in Print Preview mode and click the **Publish It in MS Word** button on the Print Preview toolbar. The report is named automatically, saved in Rich Text Format, and loaded into Word.

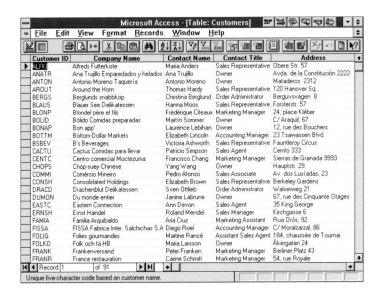

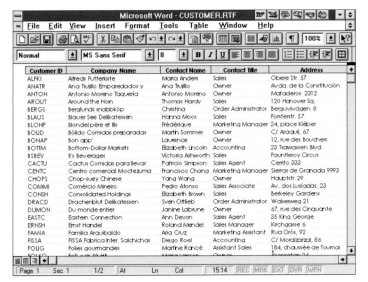

Use the Output To command to transfer information from Access to Word and maintain a great deal of Access table formatting in Word.

Chapter 7

Bringing Information into Excel

Cell Mates

OLE makes it possible to introduce a great assortment of objects into a Microsoft Excel worksheet. From within the Microsoft Office suite, you can embed such objects as clip art, equations, and WordArt effects in Excel using the various shared applications; and you can link and embed objects from Microsoft Word and Microsoft PowerPoint. In addition, you can export information from Microsoft Access for analysis in a worksheet. In this chapter, we'll focus on information sharing—especially OLE interactions—between Excel and the other major Office applications.

You can actually link information from one Excel worksheet to another or from one workbook to another without explicitly involving OLE (or even DDE). You simply copy a cell or a block of cells to the Clipboard, switch to a different worksheet or workbook, and choose Paste Special from the Edit menu. The dialog box that appears isn't the same one that you see for OLE linking, but it has a Paste Link option that you can select, and the result is similar. In the formula bar, you'll find what's called an *external reference*—similar

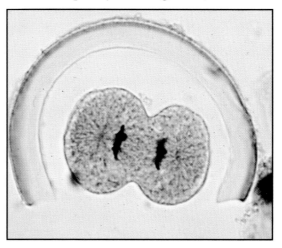

DDE

DDE, or dynamic data exchange, is a technology that predates OLE and still underlies the updating that occurs between an object in a destination document and the information in a source file. OLE has improved on DDE by providing easier commerce between the destination and the server and by adding the option of embedding objects from other applications.

to what you find in the formula bar that accompanies an OLE object (as you'll see later in this chapter). The external reference specifies a different location and perhaps a different filename from the current worksheet, but the server application is still Excel.

You can also embed information in Excel without direct reference to OLE. For example, you can create a chart on its own chart sheet in a workbook, or you can embed it in a worksheet so that it can be viewed with the data it graphically depicts. The chart is not embedded in exactly the same way that an OLE object is embedded in a worksheet, but the behavior of the chart is similar.

As you work with OLE objects in Excel, you'll find that they are easy to move on the screen and incorporate in the layout of your worksheets or in your charted information. And if you are distributing a workbook on line, you have the usual option of displaying an OLE object as an icon, whether it's a linked Word document or an embedded PowerPoint presentation. Icons are especially appropriate if the information they represent expands on the chart or the worksheet but would be distracting if it were always visible.

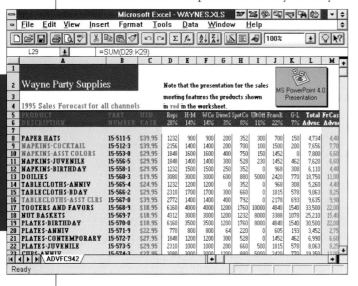

How Excel Stores an Object

When you link to an object from an Excel worksheet or embed an object in an Excel worksheet, the object appears in the worksheet with a formula that contains the critical information for connecting the object to its source application or source document. The formula appears in the formula bar when you click the object. Much as the field codes in Word reveal the source of an object in a Word document, these formulas provide a glimpse into Excel's way of handling OLE objects.

Links, Up Close   Scrutinize a link and you'll find a formula. The link formula supplies a remote reference to the item in the source file to which you've established the link. To understand how the reference is constructed, look at the formula shown here. It's the same one that appears in the formula bar for the linked object in the sample figure shown below.

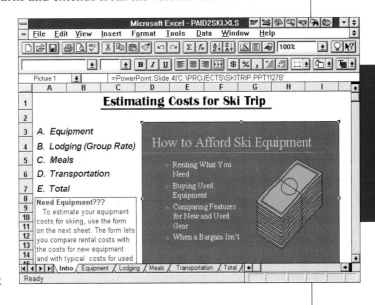

The remote reference has three arguments. The first argument, which extends from the equal sign to the vertical line, identifies the type of object—the source application, the type of application object, and the version of the application. In the figure below, for instance, the source application is PowerPoint, the application object type is Slide, and the application version is 4. If the listed object included multiple slides, the application object type would be Presentation. The second argument is the filename, which includes the drive and the pathname. It appears within single quotation marks and extends from the vertical bar to the first exclamation point. The third argument, also within single quotation marks, identifies the specific part of the file that's linked to the destination document. This might be a bookmark or a cell range or some other indicator, internal to the source program, that locates the linked item.

The link formula is generated when you use Paste Special to paste link an object into an Excel document. You *can* enter a link manually if, say, the source application is temporarily unavailable. But coming up with the appropriate item name is, in many circumstances, far from straightforward. As a rule, let the program insert the formula—you'll rarely have reason to do it the hard way.

Although you're unlikely to create links by entering a formula, you might find yourself needing to edit an existing formula—to reflect a change in the name or location of the source file, or to delete the formula entirely if you want to break the link. If the occasion arises, make changes carefully so that the pathnames and filenames are accurate and single quotation marks don't get deleted.

Pulling Back the Covers on Embedding   For embedded objects, the formula bar shows an expression based on an Excel function, EMBED. Excel inserts the formula and its function when you embed an object (using Paste Special or some other means). You can't enter an EMBED function directly; in fact, if you use the Function Wizard to look for the EMBED function, you won't even find it. Let Excel insert the function.

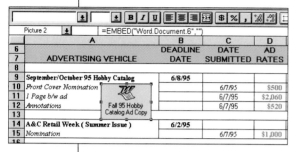

The EMBED function has two arguments, listed within the parentheses that follow the function name. You can display the formula associated with an object simply by clicking the object. Notice the formula in the following sample (from the formula bar in the figure above):

```
=EMBED("Word.Document.6","")
```

Each argument is surrounded by quotation marks, and the two arguments are separated by a comma. The first argument identifies the type of object that is embedded—the name of the server application, the type of application object, and the version of the application. In this example, the object type is Word.Document.6.

The second argument is generally empty (an empty pair of quotation marks). It determines the view of the embedded document—not the source document from which you initially copied it, but the object document that's embedded in the worksheet. The empty argument means that you're getting the full view, not a partial view.

If you use Paste Special but specify a format (such as Picture or Text) that's different from the format for the object in its server application, you won't find a formula associated with the embedded object. Only the format (in the Paste Special dialog box) that contains the word *Object* has an associated EMBED expression. For those other formats, there's no need for a formula to identify the original application, because in choosing them you forfeit the ability to reopen and edit the object in its server application.

There's little that you can do to affect the object by editing the EMBED formula. You can delete the formula entirely, leaving only a picture of the previously embedded information, but that's about it. The resulting graphic requires less storage space than the embedded object does, but it can no longer be edited in the original application. If you accidentally make other (less drastic) edits to the formula, you'll probably run up against a confused Excel, which will provide you with a barrage of error notifications. Press Esc to restore the pre-edited formula.

Working with Linked and Embedded Objects

The techniques for working with OLE objects in Excel are consistent with those for the other major Office applications. Naturally, you'll find idiosyn-

crasies related to the design of the Excel interface and to the specific tasks for which the program was developed. Here are some highlights:

Editing an OLE Object   The procedures for activating an object in Excel for editing are similar to the procedures in the other Office applications. Double-clicking an OLE object within a worksheet generally opens it in its original application—assuming that you linked or embedded it in the native format of the original application. Double-clicking an object that was pasted in a different format, such as the Picture format, displays the Format Object

dialog box. And depending on the object type, double-clicking can have still other effects. For example, it can cause a PowerPoint presentation object to launch a slide show.

The reliable standby technique for activating an object is to click the object (so that its border and sizing handles are visible), open the Edit menu, and choose Edit from the submenu that appears when you select the command at the bottom of the menu, which names the selected object. You can also point to the object and click the right mouse button to display the shortcut menu. On that menu (or on a submenu, depending on the object type), you'll generally find an Edit command for editing the object.

After you finish editing, click outside the object or close the source application. If you're editing a linked object, you can simply switch back to Excel (using the Microsoft Office Manager toolbar) if you want to leave the source application open.

Formatting an Object in Excel   You can make certain changes to an object without having to edit it with its source application. You can, for example, change colors and fill patterns for a Word object without leaving Excel. What's more, these changes "stick," in the sense that Excel retains the formatting and reapplies it when the link is updated.

We'll look at a specific example in the upcoming section titled "Linking to a Word Document." For now, simply take note of the dialog box that produces

SOURCE WON'T START

Double-clicking a linked object to edit the source document can result in an error message that says *Cannot start the source application for this document*. This might be due to insufficient computer memory or to the file being already open. If neither of these conditions can be blamed, check the filename in the formula bar. This error message can also appear if the source file no longer exists as indicated in the remote reference. You might need to correct the source location or the filename.

the changes. To display it, point to an OLE object in a worksheet, display the shortcut menu, and choose Format Object. Survey the options on the Patterns tab of the Format Object dialog box: They enable you to modify or eliminate the automatic border that Excel places around graphic ob-

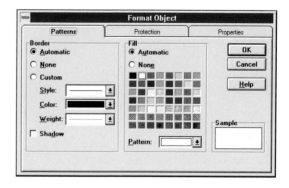

jects and to specify the background colors and fill patterns.

Updating Linked Information   By default, a linked object in Excel is updated automatically—whenever you open the destination document and whenever you change information in the source document (if the destination document is open at the same time). When you open an Excel workbook that contains links to other documents, the program asks whether you want to update the linked information. If you choose No, Excel does not reestablish the links to refresh the information displayed in the workbook.

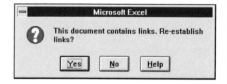

The Links command on the Edit menu is your ticket to modifying the behavior of the link. In the Links dialog box, you can select one or more links and use the option buttons to set either manual or automatic updating. When the Manual option button is selected, the corresponding link is not updated to match the source file unless you return to the Links dialog box, select the link, and choose the Update Now button.

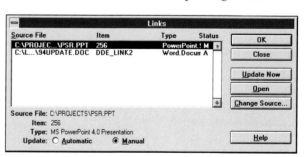

Changing the Source for a Link   If you rename or relocate a file that supplies information to other linked destination documents, the links are no longer effective. By correcting the remote reference, however, you can restore the links and revive the updating process. All in a day's work.

Correcting the reference boils down to checking the pathname and filename. It's unlikely that you'll need to make changes to other parts of the remote

QUICK UPDATE

If you want links to be reestablished automatically when you open a file—with no prompting for your OK—choose Options from the Tools menu, select the Edit tab of the Options dialog box, and deselect the Ask to Update Automatic Links check box.

INCALCULABLE LINKS

Although Excel seems to implement links as formulas, it does not treat them as formulas in all of the ways that you might expect. For example, if you press F9 to execute the Calculate Now command, Excel does not update a manual link. You still have to choose the Edit Links command and the Update Now button.

reference—the application or item identifiers—but it's possible. (See the Power Play on the next page, "Tearing and Repairing Bookmarks.") The path in the formula bar is expressed normally (no double backslashes or other quirkiness), but it must appear within single quotation marks. You can edit the formula in the formula bar: Click the object, click in the formula bar, edit the reference, and press Enter. You can also display the Links dialog box, choose the Change Source button, and edit the reference in the text box. Alas, this often seems to produce errors, so it's better to edit directly in the formula bar.

Locking and Unlocking an Object   To lock an object, whether it's linked or embedded, is simple: Select it, choose the Format Object command, select the Locked check box on the Protection tab of the Format Object dialog box, and click OK. Understanding what you've just done is only slightly more difficult.

You see, selecting Locked doesn't lock an object in the way that you might expect. Locking *identifies* the object as one that you'd like to prevent other people from changing. But the protection is not actually initiated by locking; you have to take the further step of opening the Tools menu, displaying its Protection submenu, and choosing Protect Sheet. In the Protect Sheet dialog box, be sure that the Objects check box is selected.

Of course, having a two-step protection process makes sense: You can protect and unprotect parts of a worksheet without having to select items repeatedly as you lock or unlock a long list of objects and ranges. But calling the first step "locking" can lead you to believe that you're finished, when you've only completed the first step.

When an object is locked and protection is turned on, you cannot select the object, much less activate it for editing. And if you select the link in the Links dialog box, the Update Now button is grayed-out to indicate that updating is not available. Nevertheless, the protection feature doesn't seem to be intended to prevent updates to the locked objects. You might not be able to open the source document with the Edit Links command, but you can switch to the source application and then open, edit, and save the source document. When you reopen the protected document (in which objects are locked), Excel still asks whether you want to reestablish the links, and it updates them if you choose Yes. Go figure.

Breaking a Link and Other Degrees of Separation   To break a link (in a civil way), select the object in the destination document, click once in the formula bar to highlight the entire formula, and press the Del key. With the disappearance of the remote reference, the picture of the information is stranded in Excel. It will remain in the document but will no longer be updated when the source file changes.

GOTTA UPDATE

The Calculation tab of the Options dialog box has a check box labeled Update Remote References. When you're dealing with remote references to Word and PowerPoint objects, deselecting the check box does not affect their updating. To prevent automatic updating, you must edit the link to select manual rather than automatic updating.

POWER PLAY

Tearing and Repairing Bookmarks

The link from an Excel document to a Word source file requires a remote reference, as you know. The item to which the link is established (in Word) is ultimately identified by a bookmark—in the remote reference and in the Word document. The bookmarks, as Word assigns them, take the form DDE_LINK1, DDE_LINK2, and so on.

To see the bookmarks in a Word document, you can display the large (nonprinting) brackets that mark the beginning and end of any bookmarked text. Think of these brackets as bookends. (Where the brackets indicate a bookmark for an insertion point rather than for a text block, the bookmark looks more like an oversized I-beam than a pair of facing brackets.) The check box that shows or hides the brackets is on the View tab of Word's Options dialog box (reached via the Tools menu). You might want to display the bookmarks when you edit a document that contains links so that you don't accidentally strand linked information somewhere by deleting the brackets.

DELETE-RESISTANT FORMULAS

When you link from a Word document using the Text format (in Paste Special), the reference in the formula bar is an array formula, enclosed in curly brackets { }. Because Excel won't let you delete the array formula directly, you must first convert the array to its values. That cancels the array formula, and with it the link. To do this, select and copy the cells containing the *entire* array to the Clipboard, choose Paste Special, select the Values option button, and click OK. The pasted values replace the array and the formula will be gone. (Press Esc to cancel the selection.)

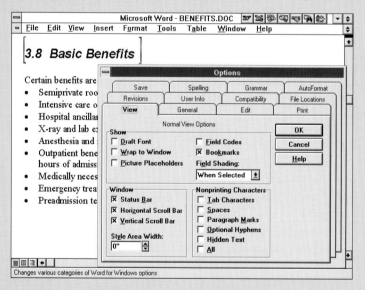

If you discover, when you try to activate a link, that the source application won't start and that the cause is a deleted bookmark, you can revive the link by noting the number of the stranded bookmark in the formula bar and inserting a bookmark with the same number in the Word document (unless it's easier to create a new link anyway). To insert a bookmark in Word, select the appropriate text, choose the Edit Bookmark command to display the Bookmark dialog box, type the bookmark name, and click the Add button. The link in Excel will subsequently be updated from the newly defined bookmark.

Links can be broken from the source end, but the result is often not what you expect, and it can be messy. Consider the following situation. While editing a Word document, you delete a large block of text. Within the deleted block was a paragraph to which an Excel document was linked. Now it's completely gone, and the destination document has nothing to which it can reestablish the link. The formula with its dead-end remote reference remains, and the graphic representation is preserved (like a memory) as it existed before the source item was deleted. Perhaps this is the outcome you want. If not, see the Power Play on the facing page ("Tearing and Repairing Bookmarks").

A similar transformation occurs when you delete the formula for an embedded object. If the object was embedded in a native format for the server—a Word item embedded as a Microsoft Word 6.0 Document Object, for example—deleting the formula means that you can no longer edit the object with the server application; instead, you're left with the graphic representation of the data, to which you can apply some formatting (with Format Object options), but little else.

CONVERTING AN OBJECT

An alternative to deleting the EMBED expression is to choose the Convert command from the Edit menu or the shortcut menu to convert a native server object to a picture. Not only can the picture be formatted (using Format Object options), but it can also be edited with the drawing tools. The Convert command is on the same submenu as the Edit command.

Embedding New Objects

To embed new information, rather than a copy of existing information, in an Excel worksheet, choose the Object command from the Insert menu. In the resulting dialog box, select the Create New tab if it's not already displayed. The other tab, Create from File, simply provides another way of embedding existing information—from a file.

You can embed new information from any of the object types listed in the Object Type list box. Selecting an object type (and clicking OK) starts the appropriate application. Before you click OK, however, give some thought to the Display as Icon check box. A worksheet is often a busy document, densely packed with figures. If the embedded information provides support for the contents of the worksheet that the reader will view on line, embedding the information so that it's displayed as an icon might be the best course.

When you finish creating the information, click outside the object to return to your worksheet, or exit the server application if it is displayed in a separate window.

Embedding a New Object

To embed new information in an Excel worksheet as an object, follow these steps:

1. Select the cell in which you want the upper left corner of the embedded object to appear.
2. From the Insert menu, choose Object.
3. On the Create New tab, select the type of object you want to embed.
4. Click OK. Depending on the application, either a separate window opens or the application's menus and toolbars temporarily replace those of Excel.
5. After you create the object you want to embed, click the worksheet outside the object or exit the server application to return to Excel.

Transferring Information from Word

OLE offers two models for transferring information from a Word document to Excel: linking the information from a separate source file, and embedding it as an object in a worksheet. Embedding can take place by way of the Clipboard or as a direct drag-and-drop action. Before we explore the OLE transfers, however, let's consider what happens when you paste information normally into a worksheet—using the Clipboard and the Paste command.

Pasting Text from a Word Document

Transferring text from Word using the Paste command is the best choice in some circumstances. But before we look at one such circumstance, let's review the limitations. If the Word document contains a discussion of some kind, arranged as a series of paragraphs, pasting the text into a cell might not be a good choice. The formatting is lost, and each paragraph from the Word document is pasted into a separate row of the worksheet. You can improve on this result by pasting the selected text into a text box: The text wraps within the text box, but the formatting is still lost. With Excel, you can achieve many of the same formatting effects that you can in a word-processed document, but the fact remains that you have to reimpose them; they don't survive normal pasting from the Clipboard.

Incidentally, when you drag and drop Word text into a cell in an Excel worksheet, the result is pasted text, as described above: no formatting, one paragraph per row. You might expect it to produce an embedded Word document—when you go in the opposite direction, it embeds an Excel object in a Word document—but from Word to Excel, it's normal pasting.

Just when things are beginning to seem uniformly bleak, here's the good news. If the information in the Word document is intended for tabular presentation, normal pasting is probably the best route for transferring it to an Excel worksheet. If the information is already formatted as a Word table, Excel pastes each table cell into a separate worksheet cell. Very neat.

If the text is not a Word table but contains other clues for defining the column boundaries, paste the text from the Clipboard, and with the pasted

If your pasted text contains delimiters, step 2 of the Convert Text to Columns Wizard lets you specify which characters they are.

Convert Text to Columns Wizard - Step 2 of 3

This screen lets you set the delimiters your data contains.
You can see how your text is affected in the preview below.

Delimiters
☐ Tab ☐ Semicolon ☐ Comma ☐ Treat consecutive delimiters as one
☐ Space ☒ Other: / Text Qualifier: "

Data Preview

FirstName	LastName	Company	Address1	Add
Paul	Martin	Astro Mountain Bike	987 1st St.	
Anne	Gabor	GG&G	123 Main	Sui
Maria	Mercier	West Coast Sales	1224 23rd Ave.	
Adam	Herder	Exotic Excursions	832 Easy St.	
Donna	Rauh	Enchantment Lakes	543 Lake St.	

Help   Cancel   < Back   Next >   Finish

information still selected, choose the Text to Columns command from the Data menu. Excel launches the Convert Text to Columns Wizard, which lets you identify the best way of parsing the pasted text into columns of cells. In most cases, you do this by setting one or more characters that are used in the text as delimiters. The wizard concludes by letting you assign a data type to the information in each column. (It even lets you eliminate entire columns from the finished data set.)

Linking to a Word Document

Linking to a Word document from a worksheet is a useful way of incorporating regularly updated information, such as a product development status report or a summary of an investment fund's quarterly performance. Text information that is best maintained in word-processed documents can, by means of the link, be repeated accurately and automatically to supplement essentially figure-driven reports and customer statements.

To establish the link using OLE, the usual procedure applies: Copy the text to the Clipboard in Word, switch to Excel, pick a location for the object, and choose Paste Special from the Edit menu. The As list box in the Paste Special dialog box provides three format choices when you're linking to text:

Linking Format	Result
Microsoft Word 6.0 Document Object	The object is represented in a picture format, but double-clicking it takes you directly to the Word source file for editing.
Picture	The object is inserted in a picture format (Windows metafile), which is similar to a bitmap but consumes less storage space and produces better printed output.
Text	The object is linked as unformatted text and is part of an array. Although that format seems native to Excel, you cannot edit the text without returning to the source file (or converting the array to values).

For most circumstances in which you want to establish a link to Word text, choosing the Word document object is best. As a practical matter, choosing Picture when you're linking has the same result: Text formatting is retained, and the source document can be readily edited in Word. You can reactivate the source file for editing by double-clicking the object.

The Text format works well for linking a Word table: Formatting is lost, but the tabular arrangement is

---

PARSE

Parsing is the process of applying rules that break up a block of selected text and differentiate one item from another. Text to be parsed normally contains one or more characters—such as tabs, spaces, or punctuation marks—that are reserved for separating, or delimiting, individual items.

Linking to a Word Document

To link an Excel worksheet to information in a Word document, open both the worksheet and the Word source document. Be sure that you've saved the Word document. Then follow these steps:

1. Select the information in the Word document and copy it to the Clipboard.
2. Switch to the Excel worksheet and select the cell in which you want the upper left corner of the information to appear.
3. From the Edit menu or the shortcut menu, choose Paste Special.
4. Select the Paste Link option button, and in the As list box, select Microsoft Word 6.0 Document Object.
5. Click OK.

translated to the cell grid. However, if you want to activate the source in that case, double-clicking the object is not helpful: It simply initiates direct editing (of the formula) in the selected cell. Instead, choose Links from the Edit menu, or point to the object and choose Edit Links from the shortcut menu. Then select the link you want to edit, and choose Open to open its source file.

Formatting an Object   Excel lets you control certain formatting and layout properties of the linked object, such as the background color, and then enforces those settings, even when the Word document updates the linked information. Here's an example:

Suppose you've got Word text linked to the bottom of a worksheet that reports quarterly financial results for a given fund. By default, Excel displays and prints the Word object with a border, but let's eliminate that border and add a light blue background using Excel's Format Object dialog box, as shown in the first figure. The result retains these formatting properties, even after the source file is edited, as shown in the second figure.

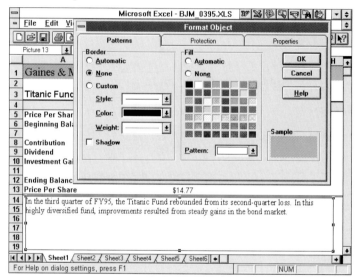

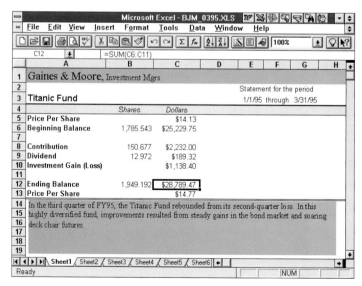

Notice that the object has been updated, but Excel has enforced its own formatting (the colored background) for the object.

POWER PLAY

Formatting Linked Information in Excel

Suppose you've created a link to information in a Word document and you want to apply special fonts and alignment that pertain in Excel but not in the source document. That is, you want the appearance, but not the content, to be independent of the source file. Here's a clever (but necessarily roundabout) way to do it.

When you select an OLE object and then choose the Format Object command, the dialog box offers three tabs: Patterns, Protection, and Properties. But if you select a text box that you created in the worksheet, the corresponding Format Object dialog box has two additional tabs: Font and Alignment. That's nice, but you can't link to the object from inside a text box. So how do these additional formatting tabs help?

You *can* display a linked paragraph in a text box—not by establishing the link from the text box directly, but by using the text box to display the contents of a cell that has a link to the text paragraph. So the text is updated (unformatted) from the Word source document, and you display the same paragraph in the text box, formatted to the extent that Excel permits in text boxes.

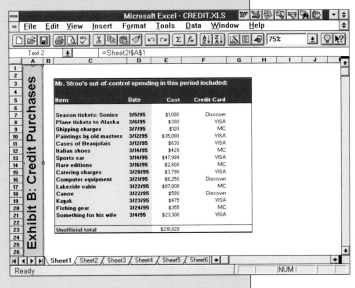

To display cell contents in the text box, select the text box but do not activate it for editing. (It has a fuzzy border with sizing handles but no blinking insertion point in the box.) Now enter a formula in the formula bar that simply references an out-of-the-way cell— behind the text box or in a different worksheet. Let's try this one: =Sheet2!$A$1. Select the referenced cell, choose the Paste Special command, and use the Paste Link option to insert the Clipboard contents (a single paragraph from a Word document) as text. Select the text box, and you can use the Format Object command to apply font and alignment options (as well as patterns and the rest), but only to the entire paragraph, not to individual words or characters.

Embedding Existing Information as a Word Object

You can embed existing information from a Word document in your Excel worksheet using the Copy and Paste Special commands. By now, you're probably familiar with this procedure. In the Paste Special dialog box, the As list box usually lists three object types you can paste. The first is Microsoft Word 6.0 Document Object, a type that carries with it all the formatting that exists in the original Word document. That's the best choice if you want the full benefits of embedding—the object remains fully editable with its server application.

If the selection in the Word document is a graphic, such as an illustration created with Word Picture or the Drawing toolbar, the As list box for Paste Special includes Microsoft Word 6.0 Picture Object (instead of Microsoft Word 6.0 Document Object). Choose this format if you want to be able to edit the object as a Word Picture in the future. Choosing Picture results in a static picture.

The first time you edit a Word object, you might find that the scaling is unworkably small, or that when you return to the Excel destination document, the object has changed size or its border has changed dimensions. You might need to resize and rescale the object each time you edit it.

EMBED + LINK = GP FAULT

If you link information from an embedded Word document object in one worksheet to another worksheet, a general protection (GP) fault occurs when you edit this linked information. You can, without this little inconvenience, link the information to the worksheet that contains the embedded object. The error occurs only when you link information from an embedded Word document object in one worksheet to *another* worksheet.

NOTHING LEFT

If your Word text is formatted to hang into the left margin, the characters that extend into the margin might be lost in the process of linking or embedding the text in a worksheet. This can occur if the negative indent places the text within the left margin of your Word document. When you make a selection for embedding, Word considers the page margins to be the left and right boundaries of the object. To avoid losing text in the process, set your margins, define your styles, and apply your paragraph formatting so that formatted text always falls within the page margins.

Embedding Existing Information

To embed existing information from a Word document in an Excel worksheet, begin by opening both the Word document and the Excel worksheet. Then follow these steps:

1. Select the text or graphic that you want to embed in the Excel worksheet.
2. Copy the selection to the Clipboard.
3. Switch to the worksheet and select the cell in which you want the upper left corner of the text or graphic to appear.
4. Choose Paste Special from the Edit menu or the shortcut menu.
5. Be sure the Paste option button (not Paste Link) is selected, and in the As list box, select Microsoft Word 6.0 Document (or Picture) Object.
6. Click OK.

Transferring Information from PowerPoint

You can paste slides from a PowerPoint presentation into an Excel worksheet in a variety of ways. You can embed a slide or multiple slides, and you can link to a slide or to a complete presentation. In the worksheet, the linked slide or complete presentation can be displayed as a slide image or as an icon.

As you'll see in the following sections, you can link or embed existing slides using the familiar Copy and Paste Special commands. Using the Paste command—or drag and drop—from a PowerPoint presentation to a worksheet results in an embedded slide or presentation object. Don't forget that you have to hold down the Ctrl key while you drag if you want to copy, not cut, the slide in the original presentation.

Once a slide is linked or embedded in your worksheet, you can drag it (or the icon) to the location that seems to fit best with the layout of the information. If the slide overlaps another object, you can use commands on the slide's shortcut menu to move the slide in front of or behind the other object. You can also resize the slide by clicking it to select it and then dragging any of its sizing handles.

IN PROPORTION
To resize a linked or embedded slide but keep its dimensions proportional to the original, hold down the Shift key while you drag one of the corner sizing handles.

Linking to a PowerPoint Slide

Use linking when you want to paste a slide into a worksheet and create a link to the source presentation. Thereafter, the slide shown in the worksheet will always match the source slide in PowerPoint. As for distributing the worksheet, you can link to a single slide and distribute copies of the worksheet in printed form or electronically. Other people who read the compound document can view the image of the slide that's included in the worksheet. But they will run up against limitations under certain circumstances:

- Editing the slide is impossible unless the user's computer has access to the source file and to PowerPoint on the local disk or at a shared location.

- Viewing the linked presentation is impossible unless the user's computer has PowerPoint or Power-Point Viewer installed locally or available at a shared location, and has access to the source file.

To prepare for the link, save your PowerPoint presentation, if it is not already saved. You cannot create a link to a presentation that has not been named and saved to a file. When you establish the link, begin by selecting a slide from the

---

Linking to a PowerPoint Slide

To link an Excel worksheet to a PowerPoint slide, begin by opening both the PowerPoint presentation and the Excel worksheet. Be sure that you've saved the presentation. Then follow these steps:

1. In PowerPoint, switch to Slide Sorter view and select the slide you want to see in your worksheet.
2. Copy the selection to the Clipboard.
3. Switch to the Excel worksheet, and select the cell in which you want the upper left corner of the slide to appear.
4. Choose Paste Special from the Edit menu or the shortcut menu.
5. Select the Paste Link option button, and in the As list box, select MS PowerPoint 4.0 Slide Object.
6. Click OK.

presentation, in Slide Sorter view. Selecting multiple slides for linking makes little difference in the result—you'll see only the first selected slide in the worksheet. And whether you link to a single slide or to multiple slides (a presentation object), the link enables you to view the complete presentation. After you switch to Excel and display the Paste Special dialog box, select the Paste Link option button. In the As list box, the first choice is MS PowerPoint 4.0 Slide Object. Select the Display as Icon check box if you want the worksheet to display an icon, rather than a slide image, to represent the linked presentation source file.

You cannot view the linked PowerPoint presentation object in a slide show directly from Excel, as you can with an embedded presentation. If you want to view the linked presentation, double-click the object to open it in PowerPoint. Then click the Slide Show button at the bottom of the window—the show starts with the first linked slide and continues through the remainder of the presentation. Press a key or click with the mouse to advance to the next slide, or press Esc to end the show.

Embedding PowerPoint Slides

To embed existing slides, open the presentation and switch to Slide Sorter view. You can select a single slide or multiple slides. Use Shift+click to select multiple slides, or choose Select All from the Edit menu to select the entire presentation. When you're embedding, as opposed to linking, the slides you choose determine the content of the presentation in the destination document, but a single slide (the lowest-numbered one) still represents the series. Copy the slide or slides to the Clipboard and then paste them into your Excel worksheet.

You can also use drag and drop to embed a single slide or a series of slides in a worksheet: Tile the presentation and worksheet windows, and be sure to hold down the Ctrl key while you drag if you want to copy the slide rather than cut it from the presentation.

Copying your selection to the Clipboard and embedding it with Paste Special gives you a wider range of options than you get with pasting or with drag and drop. Be sure to select the Paste option button to embed, instead of link, the object. Here are the formats you'll find in the As list box:

Embedding Format	Result
MS PowerPoint 4.0 Slide Object	This format is available if you're pasting a single slide, rather than a series of slides. Double-click the resulting object to edit it in PowerPoint.
MS PowerPoint 4.0 Presentation Object	This format is available if you've copied multiple slides—from two slides to a complete presentation. All of the selected slides remain editable in PowerPoint. Double-click the resulting object to view a full-screen slide show that consists of the slides you selected.
Picture	This format embeds a static image of a single slide. It requires less storage space than a bitmap and far less than a PowerPoint object.

Embedding PowerPoint Slides

To embed one or more PowerPoint slides in an Excel worksheet, begin by opening both the PowerPoint presentation and the Excel worksheet. Be sure that you've saved the presentation. Then follow these steps:

1. In PowerPoint, switch to Slide Sorter view and select the slide or slides that you want to embed in the worksheet.
2. Copy the selection to the Clipboard.
3. Switch to the Excel worksheet and select the cell in which you want the upper left corner of the (representative) slide to appear.
4. Choose Paste Special from the Edit menu or the shortcut menu.
5. Be sure that the Paste option button (not Paste Link) is selected, and in the As list box, select MS PowerPoint 4.0 Slide (or Presentation) Object.
6. Click OK.

Click OK after you select a format. Of course, if you want the presentation to appear in the worksheet as an icon, select the Display as Icon check box before you click OK. Representing the embedded object as an icon makes sense if you're distributing the compound document on line and you think that some readers will find the slides distracting.

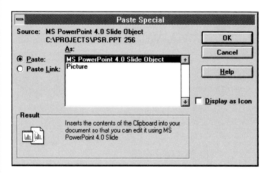

You can edit an embedded PowerPoint object (a slide or a presentation) by pointing to it, displaying the shortcut menu, and choosing Edit from the PowerPoint object's submenu. After you finish editing, choose Close from PowerPoint's File menu to (simultaneously) return to Excel and update the object in the worksheet.

OBJECT SHUFFLE
You can convert a single embedded slide to a presentation by pointing to the slide (or icon), displaying the shortcut menu, and choosing Convert from the Power-Point object's submenu. In the As list box, select MS PowerPoint 4.0 Presentation Object and click OK. Once you've converted the slide to a presentation, you can double-click the slide (or the icon) to have it appear as a one-slide full-screen show.

Transferring Information from Access

The information-sharing possibilities with Access do not include linking or embedding Access objects, since Access is not an OLE server application. What you can do, and do handily, is output information to Excel from the Database window of a table, query, form, or report. Commonly, the reason for outputting the database information to Excel is to take advantage of Excel's analytic tools. Let's see what's involved in outputting Access objects of various types and then using the exported information in a pivot table, one of Excel's powerful data analysis tools.

Outputting to a Worksheet

The Output To command on the File menu can save the output of a table, query, form, or report to a file in Excel (XLS) format. The output file resembles Datasheet view in Access and preserves most formatting elements—fonts, layout, and the like. The worksheet omits subforms and subreports and excludes the contents of any OLE fields.

BEFORE YOU SELECT

You can use the Show Columns command to show and hide columns in a table, query, or form if you want to select (and output) a block of fields that are not otherwise adjacent.

To use the Output To command, load the database and select the item you want to save. For a table or a query, you can first open the item to select the (adjacent) rows or columns you want to save. After you've made your selection (an entire item or a part), choose Output To from the File menu to display your options.

Select Microsoft Excel as the destination file type. If you selected specific rows, the small option panel in the dialog box is active: You can decide to output either the selected information or the entire table or query. Click OK after you finish.

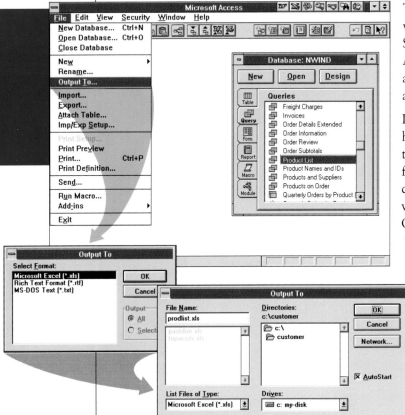

The next Output To window is basically a Save As dialog box: Assign the output file a name and a location, and click OK.

In the example shown here, we're outputting the Product List query from the NWIND.MDB database that is included with Access. In the second Output To dialog box, we assigned a filename, PRODLIST.XLS, in the CUSTOMER directory, and we selected the AutoStart check box to open the newly saved workbook in Excel.

When you click OK, Access outputs the query as a new file and automatically starts Excel with the new file open. The output process is fairly rapid because the number of records (69) is relatively small.

Generating a Pivot Table from Access Data

To demonstrate Excel's data analysis resources, let's create a simple pivot table with information exported from Access. Pivot tables provide a powerful means of manipulating and summarizing data flexibly. By shifting information back and forth between columns and rows, you can produce interesting sums and comparisons at the intersection points.

Using the PivotTable Wizard   For our sample pivot table, we'll work with PRODLIST.XLS, the worksheet we created in the previous section from the Product List query in NWIND.MDB. With the new file open, select any cell that contains data, and then execute the PivotTable Wizard, as described here:

1. Choose PivotTable from the Data menu. Excel displays the first of four steps for the PivotTable Wizard.

2. The first step asks you what type of data the table is to be built from. Click the Next button to use the default choice, an Excel list.

3. In step 2, the dialog box already displays a range to use for building the table. This range represents the entire table, $A$1:$J$70. Click Next to accept this range.

4. In step 3, you lay out the pivot table. The information fields, extracted from the column headings in the worksheet, are arranged in stacks of rectangles on the right side of the dialog box. The scheme for your pivot table is displayed to the left, with placeholders labeling its key components.

   Drag the Category field to the Page placeholder. Drag the Product Name field to the Row placeholder. Drag the Units In Stock and the Units On Order fields to the Data placeholder. (When you drop them there, the

   wizard displays Sum of Units In Stock and Sum of Units On Order, as shown here.)

   Click Next to move to the final step of the wizard.

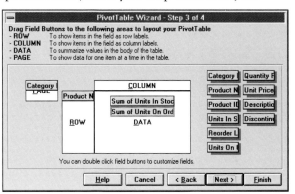

SNAP ANALYSIS
As an alternative to the Output To command on the File menu, you can use the Analyze It with MS Excel toolbar button. Clicking the button saves the selection to an XLS file (located in the Access working directory) and opens the worksheet in Excel.

DETAILS, DETAILS
Double-clicking any of the field rectangles brings up a dialog box that shows the full name of the field (which you can customize for your table). Other options depend on the area of the table to which you've dragged the field. In the Data area, for example, you can choose how you want to summarize the information that's compressed into a cell—as a count of entries, a sum of their values, or an average of their values (among other options).

5. In the final dialog box, you can specify the PivotTable Starting Cell by pointing to or typing a cell location for the upper left corner of the pivot table. If you leave the box empty, the wizard creates the pivot table in a blank worksheet in front of the current worksheet (the one that displays

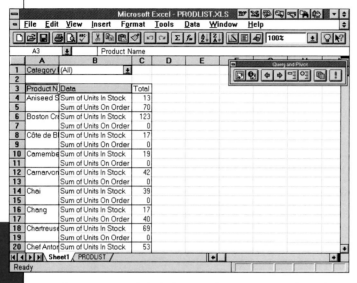

your exported Access data). Leave the box empty and click Finish to accept the default settings. The result is shown at left.

As you can see, each pair of rows is now given to one product, and the list is re-sorted by product name rather than by category. For each product, the data area has one row labeled Sum of Units In Stock and another labeled Sum of Units On Order. The third column, Total, is the sum of units in stock and the sum of units on order for each product. If you pull down the list of Categories at the top of the worksheet, you can choose among the different product categories. Initially, the pivot table contains entries for all of the categories, but you can limit the table to any of the categories in the drop-down list box.

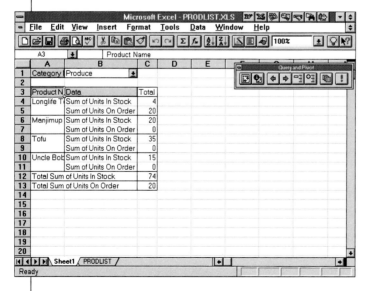

These subsets are considered separate pages of the pivot table. If you select Produce from the Category Name list, for example, you'll see the subset of the table entries, as shown in the figure at left.

Notice, too, that the Query and Pivot toolbar is displayed. Among other things, it lets you return to the wizard to rearrange rows and columns and to redefine any of the other options you set.

Showing Detail and Formatting   Pivot tables are wonderfully dynamic. You can display various pages of the table, drag fields around to view the information differently, reformat cells, and create charts. You can even expand the information that's been summarized in a given cell to see the details in the original worksheet. Even with the simple pivot table we've created, we can demonstrate a few of these options.

First, let's see how easily you can reformat the pivot table. We have columns too narrow for the data they contain, and for on-screen viewing we might as well take advantage of the available colors. Oh, and there's no reason to keep the generic name for this sheet—let's call it Unit Levels.

1. Drag the divider between column A and column B to the right until column A accommodates the longest product name, Jack's New England Clam Chowder.

2. Choose the AutoFormat command from the Format menu.

3. In the AutoFormat dialog box, select Colorful 2 in the Table Format list, and then click OK. Voilà—a handsome change.

4. To rename the worksheet, double-click the worksheet tab at the bottom of the window. In the dialog box, type *Unit Levels* and click Enter. The completed worksheet is shown below.

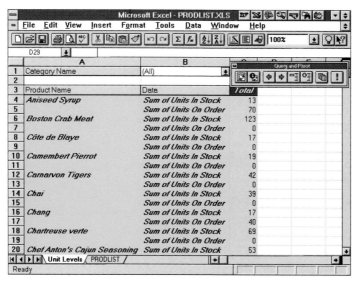

Our pivot table, reformatted and renamed.

Next, we'll look at techniques for showing additional details in the table. We'll start by including the reorder level for Longlife Tofu, information that is included in the PRODLIST.XLS worksheet but is not part of the pivot table.

We'll also break down the summed value for units on order into its component entries. In the Category Name drop-down list, select Produce to display the pivot table data for the four items in this category.

1. Double-click the first item, Longlife Tofu. Excel displays the Show Detail dialog box for that row label.

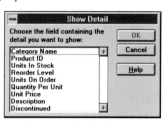

2. Select Reorder Level and click OK. The pivot table inserts the reorder level (and the corresponding heading) for Longlife Tofu.

3. After you check this information (as shown in the worksheet at right), click the Undo button on the Standard toolbar to eliminate it.

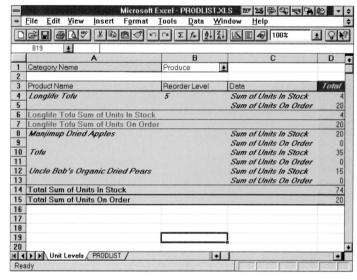

4. Point to the last entry in the Total column—the cell opposite the label Total Sum of Units On Order. Double-click the cell to show the full details for the field entries that constitute this sum. The result is inserted in a new worksheet. As you can see, it comprises all of the Produce entries and shows all of the fields from the exported worksheet. Full details—at the (double) click of a button.

Chapter 8

Bringing Information into PowerPoint

Power Sharing

In a good presentation, the speaker's command of the subject is established immediately and is never in question from that point on. And since nothing contributes to a speaker's authority like clearly presented information, you'll appreciate Microsoft PowerPoint's ability to merge a variety of objects— including documents, tables, worksheets, charts and graphics, and even sounds and animation—from a wide range of sources. You can choose the best way to support your points regardless of the originating application.

The supporting evidence that you introduce from other applications can be placed directly on a slide—for example, you can insert a chart alongside a bulleted list of key points. Or it can appear as an icon that you can activate during the presentation to "drill down" to the additional information. In this chapter, we'll explore the techniques for transferring information to PowerPoint from the other major Microsoft Office applications.

First, we'll look at ways to share information from Microsoft Word and Microsoft Excel documents. We'll focus mainly on OLE techniques, but we'll also touch on importing information from other applications. We'll skip Microsoft Access in this chapter: Beyond normal copying and pasting, there's little to report. But PowerPoint itself can serve up some interesting objects from one presentation to another, so this chapter concludes with a look at branching within a presentation.

One other thing: Because PowerPoint is presentation oriented, it offers plenty of formatting options for the objects that you introduce from other applications. This chapter will acquaint you with many of those options. The idea, of course, is to make the linked and embedded objects blend harmoniously with the design and color scheme of the overall presentation.

OLE Objects on Slides

OLE objects don't appear to be much different from the other components that you assemble on your PowerPoint slides. In fact, most of the slide components look a lot like items in a scrapbook—photos, clippings, ticket stubs, and the like. They all seem to reside in their own rectangular spaces, which you can resize, arrange, and overlap on the slide. The OLE objects are not editable immediately, as is, say, the text in the title box or in a bulleted list: When you click a linked or embedded object, sizing handles generally appear along the perimeter of the object, but no insertion point appears within the object to await the changes you type.

In PowerPoint, the linking and embedding codes or references are not as apparent as they are in Word and Excel. To identify a linked object, select it

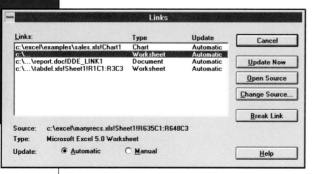

and then display the Edit menu. The last command on the menu will identify the selected object as a linked object and offer a means of editing it. To see descriptions of the existing links, choose Links from the Edit menu. In the Links dialog box, select any link in the list to identify its source in full.

Embedded objects are distinguishable from linked ones on the Edit menu. Again, look at the bottom of the menu for a command such as Microsoft ClipArt Gallery Object. An object is embedded unless it is specifically identified as linked.

Editing an OLE Object To edit a linked or embedded object, you have to activate it. This launches the original application and loads the source file (for a linked object) or the embedded object. Generally, double-clicking activates an object, but there are exceptions. A more reliable technique is to click the object with the right mouse button to display its shortcut menu, and then choose the editing command—Edit Document Link or Edit Chart Object, for example.

The server application presents itself either as a separate window or as a set of menus and toolbars that temporarily replace those of PowerPoint (except the File menu and the Window menu). After you edit the information in the

REVEALING SHORTCUT

The shortcut menu for a linked or embedded object includes an editing command that also identifies the object type. If there's a link, the command will say so.

object, click outside the object to return to PowerPoint—or, if the server is a separate window, update the object and then exit the application.

If you're editing linked information (in which case the source file is open in a separate window), you can simply switch back to PowerPoint—using the Microsoft Office Manager toolbar, for example—without closing the other application. Be careful about doing this, however: You're devoting memory resources to keeping the server open, and PowerPoint can be greedy with available resources. Also, the changes are not permanent until you save the source file.

Updating a Link When you update a link, you refresh the information on the slide that is supposed to reflect the content of the linked source file. By default, updating occurs automatically when you open a presentation that contains links—you see a dialog box that tells you that links are being updated. If you don't want to wait while links are updated, click the Stop button. After the initial update, the links in an open presentation continue to update if the linked information in the source file changes.

To change from automatic to manual updating, choose Links from the Edit menu. In the Links dialog box, select the link and then select the Manual option button. You can revert to the default setting at any time by returning to the Links dialog box and selecting Automatic.

You can cause a manual link to update by displaying the Links dialog box and choosing the Update Now button. Easier yet (if the slide is displayed), you can point to the object, display its shortcut menu, and choose Update Link.

Changing the Source for a Link If the filename or location of a linked source file changes, the link will fail until you create a new link or correct the reference. To correct the reference, you have to look at the string of names and locations that the program maintains to locate the linked item in the source file. Then you simply edit the part that's changed, and the program makes the adjustment right away.

From the Edit menu, choose Links. PowerPoint displays the Links dialog box, which lists the links for the current presentation. Select the link you want to modify and choose the Change Source button. Using the list boxes, navigate to the correct source file. PowerPoint makes the corresponding changes in the Source box as you select a different drive, pathname, or filename. Note that you can use the Network button to specify a link to a shared network location.

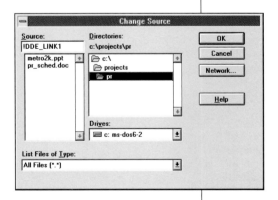

145

After you modify the source reference, click OK. The program checks the validity of the new reference. If other links in the current presentation were made to the source file you just changed, the program asks whether they should be changed as well. A nice feature.

Controlling a Link PowerPoint provides no way of locking links. Is this a big shortcoming? Not in most circumstances. You can still avoid unwelcome updates by setting links for manual updating (as described on the preceding page, in the section titled "Updating a Link"). In a group work situation, locking a link would be a drastic move anyway—too drastic, perhaps, if you simply wanted to postpone updates because of the interruption they might cause.

Breaking a Link To eliminate a link to a source document, use the Links command on the Edit menu. In the Links dialog box, select the link you want to break from the list and then choose the Break Link button. A dialog box appears, warning you that the break is permanent. Click OK to proceed. If you regret the decision later, your only recourse is to delete the former object in the destination file and re-create the link from scratch.

Appearance Counts

Many formatting changes can be made only by activating the object with its original application. To change line breaks in embedded text, for example, you have to activate the server application. But for other changes, PowerPoint provides the appropriate tools—very helpful when you're struggling to integrate a lot of unmatched objects into a consistent and coherent presentation.

Don't forget that with most of these techniques, you start by selecting the object. For our present purposes, selecting the object is simply a matter of clicking once within the region it occupies. You know that you've selected the object when the sizing handles appear.

Cropping and Resizing PowerPoint has a convenient resource for cropping objects. You might even find yourself wishing that cropping were as easy to do in other applications. To crop, point to the object, display the Tools menu or the shortcut menu, and choose Crop Picture. (Even if the object is not a picture per se, it is represented and formatted as a picture on the slide.)

THE ICON SHUFFLE

If you want to switch between displaying an OLE object on a slide as an icon and showing a picture of the object itself, select the object, display the Edit menu, and choose Convert from the object's submenu.

POWER PLAY

Honey, Who Shrunk the Embedded Objects?

After you embed an existing object, particularly a Word document or an Excel worksheet, resizing is generally the next order of business. The typical document scale for Word and Excel data is far too small for presenting on a slide. For example, consider the fact that bulleted text on a projected slide is 20 to 32 points in size, versus 10 to 12 points for data in a typical Word or Excel document.

Expanding the embedded object often requires a combination of cropping and resizing. Select the object and then drag a corner sizing handle outward from the center. Hold down the Ctrl key as you drag to expand the object from its midpoint. Release the border and then use the Crop Picture command on the shortcut menu to contract the borders around the specific information you want to show on the slide. Then resize again, using a corner handle, to expand the object to an appropriate size.

If visibility is still a problem, try formatting the characters in boldface (in the original application) or changing the text color using the Recolor command on the shortcut menu. You can also add a solid, contrasting fill in PowerPoint using the Lines and Colors command on the Format menu.

You might run into problems coloring objects with the fill tools on your Drawing toolbars, especially with Excel charts and worksheets that contain their own shading. For some helpful advice, see question 39 in Chapter 15, "Real Questions, Real Answers."

1995 Ridership Statistics

1995	Average Ridership		Scheduled Routes		% Seats Occupied	
Zone	Weekday	Sat/Sunday	Weekday	Sat/Sunday	Weekday	Sat/Sunday
Poly	678	503	38	25	27%	30%
Downtown	1278	609	77	40	25%	23%
Davidson	943	540	48	29	30%	28%
Vista	388	281	20	17	29%	25%
Olympic	578	193	33	13	27%	22%
Heights	921	472	54	30	26%	24%
Duvall	835	319	56	28	23%	17%
Southwest	678	503	38	25	27%	30%
Cen. Park	1278	609	77	40	25%	23%
Franklin	943	540	48	29	30%	28%
Arlington	388	281	20	17	29%	25%
West Lake	578	193	33	13	27%	22%

1995 Ridership Statistics

1995	Average Ridership		Scheduled Routes		% Seats Occupied	
Zone	Weekday	Sat/Sunday	Weekday	Sat/Sunday	Weekday	Sat/Sunday
Poly	678	503	38	25	27%	30%
Downtown	1278	609	77	40	25%	23%
Davidson	943	540	48	29	30%	28%
Vista	388	281	20	17	29%	25%
Olympic	578	193	33	13	27%	22%
Heights	921	472	54	30	26%	24%
Duvall	835	319	56	28	23%	17%
Southwest	678	503	38	25	27%	30%

The mouse pointer then changes to a cropping tool (a pair of interlocked *L*'s). Place this tool over a sizing handle, and click and drag the handle toward the center of the object. Rather than resizing the picture with the contracting border, the cropping tool trims away the outer part of the picture when you release the mouse button. Clicking somewhere other than a sizing

handle returns the pointer to normal so that you can reposition or resize the cropped picture.

Resizing an object on a slide is even more straightforward than cropping. To maintain the proportions of the image, drag a corner sizing handle toward or away from the center. To control sizing as a percentage of the original size, you can also use the Scale command on the Draw menu. If the object has wide margins, you might have to use a combination of cropping and resizing to expand the text to a legible size. (See the Power Play on the preceding page.)

Color Coordination   The commands that control object colors are scattered throughout different menus. On the Tools menu (and on the shortcut menu), you'll find the Recolor command. As you'd guess, this command lets you substitute new colors for the ones currently applied to the linked or embedded object. (The command is grayed-out if the object is displayed as an icon.) The resulting dialog box takes different forms, depending on the type of

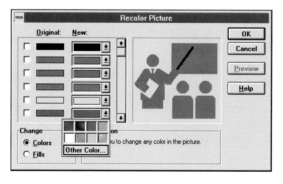

object selected, but it usually displays a column containing the original colors of the object, and a second column containing a corresponding series of drop-down boxes in which you can define replacement colors. If the Fills option button is available (below the Colors option button), you can select it to have color changes affect the interior but not the outline of a colored region.

Drop down any of the boxes in the New color column to see PowerPoint's design consultant in action. The replacement colors represent the color scheme that's associated with the template—they're carefully balanced to save you from a color-coordination gaffe. (If, despite everything, you show up for your presentation wearing brown with navy blue, you're on your own.) By choosing Other Color, you can expand the palette of color choices. If those aren't enough, you can go a step further by choosing More Colors, and your choices shoot up into the hundreds of thousands.

By testing your color changes in the Preview window, you can see the result of various color replacements and then modify the losers: Deselect the check box opposite the original color to deactivate the color substitution, or peruse the drop-down box in the New column to search for a better replacement.

Within PowerPoint, you can also modify the colors of lines and backgrounds using a couple of commands on the Format menu: the Colors and Lines command and the Shadow command. Each command displays a dialog box that lets you set options for weights and colors, guided by the prevailing color scheme. Together, these settings define a graphic style for an object. The style consists of line color and line weight (including a rectangular border for the object), fill (background), and shadows (for the border as well as for the contents). The style does not include color substitutions you might have made with the Recolor command, mentioned on the preceding page.

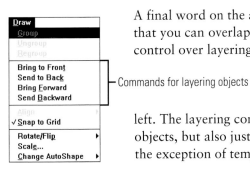

Commands for layering objects

A final word on the appearance of objects: Remember that you can overlap objects. PowerPoint gives you control over layering. You simply select an object and then use any of the front-to-back ordering commands on the Draw menu, shown at left. The layering commands affect not only the OLE objects, but also just about everything on the slide, with the exception of template items.

Activating Objects in a Slide Show

In Slide view, double-clicking an OLE object lets you edit the information in its native application or (with some object types) play the associated slide show, sound clip, or whatever. In Slide Show view, however, clicking the mouse advances you to the next slide (and double-clicking advances you two slides!). This is a problem if you're not ready to advance: Instead of advancing, you might want to "play" the embedded object during the slide show. Or perhaps you want to display a backup spreadsheet for your audience and demonstrate the effect of changing one factor and recalculating the sheet.

The secret here lies in PowerPoint's Play Settings command. To use it, first click a linked or embedded object (in Slide view), and then choose Play Settings from the Tools menu. (The command is grayed-out until you select an appropriate object.) The Play Settings dialog box identifies the current

COLOR POLICE

To maintain the color scheme of your presentation, PowerPoint often substitutes colors for the ones you've already carefully applied to an item (such as a Word table you're embedding). Despite the program's good intentions, you might not care for its attempt to enforce the template's color scheme. What can you do? You can change templates or use the Recolor command to reapply the colors you want.

STYLE SETTERS

You can reuse the style settings that you've applied to an object in either of two ways. Whichever method you choose, first click the object whose style settings you want to copy. You can then use the Format Painter button on the Standard toolbar to copy these settings to one other object, or you can choose Pick Up Object Style from the Format menu and then transfer the settings to a series of objects using the Apply Object Settings command (on the same menu).

object—for example, a document. Various controls let you identify the category of the object and select the action that constitutes playing the object. The Action list varies with the object type: For a linked or embedded document, the actions

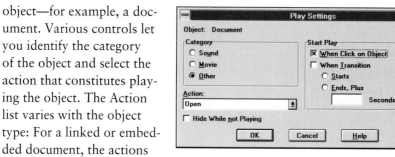

are Open and Edit; for an embedded sound, the actions are Play and Edit.

In the Start Play section, you can specify which conditions trigger the playback action you selected. The trigger might be manual—clicking the object—or it might occur automatically, at the end of the transition to the current slide, for instance. If you want the object (which might be displayed as an icon) to be invisible until its playback is triggered, select the Hide While not Playing check box.

TO, NOT FROM

Note that Power-Point considers the transition associated with a slide to be the transition *to* that slide, not the transition *from* that slide to the next slide.

Embedding New Objects

PowerPoint makes it very convenient to embed a new object. A "new" object is one that you create after you embed it, as opposed to existing information pasted as an embedded object. Among the new objects you can embed easily, four are available from a series of buttons on the Standard toolbar. You can insert a new object by choosing the object from the Insert menu or from the appropriate autolayout in the New Slide dialog box. The ease of inserting an object demonstrates the close integration of PowerPoint and the allied application.

You can also embed a new object with the standard procedure, using the Object command on the Insert menu. This approach gives you the widest range of options, but it involves more steps than the other, built-in techniques described in the following sections.

Using the Standard Toolbar Buttons

By clicking the corresponding button on the Standard toolbar, you can launch the server application to create and embed a new Word table, Excel worksheet, graph, or organization chart. A fifth button, Insert Clip Art, embeds a picture from the Microsoft ClipArt Gallery—an existing object rather than a newly created one.

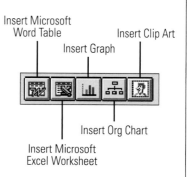

Insert Microsoft Word Table
Insert Graph
Insert Clip Art
Insert Org Chart
Insert Microsoft Excel Worksheet

MORE BUTTONS

By customizing a toolbar, you can make other types of objects as simple to embed as a table or a worksheet. The Customize dialog box contains additional buttons that are preprogrammed and ready to serve. If you're not sure of the procedure, compare it to the Power Play titled "Push-Button Presentations," later in this chapter.

When you use either the Insert Microsoft Word Table button or the Insert Microsoft Excel Worksheet button to embed a new object, an array of boxes drops down. Drag from the upper left box to define the grid for the table or the spreadsheet. The array expands as necessary. Don't forget to include rows and columns for headings.

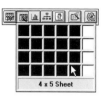

Using the Autolayout Options

PowerPoint supplies an assortment of standard layouts, called autolayouts, that you can select for a new slide or apply to an existing slide. Some layout options contain text only—in various arrangements—and others combine text with a picture, a chart, or a table. Let's look at the autolayout for a table slide to see how it facilitates embedding a Word object.

The autolayout options appear when you choose New Slide from the Insert menu. You can also display the options by choosing Slide Layout from the Format menu if you want to apply a layout option to an existing slide.

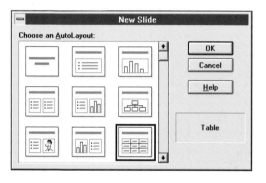

Select the Table layout option (bottom right) and click OK. The resulting new slide contains a placeholder for embedding a table. Double-click the placeholder, and then specify the dimensions of the table (columns and rows) in the Insert Word Table dialog box. Click OK.

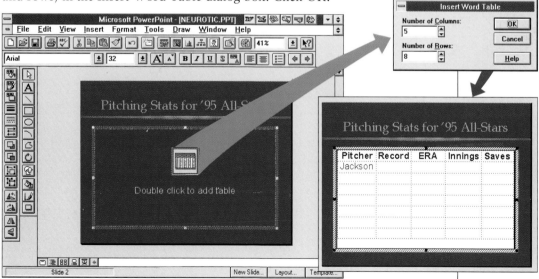

Tip!

WHAT'S ART, ANYWAY?

On the Insert menu, you'll notice distinct commands for inserting a picture and inserting clip art. Both commands let you insert existing pictures, and both handle the same list of graphic types (filename extensions). The big difference is the ClipArt Gallery, which organizes its contents for easy browsing and previewing. Use Insert Picture if the picture has not been added to the ClipArt Gallery, if you know its filename and location without needing to browse the images, or if you want to link to the file instead of embed the graphic.

POWER PLAY

Cruising for Icons

When you're linking or embedding an object as an icon, don't forget that you can substitute other icons for the standard image. In the Insert Object dialog box, click the Change Icon button that appears when you select the Display as Icon check box. If you don't see any options that appeal to you in the Change Icon dialog box, select the From File option button and then choose Browse.

Browsing is not quite a science. When Icon Files is the highlighted entry in the List Files of Type list box, the list of files includes all those that typically contain icons: filenames with the extensions ICO, EXE, or DLL. The ICO files are specifically icon images, whereas EXE and DLL files are part of a program's executable apparatus—they might contain icons as resources, or they might not.

After you select a file to mine for icons, click OK. The icons available from the file are displayed below the filename. If you choose an EXE or DLL file, you might get this message: *There are no icons in* Pathname\Filename. Back to the browsing box.

Notice, too, that in the Change Icon dialog box you can modify the label that appears with the icon. The limit for the label is 40 characters. After you have inserted the icon in the slide, you can use various menu commands to crop the icon and to add background colors, shadows, and the like.

The inserted table has the number of columns and rows you specified (separated by nonprinting gridlines). Type the information you want to appear in the table. While you are working on the embedded table, Word's toolbars and menus (except the File menu and the Window menu) replace those of PowerPoint. Click outside the table when you want to update the slide and resume work in PowerPoint.

Using the Insert Object Command

For the widest selection of object types to create and embed, choose the Object command from the Insert menu to display the Insert Object dialog box. This dialog box has option buttons (rather than the individual tabs used in Word and Excel) for switching between Create New (to embed a new object) and

Create From File (to embed an existing file). When you embed a new object, select an object type in the list. If the presentation is to be created or distributed in electronic form, consider displaying the object as an icon, particularly if the object supplies information that's difficult to read and digest when squeezed onto a slide.

Embedding a New Object on a Slide

To embed new information on a PowerPoint slide, follow these steps:

1. In Slide view, display the slide on which you want to embed an object.
2. Choose Object from the Insert menu.
3. In the Insert Object dialog box, select the Create New option button, and in the Object Type list box, select the type of object you want to insert.
4. Click OK. The other application makes its resources available, either in a separate window or by temporarily replacing PowerPoint's menus and toolbars.
5. After you create the object, return to PowerPoint either by exiting the other application (if it is a separate window) or by clicking outside the object.

Transferring Information from Word

One of the most effective ways to transfer information from a Word document to a presentation does not involve OLE. You simply take advantage of the conversion tools that transfer a Word document to PowerPoint so that the headings in Word become outline entries and slide text in the presentation. You can create a new presentation in this fashion, or you can insert the information in an existing presentation.

Move on to OLE, and you have a number of options for linking and embedding objects. You've already seen how easily PowerPoint lets you embed a new Word table. In this section, we'll focus on transferring existing text and graphics.

Importing a Word Document

If the information you want to present already exists in a Word document, you can create slides automatically by simply opening the Word document in PowerPoint. When you do, PowerPoint imports the headings from the document as text on the slides. It creates a separate slide for each paragraph formatted with the heading 1 style. It imports paragraphs formatted with other heading levels (2 through 9) as successive indent levels—subordinate points under the title (heading 1) text for each slide. Paragraphs formatted with a style other than a heading style are not imported.

Once the document is imported, you can begin editing and augmenting the initial presentation.

Creating a Presentation from a Word Outline

To create a PowerPoint presentation from a Word outline:

1. In PowerPoint, choose Open from the File menu.
2. In the List Files of Type list box, select Outlines.
3. Type or select the filename of the Word document, and then click OK.

HEADS STRAIGHT

To check the heading levels before you create a presentation, display the document in Outline view in Word. Word outlines can use up to nine heading levels, while PowerPoint stops at six (which is plenty for most situations). When PowerPoint imports a Word document, it treats the heading levels 7, 8, and 9 as if they were all level 6 headings.

When you save your work, PowerPoint treats it as a presentation file (with a PPT extension) so you won't overwrite your original Word document or change it in any way.

To insert a Word file in an existing presentation, you don't have to open the Word document and then copy and paste slides. Instead, open your presentation and display the slide that will precede the inserted slides (or select that slide in Slide Sorter view). Now choose Slides From Outline from the Insert menu, select the document you want to import, and click OK. The command opens the document you specified, imports the headings, and inserts the corresponding slides in your existing presentation.

> **Inserting Slides from a Word Outline**
>
> To insert slides from a Word document into an existing PowerPoint presentation:
> 1. In PowerPoint, display or select the slide that will precede the inserted slides.
> 2. From the Insert menu, choose Slides From Outline.
> 3. Select the Word document you want, and then click OK.

POWER PLAY

Push-Button Presentations

Microsoft Word supplies a macro, called PresentIt, that you can use to open your current Word document as an outline for a PowerPoint presentation. It complements the Report It button in PowerPoint, which exports a presentation outline as a formatted Word document (using Rich Text Format). But while PowerPoint provides the Report It button on its Standard toolbar, Word does not return the favor. You'll find the PresentIt macro in either the CONVERT.DOT template or the PRESENT.DOT template. Which template and the location of that template depend on the version of Word you have. You might have to do a little poking around to find the macro.

After you locate the macro, copy it to the NORMAL.DOT (global) template. See question 40 in Chapter 15, "Real Questions, Real Answers," for help on finding the macro and for step-by-step instructions on copying the macro using the Organizer dialog box.

Once the macro is available globally, you can make it available as a toolbar button. (We've customized toolbars in similar ways elsewhere in this book.) In brief, the procedure requires you to choose Customize from the Tools menu. Then, on the Toolbars tab, you select Macros in the Categories list box and drag PresentIt from the Macros list box to the toolbar it will reside on. Select a button image in the Custom Button dialog box—preferably the PowerPoint button shown here—and then choose Assign. That's it. Click Close, and you're equipped to create presentations with the push of a button.

Linking to a Word Object

Public speakers know that they never repeat the same presentation exactly: Various factors—the hour, the audience, the atmosphere—make each presentation unique. Given the pace of change in most businesses, that truism becomes all the truer. Linking can help. It lets you insert material from a source document that is subject to further change. You can be secure in the knowledge that the updated version of the source document will be included automatically in your presentation.

The procedure for linking to a Word object—a selection or an entire file—is straightforward. Use the Clipboard with Paste Special, as described in the quick reference card below, to link to a selection in the Word document. Use the Insert Object dialog box to create a linked object from an entire existing file. With either method, the only formats for the linked object are Microsoft Word 6.0 Picture Object (for a Word drawing) and Microsoft Word 6.0 Document Object (for text or combined text and pictures). Also, remember that selecting Paste Link (or Link) is critical.

Linking to a Word Object

To link to information in a Word document, open both the PowerPoint presentation and the Word source document. Be sure that you've saved the Word document. Then follow these steps:

1. Select the information in the Word document and copy it to the Clipboard.
2. Switch to the PowerPoint presentation and display the slide on which you want the linked information to appear.
3. From the Edit menu, choose Paste Special.
4. Select the Paste Link option button, and in the As list box, select Microsoft Word 6.0 Document Object.
5. Click OK.

In any of the linking situations, you can choose to display the linked object on your slide as an icon: Select the Display as Icon check box, and then choose the Change Icon button if you want to modify the icon image or change its label.

Embedding a Word Object

Pasting is all that's required to embed information from a Word document into PowerPoint as a Word object. Using drag and drop between the two applications has the same result as pasting. Remember, however, to hold down the Ctrl key while you drag if you want to copy (and not cut) the selection in the Word document. You can follow all the steps for using Paste Special, but if you're going to select the Word object (Microsoft Word 6.0 Document Object or Microsoft Word 6.0 Picture Object) in the As list box, normal pasting or drag and drop accomplishes the same thing.

If you want to embed text as an icon, you have to use the Copy and Paste Special procedure outlined on the quick reference card on the next page. In

LINK IS GRAY

In the Paste Special dialog box, the Paste Link option is grayed-out in some circumstances. For example, if you're trying to link to an embedded object in a Word document—such as a Microsoft Word 6.0 Picture Object—linking is not available. To create the link, return to the Word document, select and copy part of the document in addition to the embedded object, and Paste Link will be an available option once again.

HANGING AND MISSING

The width of a Word document object is determined by the page margins. If you've formatted an element, such as a hanging indent, that extends into the page margin, the linked or embedded object in PowerPoint will be cut off.

ZOOM CONTROL

If the small size of the embedded text makes it difficult to edit when you activate it in Slide view, adjust the Zoom Control on the Standard toolbar before you double-click the object. The Zoom Control is not available after you activate the object.

the Paste Special dialog box, be sure to select the Display as Icon check box.

For very short documents, the most convenient technique is often to embed the entire document: The activated file is easy to edit and view in a separate Word window. To embed the file, display the destination slide in Slide View and choose the Insert Object command. In the Insert Object dialog box, select Create From File. Then type the filename or choose Browse to identify the file by navigating the drive and

Embedding Existing Information from Word

To embed existing information from a Word document into PowerPoint, use the Copy and Paste Special commands. Begin by opening both the Word document and the PowerPoint presentation. Then follow these steps:

1. Select the text or graphic you want to embed in the PowerPoint presentation.
2. Copy the selection to the Clipboard.
3. Switch to the presentation and display the slide on which you want the text or graphic to appear.
4. Choose Paste Special from the Edit menu.
5. Be sure the Paste option button (not Paste Link) is selected, and in the As list box, select Microsoft Word 6.0 Document (or Picture) Object.
6. Click OK.

directory structure and clicking OK. In the Insert Object dialog box, be sure to select Display as Icon. Use the Change Icon button to change the icon or its label.

Transferring Information from Excel

Excel's ability to analyze and present numeric information makes it an excellent source of supporting evidence for your PowerPoint slides. You can link or embed Excel charts and worksheet ranges that summarize data effectively. For example, the slide shown here demonstrates the use of a pivot table (the one we constructed at the end of the preceding chapter) inserted as a linked worksheet object.

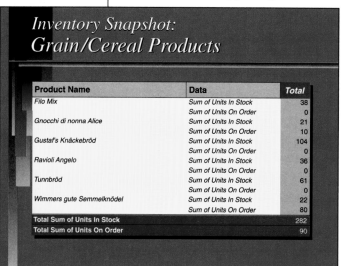

Linking to an Excel Object

The procedure for linking to an Excel object—a selection or an entire file—is not exceptional. To link to a chart or worksheet range in an Excel document, use the Clipboard with Paste Special, as described on the quick reference card shown here. To link to an entire Excel workbook, use the Insert Object command, which lets you create an object from an existing file even though only one sheet of the workbook is displayed. When data or formatting is changed in the source chart or the worksheet, the PowerPoint slide is updated automatically.

If you are linking to a chart, the only format available for the linked object is Microsoft Excel 5.0 Chart Object. When you link a range of cells, the sole format for linking is Microsoft Excel 5.0 Worksheet Object. Of course, selecting Paste Link (in the Paste Special dialog box) or Link (in the Insert Object dialog box) is critical.

In any of the linking situations, you can choose to display the linked object—a chart, worksheet, or complete file—on your slide as an icon: Select the Display as Icon check box, and then choose the Change Icon button if you want to modify the icon image or its label.

Linking to an Excel Chart or Worksheet

To link to an Excel workbook, open both the PowerPoint presentation and the source workbook. Be sure that you've saved the workbook. Then follow these steps:

1. In the Excel workbook, select the cells or the chart you want to link.
2. Copy the selection to the Clipboard.
3. Switch to the PowerPoint presentation and display the slide on which you want the linked object to appear.
4. Choose Paste Special from the Edit menu.
5. Select the Paste Link option button, and in the As list box, select Microsoft Excel 5.0 Chart (or Worksheet) Object.
6. Click OK.

Embedding an Excel Object

You can embed an object from an Excel workbook using any of a number of methods. You can drag and drop a chart or a worksheet range from Excel to the current slide in your PowerPoint presentation; you can copy and paste with the Clipboard; or you can embed an entire Excel file using the Insert Object command.

If you are embedding any part of a workbook, begin by selecting the chart or the worksheet range in Excel. Then, with the destination slide displayed, drag the selection from the workbook to the slide and drop it. Hold down the Ctrl key as you drag if you want to copy rather than cut the selection from your workbook. PowerPoint creates an embedded object wherever you drop the object on your slide. You can resize and relocate it as you see fit. The result is the same as when you use Copy and Paste Special to embed the selection as a Microsoft Excel 5.0 Chart (or Worksheet) Object.

Copying and pasting with the Clipboard has the same effect as using the drag-and-drop technique, with one exception. If you paste a worksheet range while a text box on the slide is activated for editing, PowerPoint pastes the Clipboard contents at the insertion point as text, one paragraph per row; drag and drop replaces the text box with the embedded Excel object.

CHARTING YOUR WAY

Need to pick a layout for a new slide? The PowerPoint interface is very helpful: Among its autolayout options are three that are specifically designed to include charts. If you want to embed an Excel chart, use the templates, but don't double-click the placeholders: They use the Microsoft Graph charting resources. Although it's possible to import an Excel chart into Graph, use Copy with Paste Special instead.

For the widest range of options, copy the Excel selection to the Clipboard and, in PowerPoint, use Paste Special (as described on the quick reference card on the preceding page). In the Paste Special dialog box, the only format that remains editable in Excel is Microsoft Excel 5.0 Chart (or Worksheet) Object. For most of the other formats, limited edits are possible, as explained here:

Embedding Format	Result
Microsoft Excel 5.0 Chart (or Worksheet) Object	The object retains all Excel formatting. You can double-click the object to edit the information in place as Excel data.
Unformatted Text	The information is placed in a PowerPoint text box. Worksheet rows are separate paragraphs, with tabs between columns. Direct character formatting is lost. This option is not available for charts.
Formatted Text (RTF)	The information is placed in a PowerPoint text box and retains direct character formatting. This option is not available for charts.
Picture	A picture of the information is placed in PowerPoint. Double-clicking the picture produces a dialog box in which you can elect to convert the picture (permanently) to a collection of PowerPoint objects. In that format, you can select various items and edit them as lines, text boxes, or whatever.
Bitmap	The result is static. You can resize, recolor, and crop the bitmap, but you can't edit its content in PowerPoint.

Transferring Information from PowerPoint?

Here's one case in which it really makes sense to link or embed a document to another one generated with the same application. Suppose you want to create a PowerPoint slide that lets the presenter choose among different presentation modules. With OLE, you can link or embed two or more presentations on the slide so that the presenter can double-click the appropriate title slide or icon to branch to the embedded module.

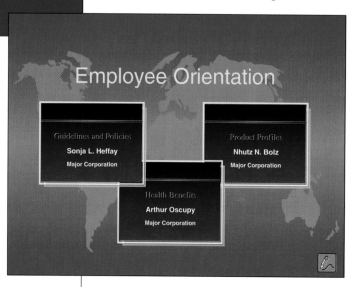

For convenience, you should probably create each module as a separate presentation file. Then you can use the Insert Object command, as described on the quick reference card on the facing page, to create each linked or embedded object from the corresponding file.

If you want to insert part of a presentation as a module, you can select the slides in Slide Sorter view (using Shift+click), copy them to the Clipboard,

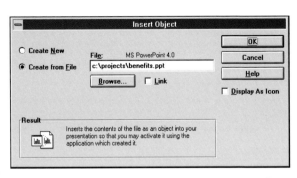

and use Paste Special to embed them on the destination slide.

Remember that you can select Display As Icon—whether you're using Insert Object or Paste Special—if you want the linked or embedded object to appear in the presentation as an icon. (To be crafty, you can hide the icon or position it behind another graphic—and activate it during a slide show.)

Keep in mind, however, that during a slide show, clicking the object does not ordinarily launch the linked or embedded presentation; it simply advances the

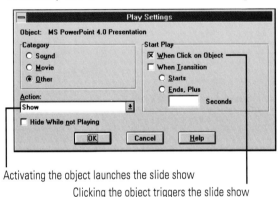

Activating the object launches the slide show

Clicking the object triggers the slide show

show to the next slide. To change this behavior, you have to select the object, choose the Play Settings command from the Tools menu, and set the options to match the figure shown below. For more details, refer to the section titled "Activating Objects in a Slide Show," earlier in this chapter.

Creating a Branching Presentation

A slide can serve as a branching point to a linked or embedded presentation. Be sure that all presentation files are saved, and then follow these steps:

1. Display the slide that will contain the linked or embedded presentation.
2. From the Insert menu, choose Object.
3. In the Insert Object dialog box, select Create From File.
4. Type the pathname and filename of the presentation to insert. You can also choose Browse to identify the file by navigating the drive and directory structure, and then click OK.
5. Click OK to embed the file as an MS PowerPoint 4.0 Presentation Object. To link (the same object format) instead, select the Link check box and then click OK. Repeat the process to link or embed other presentations on the same slide.

Chapter 9

Bringing Information into Access

The Field Is Wide Open

As we discussed in Chapter 5, "Office Connections," Microsoft Access cannot act as an OLE server, but it is fully equipped to be an OLE client. That is, an Access database can contain linked and embedded objects from a wide range of OLE server applications. The results in Access are identical to what you find with the other Microsoft Office client applications we've looked at: Linked and embedded objects can retain their original file formats; you can activate them for editing with all the resources of the server application; and with linked objects, you can take advantage of the fact that updates to the source object can be transferred to all locations linked to that source.

In this chapter, we'll look at some common scenarios that involve bringing information from the other major Office applications into Access. The linked or embedded object might be a Microsoft Word document, a Microsoft Excel worksheet or chart, or a slide or presentation created with Microsoft PowerPoint. (In Chapter 11, "Mastering Mergers," we'll look at transferring information from an Access database, such as names and addresses, to a Word form letter or catalog.)

OLE Objects in a Database

In a database, the underlying unit of information is the *field*. A field is, in turn, distinguished by its type and its properties, but it is the basic unit of information. Tables, queries, forms, reports—all are fundamentally groupings and arrangements of fields that are selected, sorted, and interrelated in various ways.

In Access, OLE objects fit, more or less, into this information management scheme. An OLE object can be stored in a field of the appropriate type—designated, as you might have guessed, as an OLE Object field. To create an OLE Object field, open a table in Design view. Enter a new field name, and tab to the Data Type column. In the drop-down list, select OLE Object, as shown at right. Only two properties apply to OLE Object fields: a caption and a Yes or No indication of whether the field is required.

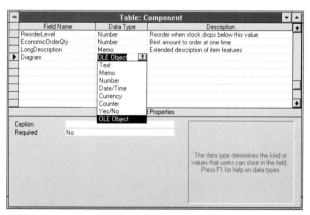

You can supply a caption for a field (up to 255 characters) to provide helpful information to the user. If you omit the caption, Access uses the field name as the caption. If you set the Required property to Yes, you cannot complete a record until you have included an entry for the OLE Object field.

Creating an OLE Object Field

You can place an OLE object in an Access database by creating an OLE Object field. Follow these steps:

1. Open a table in Design view.
2. In the Field Name column, enter a unique field name.
3. In the Data Type column, select OLE Object in the drop-down list box.
4. Complete the Caption and Required field properties.

You can insert information into an OLE Object field in a table, a form, or a report. In a table or in any other Datasheet view, the contents of the OLE Object field are represented by a phrase that identifies the source of the object, such as *Word 6.0 Document*. So where do you go to see the object itself? To view the object—whether it's a linked or embedded range of cells, an icon for a linked PowerPoint document, or something else—you have to create a form or a report in which the field contents are displayed in a bound object frame.

After you create a field for an OLE object (and display its contents in a bound object frame in a form), you might get the impression that Access manages OLE objects only as fields—incorporated into a data table and thus bound to the database. But you'd be leaving out one of the common ways that OLE objects figure in forms and reports: as unbound objects. In that guise, the object is added to a form or a report (in Design view) but remains independent of the data tables. Unbound object frames enhance the design of a form or a report; their contents might provide instructions for completing a part of the form, creating a special text treatment in a logo or a masthead, or something of that sort.

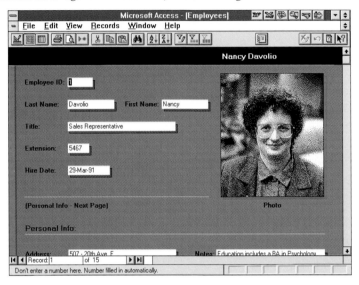

Editing an Object

Whether an object is linked or embedded, you can activate it for editing with its original application. As a rule, activating a linked object opens the source document in its original application. An embedded object is loaded by the associated application—either in a separate window or in a hybrid window—that temporarily transforms the Access window by adding toolbars from a different OLE-supporting application.

To edit an OLE object, display its shortcut menu and choose Edit from the submenu that appears alongside the object name. Linked objects are identified as such in the object name on the shortcut menu. After you finish editing, return to the database. The procedure for returning to Access depends on the application that was launched to modify the object. Often you'll find a command on the File menu for updating the (embedded) object, but if you quit before updating, the program asks if you want to update before you close the connection between the editing session and the destination document. Click OK to record your changes in the Access file.

BOUND OBJECT

A *bound object*—in a form or a report—is an object whose content derives from the information in one or more fields in the underlying tables. The bitmapped image of an employee, for example, might appear on an employee information form and derive from an OLE Object field in a table of employee records. By contrast, unbound objects are independent of the information stored in the underlying tables.

VIEWS AND WINDOWS

If you're editing a linked or embedded object in Design view, the object's original application opens in a separate window. If you're editing an embedded object in Form view, you might be able to edit in place (if the server application supports OLE).

You can also adjust the size and proportions of the bound or unbound object frame after you've inserted it in a form or a report. To do so, display the form or the report in Design view and select the object frame so that its sizing handles appear. But before you grab a handle and start tugging, click the Properties button on the Form Design toolbar (or choose Properties from the shortcut menu).

The Layout Properties section, shown at left, is displayed by default; it lets you modify various aspects of the object's appearance. To start, you can select a Size Mode option. The options—Clip, Stretch, and Zoom—let you crop the object (from the bottom or the right side), distort it to fit its frame, or enlarge or reduce it for the best fit in its frame while maintaining its proportions.

Other layout properties affect the background and border colors, the weight and style of the border, and the border's location. You can even add a special 3-D effect—a shadow that gives the frame a slightly raised or sunken appearance.

Managing Linked Information

In most respects, you manage linked information in Access—including updating and modifying links—in much the same way as you do in the other Office applications. Notice, however, as you examine and modify links with the Edit Links command, that the various forms, reports, queries, tables, and modules—though they exist within a single database—have a certain amount of independence. And each has peculiarities of its own. To list the links for unbound object frames in a form, for instance, display the form in Design view. In a table, you have to select the OLE Object field in Datasheet view before you can examine the link for that field alone. You'll get used to the various restrictions, but while you're adjusting, the best advice is simply to experiment: If you don't see the link that you expected to find listed in the Links dialog box, try selecting the specific field or frame, or try a different view.

Updating a Link As they are in the other Office applications, links in Access are updated automatically, by default. The information is refreshed when you open a file that contains links, and it is refreshed again if the linked object changes while the Access database is open. You can change the update setting from Automatic to Manual if you want more control over the link: With manual updating, the information in the database might be less current, but this setting can be helpful if you want to freeze the information or simply avoid the delays that result from constant updating.

To change link settings or to update a manual link, open the database component (the table, query, or whatever) that contains the link and then choose Links from the Edit menu. Access displays the Links dialog box, shown at the top of the facing page.

PROPERTY SETTLEMENT

You can use a property setting instead of the setting in the Links dialog box for determining how updating occurs. Select an object frame control in Design view, and then choose the View Properties command. Display all of the properties and click the setting for the Update Options property. In its drop-down box, you'll notice two settings—Automatic and Manual. Life is good.

In the Link Group drop-down list box, you can choose the type of links to display in the dialog box: OLE links or DDE links. Select OLE links if it isn't already selected. Then select the link you want to modify. (If the link you expected to see is not listed, you might have to try a different view or selection.) To change the link so that it updates only when you give the command, select the Manual option button.

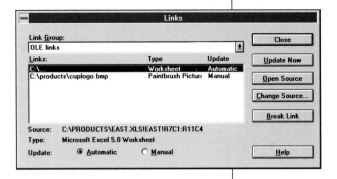

After you select a link, you'll notice that the Update Now button becomes available. Click the button to refresh the information in the database object so that it matches the source file. If a link is set for manual updating, this is the only way it can be refreshed. Of course, the source file must still exist at the referenced location. If the source file is open, certain factors can block updating—if a dialog box is open or if cell editing (in Excel) is under way, for example.

Changing the Source for a Link   As you know, a link fails if the filename or the location of the linked source file is invalid. You can create a new link, but it's often easier to repair the existing link by modifying the reference so that it points to the correct file once again.

To change the source for a link, select the link in the Links dialog box, and then choose the Change Source button. In the Change Source dialog box, shown at right, you can type a new pathname or navigate to the correct source file. Note that you can choose the Network button (if your computer is attached to a network) to specify a link to a shared network location. After you modify the source reference, click OK.

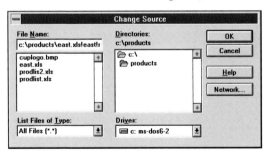

Locking a Link   As for locking, Access has a handy provision for preventing changes to linked information. In a form or a report, select the linked object in Design view and click the Properties button. Among the Data Properties, you'll find the Enabled and Locked settings. The Enabled setting determines whether you can move the focus to that control or field in Form view or in Datasheet view. For an unbound object frame, the Enabled setting is No by default.

If the Locked setting is Yes, you cannot change the information in the frame while you are working in Form view or Datasheet view. In a form, you can activate the source file from Access (if the control is enabled) and edit it—you'll even see the updates. But the changes will not be saved when you close the form.

To make changes to the contents of a locked control, return to Design view, display the properties, and change the Locked setting to No. You can also make the changes while you are in Design view. In that view, the Enabled and Locked settings do not prevent you from activating or changing the object.

Breaking a Link   Unlike rules, links were not made to be broken. You *can* break them, but you have to be deliberate about it. Even if the source for a link changes location, the link continues to exist, although it cannot be updated.

To break a link, open the table, form, or report that contains the link, and then choose Links from the Edit menu to display the Links dialog box. Select the appropriate OLE link in the list, choose the Break Link button, and then click Close. That's it: Once you break a link, you can't "unbreak" it.

Embedding a New Object

You can embed a new object created in any of the server applications that are registered with Office. Most often, you'll embed the new information in an Access form or report. That way, you can see the object or icon after it's embedded. If the object you want to embed is not stored in a table, you can insert the object in an unbound object frame to make it part of the form or the report itself.

When you embed new information that is stored in a table, you can use a bound object frame in a form, or you can insert the new object directly in a field. Of course, in a datasheet the field does not display the object content (or an icon); it merely identifies the object type. You'll probably find the process more satisfying if you can embed the new object in a bound object frame—and see what results you're getting!

Embedding a New Object in a Form or Report

To embed new information from another application in an Access form or report, open the form or the report in Design view and insert a new object in an unbound object frame. To insert the right kind of object frame, be sure to click the Object Frame button in the Toolbox—not the Bound Object

Click this button to insert an unbound object frame

Frame button immediately to the right of it. If the Toolbox is not visible, click the Toolbox button on the Standard toolbar.

The Insert Object dialog box, shown on the facing page, appears automatically after you create the unbound object frame. If you select the Create New option button, you can scan the list of object types to determine which server application you'll use to create the object. Select an object type in the list. If you want to display the object as an icon in your form or report, select the Display As Icon check

A PICTURE IS FOREVER

You can freeze linked or embedded information by converting it to a picture. Point to the frame or the field in which the OLE object is stored, display the shortcut menu, and choose Convert to Picture from the submenu alongside the object name. A message appears warning you that this step cannot be reversed. Choose Yes if you're resigned to editing no more.

NO OLE 1 ICON

Objects created with OLE 1 applications cannot be displayed as icons in Access forms and reports. If the server application does not support OLE 2, Access displays an error message and inserts the object content rather than an icon.

box; then you can choose the Change Icon button to replace the default icon or to modify the label.

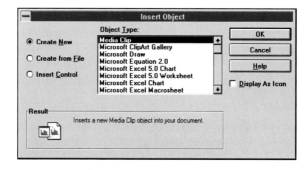

When you click OK, the server application opens in a separate window. Create the object you want to embed. After you finish using the server application, close the application. If a subsequent message asks you whether you want to update the information, choose Yes.

Embedding a New Object in

a Field You can create a new picture, spreadsheet, word-processing document, or other object in your database that you can embed in an OLE Object field. You can insert the object in a field directly—by opening a table, query, or form in Datasheet view—or you can insert it in a bound object frame in Form view. After the object is inserted, you can display it in a bound object frame in a form or a report.

When you use the procedure described on the quick reference card on the next page, don't be thrown by the fact that Access lacks an Insert menu. In this case, the Insert Object command is on the Edit menu, but the resulting dialog box is similar to those in the other Office applications. The Insert Object command is also on the shortcut menu any time you have an OLE Object field selected.

In the Insert Object dialog box, select the Display As Icon check box if you want the object to be displayed as an icon in a form or a report. Regardless of whether it is to be displayed in full or as an icon, the field (in a datasheet) merely identifies the object type.

After you create the object using the resources of the server application, exit the server. If a dialog box appears asking whether you want to close the connection and update the object, choose Yes.

Embedding a New Object in a Form or Report

To embed a new object in an Access form or report so that the object becomes part of the form or the report, follow the procedure below:

1. Open the Access form or report in Design view.
2. Create a control using the Object Frame tool.
3. In the Insert Object dialog box, select the Create New option button. Then, in the Object Type list, select the type of object you want to embed.
4. Click OK. The server application opens, enabling you to create the object.
5. After you create the object, return to Access by exiting the server application.

HATCHING AN OBJECT

If the server application has an Update command on its File menu, you can preview the result in Access (before you exit the server). Choose the Update command and then minimize the server application or switch tasks to display the Access window. The framed object is covered with hatch marks to remind you that you have not yet stored the object. Return to the server, finish creating the object, and choose the Exit command.

NOT MY TYPE

If you're trying to embed an object but the Insert Object command is dimmed, check to be sure that the data type of the selected field is OLE Object.

Transferring Information from Other Office Applications

The following sections explain the procedures for linking and embedding objects that were created in Word, Excel, and PowerPoint. For the moment, we'll overlook importing, although you can certainly import text files and Excel tables into Access. When you import an Excel worksheet, Access creates a new table in which to store the imported data. Look for more information on these topics in Chapter 14, "Importing and Exporting."

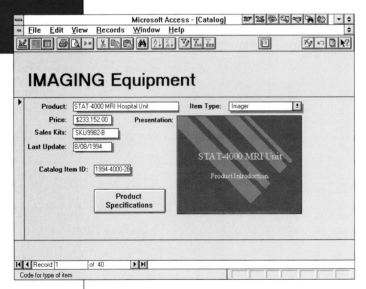

Linking to a Document

When you're working with an Access database, you can establish links to documents created with other Office applications. You can link to an entire document, such as a complete PowerPoint presentation, as shown in the figure at left. You can modify the object in the database by opening the source file for editing (using the resources of its original application). By default, changes to the linked source file are reflected automatically in the database. The link in the database can be from an unbound object frame or from a bound object frame (or its associated field).

Linking to a PowerPoint file displays the first slide of the presentation.

Linking to an Entire Document   The process for linking to an entire document from an Access form or report originates with the database. Open the database, and then follow the steps on the quick reference card shown at right.

The procedure on the quick reference card applies to linking from an unbound object frame. To link from a bound object frame (in Form view) or directly from a field, you have to adjust the procedure slightly. Select the bound object frame in Form view or select the OLE Object field in Datasheet view (for a table, query, or form). Then choose the Insert Object command from the Edit menu (or the object's shortcut menu), and follow the procedure on the quick reference card, beginning with step 3.

In the Insert Object dialog box, you can choose the Browse button if you're unsure of the pathname or the precise filename. After the linked object or the icon is visible, you can adjust the size and location of its frame in your form or report. In the last step, remember that you can select the Display As Icon check box if you want the file to appear as an icon in the object frame. When you are linking to an entire file, displaying the file as an icon might be a sensible use of space in the form or the report.

Linking to an Object   When you're linking to part of a document in one of the other major Office applications, open both the Access database and the document in the other application. You begin the procedure, summarized on the quick reference card below, by selecting the part of the document to which you're establishing the link. When you select the Paste Link option button in the Paste Special dialog box, the only format Access provides for OLE links (in the As list box) is the native format for the particular Office application. (See the Power Play on the next page for what seems to be an exception for Excel objects.) You can select the Display As Icon check box if you want to display an icon rather than the selected object.

After you click OK, Access creates an unbound object frame and

---

Linking to an Entire Document

To link to an entire document in an Office application from an unbound object frame, follow these steps:

1. Open the form or the report in Design view.
2. Click the Object Frame tool in the Toolbox, and then drag to create the object in the form or the report.
3. In the Insert Object dialog box that appears, select the Create From File option button, and then specify the pathname and filename to which you want to link.
4. Select the Link check box, and then click OK.

Linking to an Object

To link to an object in an Office document from an unbound object frame, open the document and the Access database. Then follow these steps:

1. Select the object in the document (such as a slide, a chart, or a range of cells) to which you want to link.
2. Copy the selection to the Clipboard.
3. Switch to Access and open the form or the report in Design view.
4. Choose Paste Special from the Edit menu.
5. In the Paste Special dialog box, select the Paste Link option button and then click OK.

THE GRAY THAT CAME TO STAY

If the Paste Link option is grayed-out, you might have neglected to save the file that contains the object to which you want to link. If you are linking to an entire file, be sure that the file is closed, and verify in Design view that OLE Type Allowed (among the data properties for the frame) is set to Linked or to Either.

POWER PLAY

Creating a DDE Link

Access can exchange information with another Windows-based application by establishing a dynamic data exchange (DDE) link. This information, which is limited to text, can be either sent or received by Access, depending on the type of DDE link created. Although DDE links can be difficult to create and maintain, this is a good method for bringing information into Access from certain applications. Outside the Office suite, numerous applications (applications that support DDE but not OLE) are candidates for DDE links. But we need not look outside the Office suite to demonstrate the creation of DDE links: We can create such a link from an Excel worksheet object.

From the Clipboard, transfer a cell (or a range of cells) to a form or a report in Design view. In the Paste Special dialog box, select the Paste Link option button, and in the As list box, select Text format. When you click OK, Access adds a text box to the form or the report. In Design view, this text box contains an expression that uses the DDE function to show where the object came from. For example, the expression might identify the source as follows:

```
=DDE("Excel","C:\PRODUCTS\[FORECAST.XLS]SHEET1","R3C3")
```

In Form view or Print Preview (for a report), Access displays the actual linked text, such as *$178,325.00*. To examine or edit the link, display the form or the report in Design view. Select the text box, choose Links from the Edit menu, display the Links dialog box, and select DDE Links in the Link Group drop-down list.

displays the object in the frame. Drag the linked object to position it where you want it in your form or report.

With a few adjustments, the same procedure applies to linking to an object from a bound object frame or from a field in a datasheet. After you've copied the selection and switched to Access, select the bound object frame in Form view or select the field directly in a datasheet (for a table, query, or form).

Embedding an Existing Object

As with linking, you can embed information in an unbound object frame or in a bound object frame or field. Embedding an object in Access is especially easy because the object format is also the default for simple pasting. You can use the Paste command or use drag and drop to embed an object from another Office application. (Before you can embed information from a document created with another application, you must save the document.)

Remember that in Access the view and the object frame are factors when you try to paste from the Clipboard. When you paste an object in Design view, Access creates an unbound object frame to house it. This is the situation to which the procedure on the quick reference card shown here applies. After you embed the object, you can relocate it in the form or the report by dragging (and resizing) the frame. Don't forget the Size Mode options and other layout properties that you can set in Design view.

> ### Embedding Information in a Form or Report
>
> You can embed information from an existing Office document so that it becomes part of an Access form or report. To insert the object in an unbound object frame, follow these steps:
>
> 1. Select the information that you want to embed.
> 2. Copy your selection to the Clipboard.
> 3. Switch to Access and open the form or the report in Design view.
> 4. From the Edit menu, choose Paste.

In Form view or in a datasheet, you can embed information directly in an existing bound object frame or an OLE field. By default, you cannot select or edit the object in an unbound object frame (unless you return to Design view). If the selected object is not appropriate for embedding, you might be able to paste the Clipboard contents as text, or the Paste command might simply be unavailable.

If you use the Paste Special command to embed the contents of the Clipboard, you can choose a format for the pasted information. Your format choices (in the Paste Special dialog box) are determined by the particular selection on the Clipboard. The following table describes the formats available with the Paste Special command.

Embed As	Result
Microsoft Word 6.0 Document (or Picture) Object or Microsoft Excel 5.0 Worksheet (or Chart) Object or MS PowerPoint 4.0 Presentation (or Slide) Object	Embedded in its native format, the object is editable using the resources of its original application; you can activate it for editing from a form, a report, or a datasheet. Access uses this format when you execute the Paste command.
Picture	The object is no longer editable, but it occupies far less storage space than a native object does. You can resize the object frame in a form or a report.
Bitmap	Like the Picture format, this format does not permit further editing. Bitmaps occupy the least amount of space, but they cannot be resized as successfully as objects in Picture format can.
Text	This format lets you embed the text from an object (for example, the text in an Excel worksheet cell) in a text box.

WHOLE FILES

Alas, you cannot use drag and drop to embed files from File Manager in frames or fields. You can, however, embed entire files in the same way that you link them: Select the Create From File option button in the Insert Object dialog box, but don't select the Link option button.

UNBOUND, STILL LOCKED

Suppose that you embed an object in an unbound object frame in an Access form (in Design view). If you want to edit or activate the object from Form view, you have to return to Design view and set the Enabled property of the unbound object frame to Yes and the Locked property to No.

④ Working Officewide

Chapter 10

Collaborating

The More We Get Together

Somewhere between old-fashioned correspondence and face-to-face encounters is a new realm of interaction made possible by computers. This realm can function as a play space, a workspace, a commuting corridor, a research arena, a shopping mall, a back alley. It has as many uses as entrepreneurs and users can dream up. With Microsoft Office, electronic interaction can help people pool their talents to refine ideas and products.

Most types of electronic collaboration rely on local area networks or similar file-sharing mechanisms. By sharing files, members of a workgroup can read and modify a single copy of a document, working on separate parts of the document or critiquing and refining the document collectively. The particular network software you use "behind" Office might be one of many brands and products; as a consequence, it's hard to be specific in this book about the network features you have available or how you can take advantage of them.

Given the wide range of file-sharing capabilities that Office users have available, what can this chapter do for you? Three things, principally. First, we'll explore some ways to take advantage of network features that are common to most network arrangements. Second, we'll discuss a few ways that Microsoft Mail can boost the collaborative possibilities of your Office suite. (Even if your office uses a different e-mail package, you might have some of the same features as Mail—and you might be able to assess the value of switching to Mail.) Third, we'll focus on some features of Microsoft Word that can help bring together the talents and expertise of a group of people. Used in concert with Mail or independently of it, these revision and annotation features stimulate collaboration.

Office Documents à la Net

ACCESS FOR THE MULTITUDES

In the context of networking, remember that Microsoft Access is a multi-user product. You can develop databases that reside at a shared location and can be opened "nonexclusively." Members of a workgroup can edit the same database (but not the same record) simultaneously.

With the increasing prevalence of local area networks, many users of the Office suite have access to shared storage locations to which they can post (copy) widely needed documents. The advantages of this arrangement are many (although the limitations of some networks might diminish some of these advantages):

- Coworkers can have access to the same document and be confident that they are looking at the same version of the file—a major concern with documents that are updated frequently.

- Members of a workgroup can take turns reviewing or editing a file by opening the file in its shared location (or by first copying the file to their own computers).

- Coworkers can post (or otherwise distribute) documents that contain links to files residing at shared locations.

If you've been using a network for a while, you know how easily you can post and open shared Office documents. Recent versions of File Manager in Microsoft Windows have increased the ease with which you can connect to network drives and copy files between your computer and a remote storage location. And with Office, the Save As command on the File menu lets you save files across the breadth of the network almost as easily as you can navigate the disks in your own PC.

If you've never clicked the Options button in the Save As dialog box in Word or Microsoft Excel, try it. The settings it provides let you protect a document at various levels: You can attach passwords that prevent other people from opening or revising a document, or you can attach a simple reminder to a file recommending that users open the file with read-only access.

The same built-in features that let you

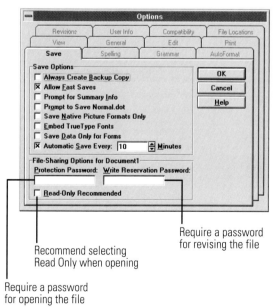

Require a password for revising the file

Recommend selecting Read Only when opening

Require a password for opening the file

save files to remote locations also let you open the files easily. Choose the File Open command; in the Open dialog box, the network drives to which you are already connected appear in the Drives box. For most networks, the Open dialog box also includes a Network button to let you connect to other network directories without having to back out of the immediate task.

When you open a document that's stored at a shared location, you normally lock out other users from everything but read-only access to the file. For that reason, people are often encouraged to copy documents to their own computers for closer scrutiny. (But you should probably open the document on the network if you want to be sure that your edits don't collide with someone else's.)

Sending and Routing Documents

In the Office suite, Word, Excel, Microsoft PowerPoint, and Microsoft Access are all equipped for direct mailing. This simply means that if you are also using Mail, you can choose the Send command from the File menu to send a copy of the current document to another Mail user. The recipient sees an icon for the document in the message area and can double-click the icon to display the document in its original application. (As you'll see shortly, we have to make a few exceptions for Access.) Of course, the recipient must have either a copy of the original application on his or her computer or access to the application at a shared location.

If you want to send a document to a number of other people, you can simply add more user addresses to the To line of your message. But to give the process a bit more structure, you can add a routing slip. The routing slip

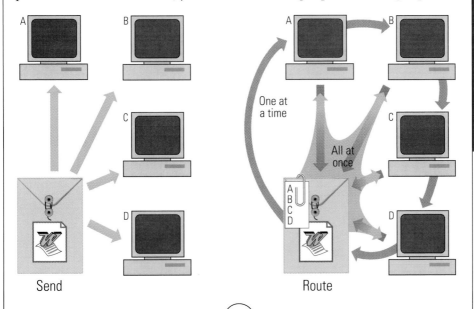

Send

Route

Tip!

WE CAN'T BOTH BE WRITE

If you're opening a file that you intend to read but not to modify, select the Read Only check box in the Open dialog box. In this way, someone else can open the file with read and write access while you have it open.

You can send your message to everyone at once or you can route it to control how it is distributed.

handles the progress of the document so that the people you specify see the attached document. You decide whether the document should route to the recipients in sequence or all at once. Either way, the reviewers are politely prodded to pass the document along so that the copy or copies return to you in the end.

Let's look first at two examples of sending a document, one in which you send an Excel workbook and one in which you mail a report from Access. Later on, in the section titled "Revising and Annotating," we'll look at an example of routing a Word document.

Let's Mail an Excel Workbook

The procedure for mailing an Excel workbook is simple, and it is nearly identical to the procedure for mailing an Office document of any other type. When the workbook is ready to be mailed, choose Send from the File menu. Excel opens a window in which you can prepare your message.

As you can see in the figure below, the window has a header area for address and subject information, and it has a message area that contains your workbook in the form of an icon. Type one or more e-mail addresses on the To line, and type addresses on the Cc line if you want to send copies of the message. (As with other types of correspondence, you can send copies to people who have an interest in the contents but from whom you do not expect a reply.) On the Subject line, Excel supplies the filename of the document you are sending. You can change this subject information if you like.

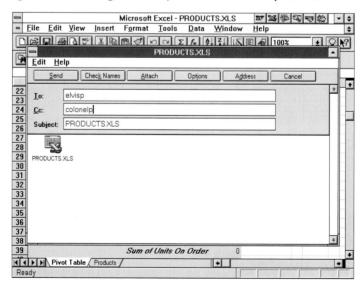

Within the message area, the workbook icon looks like an icon for an embedded object—the sort that you'd find in any other compound document. It's

WORKGROUP TOOLBAR

Excel has a separate WorkGroup toolbar devoted to workgroup features, such as sending and routing. To display it, choose the Toolbars command from the View menu, select WorkGroup, and click OK.

UNATTACHED

If you receive a message with an attached file, you can store a separate copy of the file on disk. Mail provides the Save Attachment command for this purpose. See the last section of this chapter, "You *Can* Take It with You," for details.

not quite the same, though. You can't drag or resize the icon; it sits in its box like an oversized character in a line of message text. You can delete it simply by backspacing over it.

Click in the message area (or tab to it) and compose whatever message you want to send with your workbook. You can move and copy text (or the icon), and you can check spelling within the message. Mercifully, the Spelling utility skips the proper nouns and cryptic addresses on the To and Cc lines. As with any other Mail message, you can attach additional files, import text files directly, and use Paste Special to embed other objects. These features are covered later in this chapter, in the section titled "Transferring Information to and from Mail."

Before sending your message, click the Options button if you want to flag the message as having high or low priority. Select the Save sent messages check box if you want to retain a copy of your outgoing message (in the Sent Mail folder). You can also request an automatic return message to indicate that your mail has been received. To send the message, click the Send button or press Alt+S.

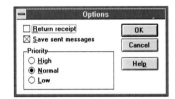

Let's Send an Access Report

Access, as you know, is not an OLE server, and that limitation is apparent when you try to send a document directly from an Access database. In the first place, you cannot simply mail an entire database file. To get around its inability to embed objects, Access sends the table, report, or other item in a converted format—to be opened and read as an Excel worksheet, a Word document, or a text file.

Let's walk through an example. We'll work with NWIND.MDB, a sample database that ships with Access. Open the database, which is located in the SAMPAPPS subdirectory in your Access directory.

1. Display the items on the Report tab, select the report titled List of Products by Category, and choose the Preview button.

2. From the File menu, choose Send.

3. In the Send dialog box, select the Microsoft Excel format. Click OK. The Send Note window appears, with an icon for the output file in its message area.

4. In the header, type the address information and a subject. The figure at the top of the following page shows an example. (Access does not gather a Subject line from the output filename.)

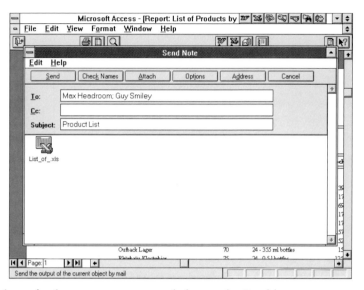

5. Add any further message text, and choose the Send button.

When the mail is delivered, the recipient can double-click the icon in the message to open the embedded document as an Excel workbook. In the output worksheet shown here, notice that the information levels in the report are converted to outline levels. By clicking the boxes that have plus and minus symbols along the left edge, you can expand and contract the outline, revealing and hiding worksheet rows.

LEFT ON THE LOADING DOCK

The restrictions that we saw with the Output To command also apply to mailing database objects with the Send command: OLE Object fields are excluded, and other fields are limited to 255 characters.

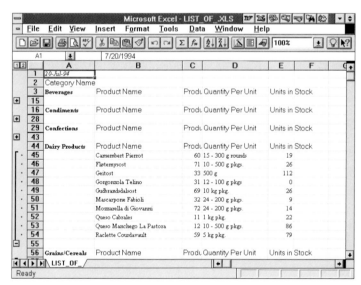

Revising and Annotating

The ability to distribute documents gains a powerful dimension when the recipient can open the document and insert comments. The document can be returned to its originator, with the comments easily distinguished from the original text. You can, of course, exchange documents using network resources, posting copies of documents and revised (renamed) versions at agreed-upon shared locations. And you can accomplish this interaction using the routing capabilities of Office with Mail, as the example later in this section demonstrates. Before taking up an example, however, let's look at Word's revision and annotation features.

With the revision and annotation features, a number of people can edit and comment on an electronic document in succession. The originator of the document can easily distinguish the revisions and accept or reject the changes individually or all at once. Likewise, the originator can read comments—separate from the text—from multiple reviewers, identify the reviewers, and respond in a variety of ways.

REVISION

In Word, a *revision* is any content change—text that is added or deleted.

Revisions and Decisions

You control Word's revision features in the Revisions dialog box. To display it, choose Revisions from the Tools menu.

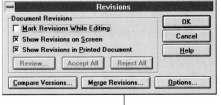

Probably the most important thing you can do in the Revisions dialog box is turn on revision marking. Select the first check box, Mark Revisions While Editing. Most of the remaining options apply only if that box is checked. When you turn on Word's revision marks, any subsequent editing will be marked, but previous edits remain unmarked. The revision marks are displayed on your screen, included in the document when it is printed, and saved with the document when the document is saved. So what do marked revisions look like on your screen?

Unless you change the default settings, the revision marking system is very simple: Inserted characters show up underlined; deleted characters have a line through them. On your screen, the revision marks are assigned a different color for each reviewer. Word adds a black vertical bar in the outside margin alongside any line that contains a revision. It adds the marks as you edit the document—all you have to do is turn on revision marking. Here's what the marks look like on your screen:

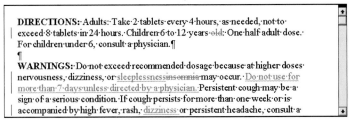

SAY WHAT?

When you use revision marking, consider the person who will be reviewing the revision-marked text to understand what is being suggested versus what was said originally. You can help by deleting and inserting entire words rather than starting an insertion in the middle of a word.

If you prefer a different system of marks or colors to indicate revisions, click the Options button in the Revisions dialog box to see what choices it provides. You can change the insertion or deletion indicators or the revised-line indicators. The changes affect the entire document, including previously saved marks.

Sets the type of mark and color of inserted text

Sets the type of mark and color of deleted text

Sets the location and color of revised-line indicators

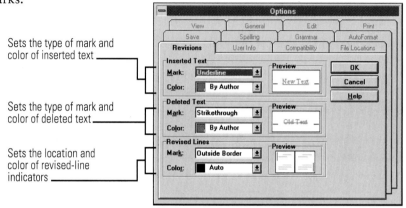

Turning on Revision Marking

To turn on revision marking, open the document you want to revise, and then follow these steps:

1. Choose Revisions from the Tools menu.
2. In the Revisions dialog box, select the check box labeled Mark Revisions While Editing.
3. Click the Options button if you want to modify the colors or character formatting that indicates insertions or deletions.

When it's time to implement the marked revisions, you can expedite the process in a number of ways. After you open the revised document, choose Revisions from the Tools menu to survey your options. You can accept or reject the whole lot of them with a single command—either Accept All or Reject All. Or you can review the changes one at a time by clicking the Review button.

The Review button gives you a chance to rule on each insertion, deletion, or replacement. To zip through a document, move the insertion point to the beginning of the document, display the Revisions dialog box, and choose Review. Select the Find Next After Accept/Reject check box (to speed up the

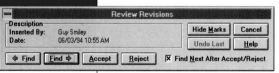

process) and click Find (with the right-pointing arrow) to visit the first revision. Word identifies the reviewer and the date of the revision; you accept or reject the change and Word then jumps to the next revision—or you simply click Find to skip the revision and move to the next decision. The Undo Last button does just what you'd expect: It retreats from the last decision you made, so the accepted or rejected change reverts to revision-marked text.

The Hide Marks button affects all of the revisions; it lets you see what the revised document would look like if you were to accept all of the changes. When you finish reviewing the document, click the Close button to return to your document.

POWER PLAY

We Used to Be So Alike

If you have two distinct versions of a Word document but you (or someone else) didn't use revision marks to show the changes, Word can point out the differences. Proceed as follows:

1. Open the edited version of the document.

2. From the Tools menu, choose Revisions.

3. In the Revisions dialog box, choose Compare Versions.

4. Supply the name of the original file in the Compare Versions dialog box, and then click OK.

Word does the rest: It displays the edited version with revision marks that show how it differs from the file you specified as the original. From there you can assess the differences and return to the Revisions dialog box to accept or reject the changes singly or wholesale.

PESKY MARKS

When you save a document, Word saves the setting for revision marking (on or off). If you want revision marking to cease, you must choose the Revisions command from the Tools menu and deselect the appropriate check box.

Say It with Annotations

Word's annotation feature lets you insert comments as you review a document. The comments, which resemble footnotes, are displayed in a separate pane. You can view them or hide them, and you can print them with the document or independently. For each comment, an annotation mark that consists of the reviewer's initials and a number is inserted in the document

(formatted as hidden text). The figure shown here contains a comment in the Annotations pane and the corresponding annotation mark in the document.

Before you insert an annotation, place the

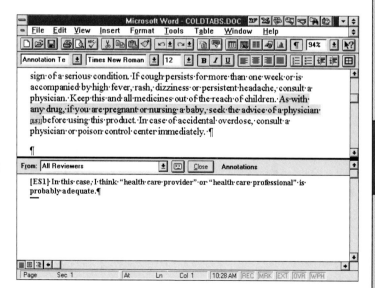

INITIALS, PLEASE

Word derives the initials in the annotation mark from the User Info tab of the Options dialog box (choose Options from the Tools menu).

NO COMMENT?

Use the Show/Hide ¶ button on the Standard toolbar to reveal or conceal annotation marks in a document.

insertion point immediately after the passage in the document on which you want to comment. Better yet, select the relevant passage; the entire passage will then appear highlighted when someone selects your comment. Next, choose Annotations from the Insert menu. The Annotations pane opens, numbered references are inserted, and the cursor blinks back at you from the appropriate spot for your comment. Go ahead. Of course, if you're equipped to use sound files, you can click the Insert Sound Object button at the top of the Annotations pane to start the Sound Recorder application and insert a sound annotation. Chapter 12, "Graphics and Other Gizmos," explains how to use Sound Recorder.

When you finish typing a comment, resume work in the document window. To reclaim space for viewing the document, close the Annotations pane by clicking its Close button. It reopens when you insert another comment. If you want to look at the comments again, choose Annotations from the View menu to display the Annotations pane.

To delete an annotation, delete the (hidden text) annotation mark in the document: Select the mark by triple-clicking it so that it has a black (not gray) highlight, and then press the Del key. Word renumbers any subsequent annotations.

POWER PLAY

Written on the Cell Walls

Excel has a feature that corresponds in many ways to the annotation feature in Word. You can add normally hidden notes to the current worksheet cell by choosing the Note command from the Insert menu or by clicking the Attach Note button on the Auditing toolbar. Type the note and click the Add button to register it in the list. In the annotated cell, a small red square in the upper left corner indicates the presence of a note.

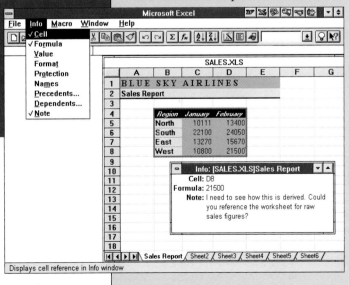

To see the note, display the Info window. You can do this in either of two ways: Choose the Options command from the Tools menu, and on the View tab select Info Window from the Show options; or click the Show Info button on the Audit toolbar. Thereafter, you can switch between the worksheet and the Info window by pressing Ctrl+Tab.

Notes are among the items you can track in the Info window. Whenever the window is active, you can select the items that it displays from the Info menu.

Let's Route a Word Document

Earlier in this chapter, we discussed how to use the Send command directly from an Office application. Now let's see how Word, Excel, and PowerPoint can take the next step by attaching a routing slip to a message. What does that achieve? Well, based on the information in the routing slip, Mail prompts each recipient to send the document to the next person on the list (or back to the original sender).

Adding a Routing Slip

Using Word's routing and annotation features, you can easily gather comments on your document from appropriate members of your workgroup. Suppose, for example, that you've written a proposal and you're ready to route it to a few coworkers for comments. After you save the document, you create a routing slip, as follows:

1. From the File menu, choose Add Routing Slip.

2. In the Routing Slip dialog box, add address information to the To list. To do that, choose the Address button to display the Address dialog box. Select from a list of available addresses and click the Add button, or type directly in the To list box. After you select or type the appropriate addresses, click OK.

3. We'll let the Subject line stand (it was gleaned from the Subject line in the document's Summary Info dialog box). In the Message Text box, add this message: *Please complete this routing by the end of the week. These guys want it yesterday.*

4. In the Route to Recipients section, select One After Another (normally the default).

5. Select the Return When Done check box so that the last recipient will be prompted to send the document back to you when the routing is finished. Deselect the Track Status check box. This option causes Mail to notify you each time the document is sent to the next recipient on the routing slip.

6. In the Protect For drop-down list, select Revisions. The recipients can annotate the document and make revisions, but all revisions will be tracked—that is, they will all be indicated with revision marks. Here's what the completed dialog box looks like:

WHO'S ON FIRST?
The Move buttons let you move the selected address up or down in the To list, which determines the order in which the document is routed.

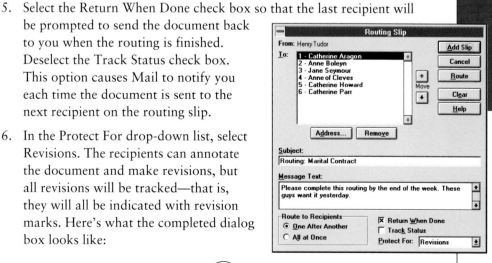

WHAT TO PROTECT
You need not protect your document before you create the routing slip. By using the protection feature in the Routing Slip dialog box, you can protect the copy, though not the original.

7. Choose the Route button to attach the slip to the document and send it on its way to the first recipient in the To list.

Editing and Removing Routing Slips

After you add a routing slip to a document, the Add Routing Slip command on the File menu becomes Edit Routing Slip. This command allows you to revise the names or the order of names, or to modify the message on the slip. Of course, editing the slip is especially useful if you have not yet routed the document (if you chose Add Slip rather than Route when you created the slip). But you can reuse the slip to route a document again—Word simply cautions you that you've used the slip already and then steps out of your way.

To delete the routing slip, choose Edit Routing Slip and click Clear to eliminate its contents—addresses, message, everything. Then choose Add Slip; because the content is now gone, the command deletes the slip.

POWER PLAY

Tamper-Proof Mail

If you have assigned a protection setting to a file on its routing slip, you might notice that the protection options on the routing slip provide only limited security. Any recipient can choose Unprotect File from the Tools menu to remove the restrictions you applied. To improve security, let's go a bit further.

You can apply protection to a Word document by choosing Protect Document from the Tools menu. The options here might be familiar to you, especially the options to protect the document from revisions or annotations. If you click OK, the document will be protected in whatever way you select. If you have

added a routing slip, the slip will also change to match the setting here.

The password is optional. It goes beyond what you have available in the Routing Slip dialog box, and it governs the protection options for routing. If you set a password (by entering it in the Password box and then confirming it at the subsequent prompt), protection options are grayed-out for the routing slip. When you send or route the document, it is protected as specified in the Protect Document dialog box. And the protection can be removed or changed only by the person who first provides the password.

Transferring Information to and from Mail

Mail messages can contain documents of any type. And there are no envelopes to lick. You've seen how Office applications can send documents directly, but you can also attach documents (and import text files) from within the Mail application. And if you aren't interested in attaching entire files, you can use the Paste Special command or the Insert Object command to include a portion of a file in a message.

On the receiving end, you can use the Clipboard to copy and move text from a message. But you can also save a message or an attached file as a separate document quite easily.

Stuff It in a Message

In Mail, the Attach command is the equivalent of the Send command on the File menu of an Office document. In fact, it's more than an equivalent: You can use Attach to send a document that has no Send command in its application interface. Access is an obvious case to consider: You can use Attach to convey an entire database file within a Mail message. Let's see how this works.

While you're composing a message in Mail, click the Attach button (at the top of the message area). The resulting Attach dialog box lets you identify a file by

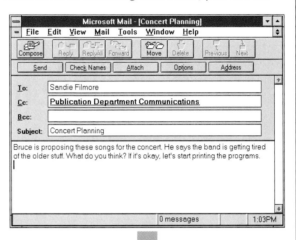

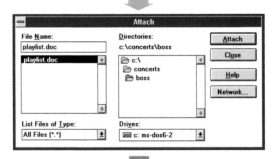

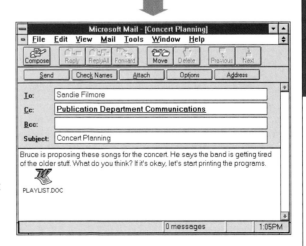

FEEL LIKE A MILLION?

With the Attach command you can attach files of any type, but size is a consideration. A database, for example, can easily run over 1 MB—the maximum that Mail can deliver.

browsing the disk and directory structure. When you locate and select the file you want to embed in the message, click Attach. Choose Close and you're done. The file appears in the message as an icon. The recipient of the message can open and edit the document simply by double-clicking the icon.

You can also insert the contents of a file directly into a Mail message, but some limitations apply. The text in a message is unformatted, so you should limit your inserts to ASCII files (conventionally, files with a TXT extension). Suppose you want to send a technical support employee in your organization a copy of a system file, CONFIG.SYS. You choose Compose to create a

message, type the header information, and tab to the message area. There you can insert CONFIG.SYS, an ASCII file, as part of the message by displaying the Edit menu and choosing Insert From File. In the resulting dialog box, navigate to the CONFIG.SYS file, and then click OK.

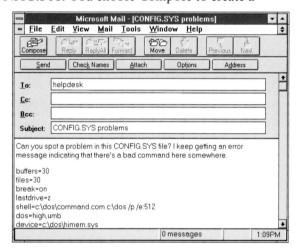

A message can contain embedded objects as well as entire files. You can use the Insert Object command (on the Edit menu) as you would in any other document to insert an embedded object from another application. The available options are far more limited, however. You'll notice that the dialog box offers no Link check box

or Display As Icon check box, nor is there a Create From File option or tab. Otherwise, the behavior is similar: Selecting a server application and clicking OK starts the application so that you can enter the information you want to embed.

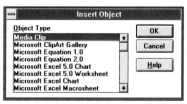

If you use the Clipboard to embed part of a document, the limitations are similar to those for Insert Object. In Mail, the Paste Special dialog box has no Paste Link check box and no Display As Icon check box. To embed, select the object format in the As list box (such as MS PowerPoint 4.0 Presentation Object) and choose the Paste button.

You *Can* Take It with You

Although Mail does not store messages as separate files, you can save them in that form; likewise, you can save the files attached to a message as separate files on your disk. The commands for these actions are quite simple.

Display the message you want to save. From the File menu, choose Save As to save the message as a text file. The resulting file, as shown in the example here, does not retain attached or embedded objects. All that remains is a reference to the filename of the attachment.

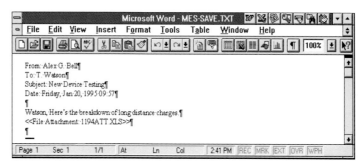

To retain a copy of the attachment, you have to save it separately. Display the message and choose Save Attachment from the File menu. The resulting dialog box lists the attachments in the current message. Select an attachment and a pathname, and choose the Save button (or choose Save All to save all of the attachments to a specified location). Each file attachment you save retains its original file format. For example, an attached Excel workbook saved to your disk can be opened and edited in Excel.

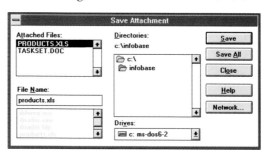

Chapter 11

Mastering Mergers

You're Already a Winner

Microsoft Word's Mail Merge feature is sophisticated. It handles spacing so well that you'll never find your merged information floating in an oversized space or truncated in an undersized space. To check for glitches before you commit yourself, you can merge to a new electronic document or simulate the merge to report errors only.

What's more, Mail Merge is easy to use. It has a Mail Merge Helper that leads you through each step—if you've tried to perform a mail merge before, you know how easily the process can get away from you. Like the sorcerer's apprentice, a mail merge can start something that quickly multiplies out of control. While you're muttering incantations, the gibberish can go off in all directions.

The Mail Merge feature is housed in Word, but you can consider it Office property. You can merge information from a data source in Word, Microsoft Excel, or Microsoft Access. And with the right equipment, you can distribute a merged document not only in printed form, but also as electronic mail or a fax.

In this chapter, we'll examine the fundamentals of performing a mail merge in Word. For simplicity,

> **MAIL MERGE**
>
> The process of integrating the entries in a data source with the information in a Word document is called a *mail merge*. (In earlier versions of Word, it was called a *print merge*.) As its name suggests, the process is often used for preparing form letters and mailing labels, but it's also useful for other types of documents—such as catalogs—that report information from a set of categories.

Mail Merge gathers information from a data source to complete the main document and create a set of new documents that you can print, fax, e-mail, or save as electronic files.

we'll start by using a Word data document as the data source. Then we'll progress to examples that use data from an Excel worksheet and from an Access table.

The mail merge process brings together information from two components, as shown in the illustration below. The first component, which Word calls the *main document*, contains the information that you want to repeat in every copy of the merged result. If you're planning to send a form letter,

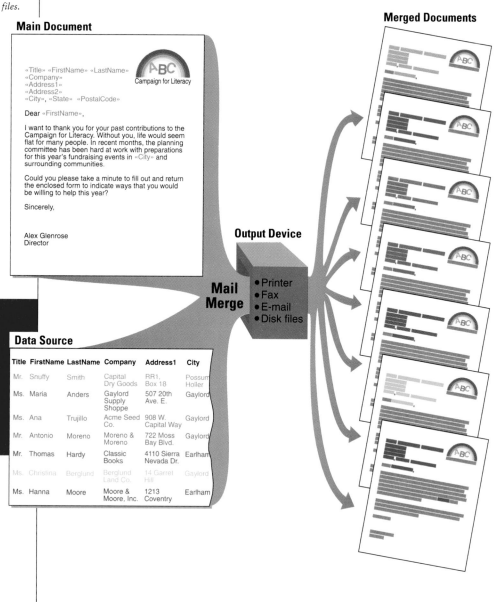

Main Document

«Title» «FirstName» «LastName»
«Company»
«Address1»
«Address2»
«City», «State» «PostalCode»

ABC
Campaign for Literacy

Dear «FirstName»,

I want to thank you for your past contributions to the Campaign for Literacy. Without you, life would seem flat for many people. In recent months, the planning committee has been hard at work with preparations for this year's fundraising events in «City» and surrounding communities.

Could you please take a minute to fill out and return the enclosed form to indicate ways that you would be willing to help this year?

Sincerely,

Alex Glenrose
Director

Output Device

Mail Merge

- Printer
- Fax
- E-mail
- Disk files

Merged Documents

Data Source

Title	FirstName	LastName	Company	Address1	City
Mr.	Snuffy	Smith	Capital Dry Goods	RR1, Box 18	Possum Holler
Ms.	Maria	Anders	Gaylord Supply Shoppe	507 20th Ave. E.	Gaylord
Ms.	Ana	Trujillo	Acme Seed Co.	908 W. Capital Way	Gaylord
Mr.	Antonio	Moreno	Moreno & Moreno	722 Moss Bay Blvd.	Gaylord
Mr.	Thomas	Hardy	Classic Books	4110 Sierra Nevada Dr.	Earlham
Ms.	Christina	Berglund	Berglund Land Co.	14 Garret Hill	Gaylord
Ms.	Hanna	Moore	Moore & Moore, Inc.	1213 Coventry	Earlham

for example, the main document is the text of your letter, which might begin as follows:

> You're probably asking yourself, "Why am *I* getting this offer? Do they think I'm some kind of *millionaire*? I couldn't *possibly* afford to have a deluxe vacation home on *every* continent! *Or could I?*"

The second component in every mail merge is the *data source*. It contains—in one tabular format or another—the information that changes with each copy of the merged document: Ms. Louise Brown, Mr. Jeremy H. Bullington, and so on. In a form letter, the data source supplies names, addresses, and the like; in a catalog, the data source supplies other facts, such as product names, descriptions, prices, and stock numbers. You can identify as your data source another (specially formatted) Word document, or you can draw from outside of Word to use information in a worksheet or a database.

The link between the two components is the *merge field*. A merge field is a placeholder inserted in the main document, as in "Dear «FirstName»," that refers to a column of information in the data source—in this case, the First-Name column. The name in the merge field in the main document matches the header for the column in the data source. Commonly, Word expects to find the headers in the first row of the data source—the column headings—and then it treats each row (after the first) as an individual data record. Each time Word moves to a new record, it goes to the next row in the data source.

What happens to the result—the merged document? Very often, you produce the merged document by directing it to the printer—such as when you create a series of personalized form letters ready for mailing. Or the printed result might be a series of envelopes, sheets of printed labels, or a catalog that comprises information in many records. The form of output need not be printed pages; the merged document might instead be distributed by e-mail or fax.

FIELDING FIELDS
Don't confuse the different types of fields: Word has its own fields—place-holders for variable text or for programming instructions—of which mail merge fields in the main document are a special case. These Word fields are different from fields in a data source, which are specific categories of information.

Making It Happen

Word provides a wizardlike tool called the Mail Merge Helper to orchestrate the process of defining a mail merge. To display the Mail Merge Helper dialog box, choose Mail Merge from the Tools menu. As you work through the process, you'll also see two special toolbars. Each is dedicated to helping you with a certain part of the overall task:

- The Mail Merge toolbar supplies tools for adding and manipulating fields in your main document.

- The Database toolbar streamlines the management of your data source.

In theory, the mail merge process consists of three sequential steps. In practice, you'll probably have to go back and forth between the steps as you develop a

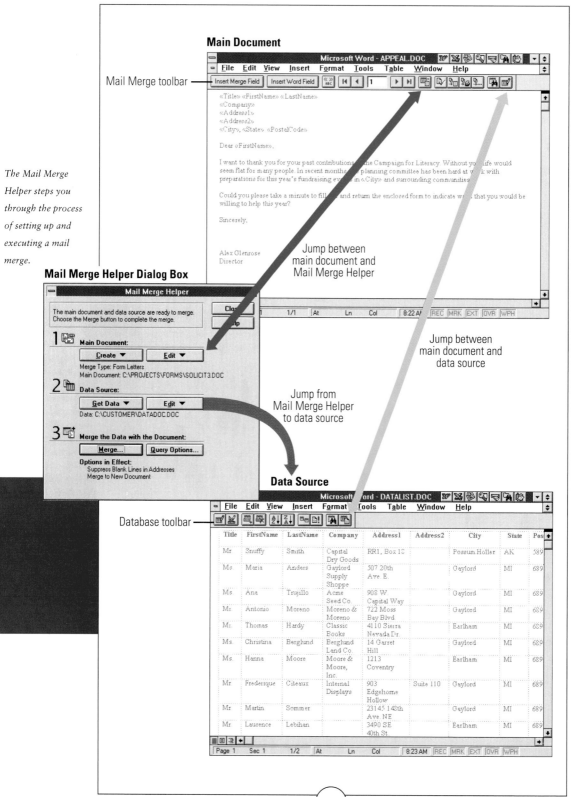

Main Document

Mail Merge toolbar

The Mail Merge Helper steps you through the process of setting up and executing a mail merge.

Jump between main document and Mail Merge Helper

Mail Merge Helper Dialog Box

Jump between main document and data source

Jump from Mail Merge Helper to data source

Data Source

Database toolbar

smooth fit between the main document and the data source. You might have to adjust spacing or modify an expression or insert a column—all varieties of wrinkles and tweaks. Word can be very helpful—the various tools it provides can hide messy details and simplify the process.

To explain the process of performing a mail merge, let's walk through the three major steps as the Mail Merge Helper outlines them: Establishing the main document, defining a data source, and merging the data into your main document. After you see what's involved in each of these steps, we'll investigate data sources outside of Word, such as Excel and Access.

Establishing the Main Document

The first thing that the Mail Merge Helper will want is a main document. Open a blank document, or if you want to use an existing document as the basis for the main document, open it (or make it the active window). Choose Mail Merge from the Tools menu to start the Mail Merge Helper. In the Mail Merge Helper dialog box, click the Create button. (Not much choice—the other steps are inactive until you designate a main document.) The Create button opens a menu of main document types; choose the one that best fits your needs.

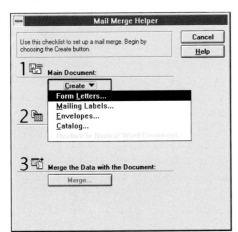

Regardless of which document type you choose, the Mail Merge Helper then asks whether you want to base your main document on the document in the active window or open a new window to work from scratch. Again, choose the one that fits your situation. Ideally, you've already started work on the main document, skipping those places at which you need to merge information from the data source. You'll add the merge fields later, after you designate the data source, but for now you do need to visualize the data source—what information it contains and how that information is broken up.

Word returns you to the Mail Merge Helper dialog box for the next step—designating a data source. The fact remains, however, that you have much more to do before the main document is complete. You have to type the text of the document, if you haven't already done so. And you have to insert the

BREAKING RECORDS

If you aren't sure which main document type fits your situation, you're probably trying to decide between Form Letters and Catalog. Here's the primary distinction: Word assumes that a form letter is based on the information in a single record, while a catalog will string together many records.

Mail Merge

The Mail Merge Helper conducts you safely through most parts of the mail merge process. Broadly speaking, these are the steps:

1. Create a normal Word document that contains the standard text. Envelopes and labels might not contain any standard text. At this point, saving your document is useful but not essential.
2. From the Tools menu, choose Mail Merge to open the Mail Merge Helper dialog box.
3. In the Main Document section (number 1), click Create and choose a document type.
4. Designate the main document as the one in the active window.
5. Click Get Data in the Data Source section (number 2) and choose to either create a data source (a Word data document) or open an existing source.
6. If you choose to create a Word data document: In the Create Data Source dialog box, add, remove, and move (reorder) entries to include the appropriate field names in the list; then click OK. If you choose to open a data source: In the Open Data Source dialog box, specify the pathname and filename and then click OK.
7. Return to your main document and introduce merge fields by clicking the Insert Merge Field button on the Mail Merge toolbar.
8. Click the Mail Merge button on the Mail Merge toolbar.
9. In the Merge To list, select a destination. Use the Query Options button if you want to sort the records, or use filters to include only specific records. Click OK to generate the mail merge.

merge fields that will place the information from the data source in the main document. These tasks, particularly inserting the merge fields, can wait until you've defined the data source.

If at any point you want to break off the engagement (to let the main document become a normal Word document again), return to the Mail Merge Helper dialog box, click Create, and choose Restore To Normal Word Document from the menu.

FROM THE SOURCE

If you need to create a data source in a different application, don't try to do it using the Mail Merge Helper. Instead, launch the application separately and create the data file. Then, in the Mail Merge Helper dialog box, click Get Data and use the Open Data Source command to attach the data source.

Defining a Data Source

The second step in the merger is to make some data available to merge into the main document. Never mind for the moment that the main document has no references to the data (or is completely blank). You'll have an easy time adding those references after you've introduced the data source.

Forging a Header   Click the Get Data button in the Mail Merge Helper dialog box (shown on the facing page) and survey your choices. In this section, you'll see what's required to execute the first command, Create Data Source.

You can choose the second command, Open Data Source, if you have an existing data file that already contains the information you want to merge. What sort of file might that be? Well, you can use a number of different types, including a Word document, an Excel worksheet, or an Access database. We'll explore these sources later in this chapter. As for the third command, Header Options, we'll leave that for the Power Play titled "Two Heads Are Better," later in this chapter. In most cases, the data source can supply

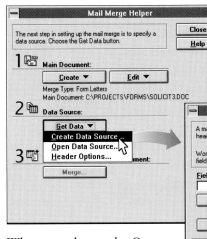

appropriate header entries—so you don't need to choose Header Options unless you want to create a header source that's distinct from the data source.

When you choose the Create Data Source command, the Mail Merge Helper displays a series of windows in which you supply the appropriate field names and enter the information that belongs in the fields. The result is saved as a table in a separate Word document.

The first window, labeled Create Data Source, is shown in the figure above. In it you insert the field names that make up the header row for your data source. To give you a head start, the header row contains a set of commonly used field names. Add to the default list, remove unnecessary field names, or move field names up or down to change the order—you can modify the header row in whatever way you want. (Just don't try adding spaces between words in a field name; that'll get you nowhere.)

When you're satisfied with the field names, click OK and proceed to the Save Data Source dialog box. Looks a lot like a Save As dialog box: You assign a filename and a location to your data source; its format (Word document) is not negotiable. When you click OK, you get the unsurprising news that your data source contains no records. You can add records at this point (by choosing Edit Data Source) or return to the main document and work there.

Adding Data When you're ready to add or edit the information in the data source, Word supplies a customized data form in the Data Form dialog box, shown on the next page. The whole idea of the form is to make your records easy to view and manage. To display the form when you first create the data source, click Edit Data Source in the message box that informs you that the data source contains no data records. The dialog box is also displayed when you click Edit in the Data Source section of the Mail Merge Helper dialog box and choose the name of the data file from the menu or when you click the Edit Data Source button on the Mail Merge toolbar.

HEADER ROW

The field names are often presented in a list in the Create Data Source window and in the Data Form window. So why refer to the field names as the *header row*? Because the data source itself is normally displayed as a table, with the field names arranged across the top row as column headings.

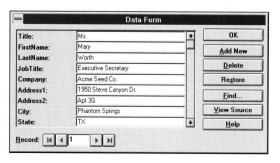

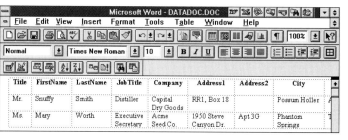

To enter information, simply type in each text box and tab from field to field. After you complete the form, choose the Add New button to enter the next record. Click OK after you add the last record. If you want to start over with the record that you are adding or modifying, choose the Restore button.

To see the Word document that contains your data table, choose the View Source button. As shown in the figure above, the first row in the table is the header row, with field names at the head of each column. Data records begin in the second row. If you like, you can edit the information in the table directly. In addition, you can open the data source using the Open command on the File menu; you needn't open it with View Source via the main document. On the Database toolbar, click the Data Form button to return to the data form. Return to the main document if you want to revisit the Mail Merge Helper dialog box.

FIELD SHIFT

To add or remove a field in your Word data source, click the Edit Data Source button on the Mail Merge toolbar. Choose the View Source button in the resulting dialog box. With patience and skill you could edit the data table directly, but here's the answer for most situations: Click the Manage Fields button on the Database toolbar. The resulting dialog box lets you add, remove, and rename fields.

Merging the Information

The third and final step of the Mail Merge Helper is entitled Merge the Data with the Document. At this stage, you insert the data from the data source in the main document. Merging the data means substituting the information from the data source at the locations specified by the merge fields in the main document. Through no fault of our own, we have not specified any of these locations yet. You might recall that we were waiting to get the data source squared away. So let's see about inserting merge fields now.

Inserting Merge Fields   To insert merge fields, switch to your main document. If your data source is the active window, you can switch to the main document by clicking the Mail Merge Main Document button on the Database toolbar. Alternatively, from the Mail Merge Helper dialog box you can choose Edit in the Main Document section and choose the filename from the menu.

Adding merge fields is a snap. Position the insertion point where you want the merged information to appear, and then click the Insert Merge Field button on the Mail Merge toolbar. A menu drops down that lists all of the field names in the data source. When you choose a name, Word inserts the corresponding merge field at the insertion point in your main document.

The figure at the top of the next page shows what merge fields look like in a main document. If you insert consecutive merge fields—FirstName and LastName, for example—remember to put any necessary blank spaces or punctuation between them. Notice that when you format a merge field, the merged information will retain the text formatting you applied.

POWER PLAY

Avoiding the Fate of the Doe Doe

Don't assume that you can change a merge field simply by typing a different field name in place of the one in your main document. For example, you might edit

«LastName» «LastName»

so that it reads

«FirstName» «LastName»

and believe that you've taken a clever shortcut. But when you execute the merge, Word ignores the change: The letter to John Doe or Jane Doe is addressed to Doe Doe. Sure, the recipient probably has a sense of humor. But you definitely want to make a better impression than that.

Recognize that a merge field is window dressing for a Word field. When you press Alt+F9 to display the field codes, a pair of merge fields such as

«LastName» «LastName»

becomes

{ MERGEFIELD LastName } { MERGEFIELD LastName }

where MERGEFIELD is the Word field name used for all merge fields, followed by its only parameter, the name of a specific merge field. So even if you edit the merge field to appear as «FirstName», the field code still has the LastName parameter. You can, however, edit the field code to change the parameter, which has a real effect on the merged outcome:

{ MERGEFIELD FirstName } { MERGEFIELD LastName }

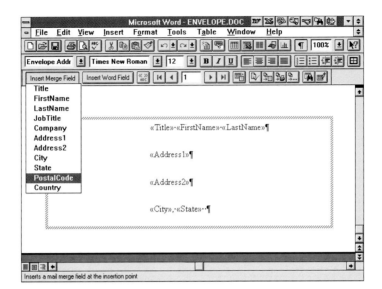

Choose a field
name to insert the
corresponding
merge field.

Sorting and Selecting Microsoft Office gives you significant flexibility as you execute a mail merge. You can control the order in which you merge records by sorting the information according to the contents of the fields. For example, you might sort a set of letters and labels by zip code to prepare a mass mailing. In addition to sorting your information, you might choose to select certain records from the entire set by indicating the appropriate criteria. You might, for example, set up a filter that targets customers in a given region who have exceeded a certain volume of orders in the past year.

To establish either a sort order or a filter, choose the Query Options button in the Mail Merge Helper dialog box. (This command is active only after you've indicated the main document and associated a data source with it.) On the Sort Records tab of the Query Options dialog box, you can define a primary sort and two subsequent sorts. For each stage in the sorting process, click the arrow alongside the drop-down list box and choose from the list of field names in your data source. For each sort, select either the Ascending or the

> **FILTER**
>
> A *filter* is one of the components of a query (along with the sort order). It establishes the selection criteria that let you define a subset of the records in your data source.

Descending option button to specify the order in which the records are to be sorted. For text, ascending order is A-to-Z alphabetic order; for numbers, it's low to high.

In the sort defined here, the records are ordered

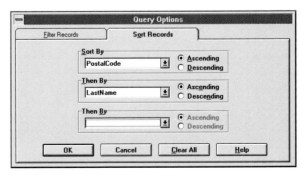

by the information in the PostalCode field (the primary sort); records with identical postal codes are then sorted alphabetically by the information in the LastName field.

The Filter Records tab lets you determine which records are included from the data source. You can set up to six criteria. For each one, you select a field and a comparison type in the drop-down list box. Then you type a value in the third box (unless it's not appropriate, as in the case of the comparisons Is Blank and Is Not Blank).

When you include multiple criteria, you must connect them logically with an And or an Or (in the boxes along the left side of the tab). The And operator constricts the filter by imposing additional conditions on each selected record; the Or operator dilates the filter by allowing different ways for a record to satisfy the selection criteria.

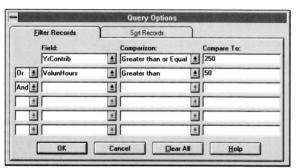

The simple filter shown in the figure at left demonstrates the use of multiple criteria. The first criterion states that the value in the YrContrib field must be greater than or equal to 250. The second criterion, joined to the first with the Or operator, states that the number of volunteer hours must exceed 50. The records that are selected will meet either or both criteria.

After you establish the sort and filter settings, click OK to apply the query. If no records meet the criteria, the program tells you so. Otherwise, you're back at the Mail Merge Helper dialog box.

Merging...Somewhere Merging can accomplish a lot in a hurry—all of it wrong, if you aren't careful. So let's take it slowly. If you simply want to see what the merged information will look like, you can display the main document (with its various merge fields inserted) and tell Word to substitute the information from your data source in place of the fields: Simply click the View Merged Data button on the Mail Merge toolbar. By clicking the

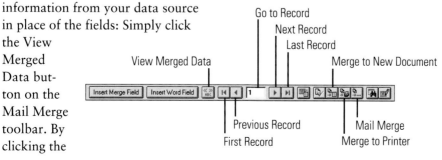

Go to Record
Next Record
Last Record
Merge to New Document
View Merged Data
Insert Merge Field Insert Word Field 1
Previous Record
First Record
Mail Merge
Merge to Printer

TORN FILTER?

Filters with many criteria that combine And and Or operators can be difficult to devise properly. If the data source is part of a database, you can use the database program, such as Access, to conduct the query. A query in a database program is usually easier to create, and you can save a complicated query and not be forced to reenter it.

MAIL MERGE DISBARRED

If the Mail Merge toolbar is not displayed, point to any toolbar, click the right mouse button, and choose Mail Merge from the shortcut menu. If Mail Merge is not among the toolbars listed, you haven't established the document in the active window as a main document (using the Mail Merge Helper). Only then does the Mail Merge toolbar become available. You might be looking at a document containing the merged results instead of at the main document.

arrow buttons on the toolbar or entering a different record number, you can skip around among the records.

Now, to get a result from the mail merge, you have to indicate a destination. One way to do that is to click the Mail Merge button on the Mail Merge toolbar. Other buttons can initiate immediate action—merging to a new document or merging directly to the printer, for example—but using the Mail Merge button is a good way to consider all of your options.

In the Merge dialog box, drop down the Merge To list, as shown at the top of the facing page. The most cautious step you can take is to select New

POWER PLAY

Merging to Electronic Mail or Electronic Fax

Merging your correspondence to output it as electronic mail messages or faxes is not difficult, provided your computer is set up for sending. To find out if Office detects the necessary hardware and software, open your main document (for which you have already made data available). Click the Mail Merge button on the Mail Merge toolbar. In the resulting Merge dialog box, drop down the Merge To list box. Word displays Electronic Mail and Electronic Fax if you are equipped to distribute your documents using these routes. Select the option you want to use.

In the same dialog box, you can click the Query Options button to select only the records that contain suitable address information for sending an e-mail message or a fax. On the Filter Records tab, specify for Field the field that contains the e-mail address or the fax number; for Comparison, select Is Not Blank. Click OK to return to the Merge dialog box.

Now click the Set Up button. In the Merge To Setup dialog box, you have to tell the program where to find the e-mail addresses or the fax numbers to use as it dispatches each letter. Select the name of the appropriate field. For e-mail messages, you can include a subject line for the message.

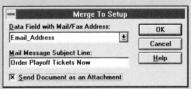

Normally, Word inserts your letter in the e-mail or fax message as unformatted text. If you want to preserve the formatting, select the Send Document as an Attachment check box. Click OK after you finish dealing with the setup options.

Finally, in the Merge dialog box, choose Merge to initiate the process of merging and distributing the letter.

Document. By merging to a document, you can review, edit, and personalize the results. The result of a merger, such as a single form letter, is separated from the next result by a section break. If you take the further step of saving the

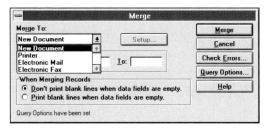

document to a disk, you can transport it for later output—perhaps to a printer that gives you faster or higher-quality results.

The other Merge To options let you send the merged document directly to a printer, to an electronic mail system, or to a fax machine. See the Power Play on the facing page for details on mailing and faxing; note that the options won't appear in your list if your computer is not appropriately equipped.

DOC HOPPING

When you merge to a new document, you can use the Window menu to move back to your main document if you need to make changes and repeat the merge (to a printer or other resource).

More Mergers

As you become comfortable with the Office suite, you'll recognize and explore the strengths of each application. Consequently, when you use Word's Mail Merge feature, you'll be more likely to fold in information that's maintained in Excel or Access. The techniques for doing so are almost identical to those for using a Word document as a data source, but you might prefer to use the superior features of Excel or Access for maintaining and manipulating your data.

FIELDS OF GRAY

You can make the merge fields more visible in your main document by displaying the View tab of the Options dialog box (reached via the Tools menu) and selecting Always in the Field Shading list.

Creating a Form Letter with Excel Data

To demonstrate a mail merge using an Excel file as the data source, let's step through a simple example: a form letter that merges information from an Excel worksheet. Suppose that you have the form letter shown here, which uses a Word document as the source for the name and address data.

You want to merge information from an Excel worksheet that another person created and sent to you as an attachment to an e-mail message. You open the worksheet, peruse it, and find

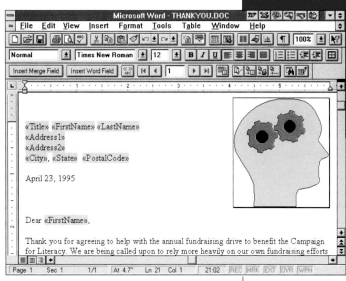

EXCEL INFO
For more information on using Excel data, see questions 45 and 47 in Chapter 15, "Real Questions, Real Answers."

that it is constructed in a similar way to the Word data source that you used previously. In Mail, choose Save Attachment from the File menu to save the attached workbook as PLEDGES.XLS, a separate file on your disk. Here's the Excel worksheet:

To merge this data, follow these steps:

1. Open the main document for the form letter in Word and click the Mail Merge Helper button on the Mail Merge toolbar. You've already registered this form letter as a main document and created a Word data source for it. What you need to do now is change the data source to the new Excel worksheet. In the Mail Merge Helper dialog box, click Get Data and choose Open Data Source.

2. The Open Data Source dialog box has the standard controls for opening a file. The List Files of Type drop-down list includes a setting for MS Excel Worksheets. Select this option, navigate the directory structure to select the filename PLEDGES.XLS, and click OK.

3. Word displays a dialog box in which you can specify the specific portion of the worksheet that contains the data to merge. Within the range, include as the first row the column headings; this is the header row and will supply the field names. Better than a specific range of cells is a named range (which you create in Excel with the Insert Name command). After you specify a range and give it a name, you can add or delete rows within the named range and it will adjust its range accordingly. If you use a named range, you must create the name in Excel before you use the worksheet as a data source.

In this example, select PledgeList (as shown in the figure below) and click OK. (The person who prepared the worksheet gave the name PledgeList to the range of cells that contains the information to merge.) As you can see, you can always select Entire Spreadsheet, a default name that includes just what it says—the whole worksheet—but the header row must be the first row of the worksheet.

NAME THAT FIELD

Word truncates field names longer than 20 characters, and it substitutes underscores for characters other than letters and numbers.

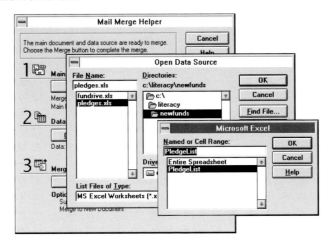

4. In the Mail Merge Helper dialog box, click the Merge button (or click the Mail Merge button on the Mail Merge toolbar). Pick a destination to merge to—let's select New Document, the default option—and click Merge.

5. Because not all of the merge field names in your main document match the Excel column headings precisely, Word displays the Invalid Merge Field dialog box and prompts you to change the names of the merge fields to match the field names it extracted from the first row of your data source.

Choose the appropriate field name. The alternative (unless you remove the offending field from your main document) is a set of merged documents littered with **boldface error statements. Ugly.**

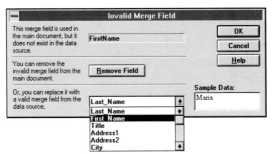

6. After you correct the invalid field names, Word completes the merge to the new document.

MERGE ERRORS

As you review your merged documents (on screen, or as they come out of the printer), you might encounter the following message: *Error! MergeField was not found in header record of data source.* Normally, the problem is a mismatch between the name of the merge field and the field name in the header record (the first row) of the data source. You can correct this by making the field names match (by changing either the merge field or the header record) or by creating a separate header file, as described in the Power Play on the next page.

POWER PLAY

Two Heads Are Better

What happens if you don't want to change your main document by modifying the names of its merge fields to match the field names in the data source, and you don't want to change the field names in the data file? Using our previous example, let's say you want to be able to use the form letter with the Excel worksheet *as well as* the Word data source you have been using happily for years. You want to leave the merge fields as they stand; you simply want Mail Merge to understand that where the main document refers to Postal-Code, it should look in the column headed Zip Code.

The solution is to create a separate header file that Mail Merge will reference instead of the first row of the data source. In that header file, the column of zip codes will have the heading PostalCode—no need to change the Excel heading and no need to monkey with the merge field. Just be sure that you put the correct field names in the header file, and be

sure that they match up with the correct columns in the worksheet. Here are the necessary steps:

1. In the Mail Merge Helper dialog box, click Get Data and choose the Header Options command.

2. In the Header Options dialog box, choose Create to create a new header file.

3. In the Create Header Source dialog box, add, remove, and move field names as necessary to provide an accurate set of column headings for your data source—headings that match the merge field names in your main document.

4. Click OK after you finish.

Note that Word refers to this header source instead of to the first row of the data source (the header record). You don't have to adjust the range of the data source to eliminate the header record.

Creating a Catalog with an Access Query

You can use the information in an Access database as your data source in much the same way that you used the information in an Excel worksheet in the previous example. There are, however, ways in which Access is even better suited than Excel to serve as a data source. Take, for instance, the fact that you can create and save queries in Access that support your mail merge needs. And Access has its own Microsoft Word Mail Merge Wizard, which builds a mail merge with considerable ease.

To demonstrate the process, let's generate a catalog for the products in NWIND.MDB, the sample database included in Access. Of course, NWIND includes its own catalog, a nicely formatted report. But we'll use the database to show how you can use a mail merge to create a simple catalog of products that have not been discontinued.

1. Begin by opening NWIND.MDB. In the Database window, select the table or query that contains the data you want to merge. We'll select the Products table.

2. Click the Merge It button on the Standard toolbar.

3. The resulting wizard asks whether you want to create a new Word document or link to an existing one. Select the option that creates a new Word document as the main document. When you click OK, the wizard launches Word, creates the document, and links the data source to it.

4. In Word, click the Mail Merge Helper button on the Mail Merge toolbar to see how much the wizard has accomplished.

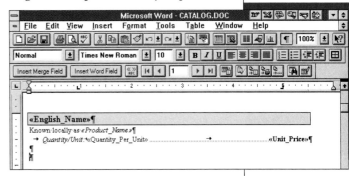

Merge It button

The main document and the data source are already set. Notice that, by default, the main document chooses the category Form Letters. Click Create and choose Catalog. Then confirm that you want to change the current document to a catalog.

5. Click Close to return to the main document. You can now add the text for your catalog and insert whichever merge fields a product entry requires. Save the document after you are finished. Here is a sample:

We have not yet made any provision for eliminating the discontinued items. NWIND.MDB includes a query that does just that: The Catalog query selects only product records that have the value No in the Discontinued field. So we can use the information from that query for the mail merge (instead of using the Products table) to get only the products we need.

If you want to get the same result from within Word, you can create the query from the Mail Merge Helper. Choose Open Data Source from the Get Data menu. Then click the MS Query button. The MS Query shared application appears and you can then set the conditions of your query.

POWER PLAY

Nonrepeating Text in a Catalog

If you'd like to have some introductory text in your catalog, you will be confronted with a problem in Mail Merge. As it merges the data to generate your catalog, Mail Merge repeats the main document for each record—including the introductory text. So if you want to include the introductory text only once, at the beginning of the document, how do you convey that? Here's one way.

Enter the introductory text as a separate document; we called our document CATINTRO.DOC, as shown below. Then switch to your main document and insert the following IF field. (Press Ctrl+F9 and enter the field instructions between the brackets. Remember that you also have to press Ctrl+F9 to enter each of the two nested fields.)

```
{ IF { MERGESEQ } = 1 { INCLUDETEXT c:\\catalog\\catintro.doc } "" }
```

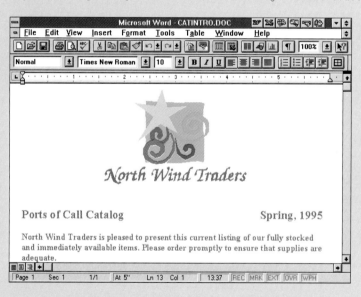

To understand how this field works, recall the syntax for an IF field:

```
{ IF Expression1 Operator Expression2 "TrueText" "FalseText" }
```

The first expression is the value of the MERGESEQ field, which Word increments for each record it merges. Therefore, the value of MERGESEQ is equal to 1 only for the first record, so the *TrueText* argument is implemented only once. At all other times, the conditional statement is false, so we're left with *FalseText*, an empty pair of quotation marks (which does nothing). The

TrueText argument is another nested field, an INCLUDETEXT field that inserts the text of the specified file. So check it out. (It's shown in full page view below.) The introductory text is followed by the merged product information.

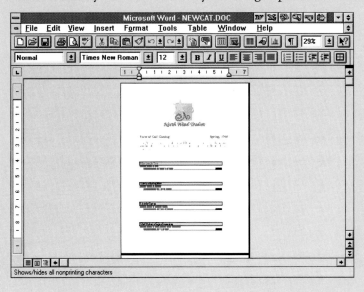

Chapter 12

Welcome to Graphics & Other Gizmos!

Beyond Text Appeal

You might think that adding graphics, sound, and animation to your files is a bit exotic, or you might be wary of the memory demands or the processing time required to incorporate these gizmos into your documents. This chapter should change your mind. Included with the Microsoft Office suite and the Microsoft Windows environment is an assortment of shared applications, utility programs, and system resources that bring this "extra-textual" realm within your grasp.

It's easy to add sound, video, clip art, and other gizmos to your documents.

A computer that can handle your Office applications—as well as frequent switching between applications that are open concurrently—can probably meet the processing and memory-management requirements of modest gizmo files. But keep in mind that as the extent and quality of graphics, sound, and animation increase, the demands they place on your hardware climb rapidly. You'll eventually discover a point at which your desire for more complex multimedia resources is offset by diminished system performance.

As for the output, the VGA and Super VGA monitors that are standard in new computer

MindScope MultiMedia

Senior High Curricula

- Excerpts from Contemporary News Programming
- Cultural Commentary

  Einstein on Nonproliferation
- Project Suggestions
- Panel Discussions

Signing of Test-Ban Treaty

Linked sound file

Embedded video sequence

Clip art from Microsoft ClipArt Gallery

systems have sufficient color range and resolution for most clip art and animated images. Sound capabilities are also built into many computers, including all machines that meet the so-called MPC (Multimedia PC) standard. In addition, upgrade kits (such as the Microsoft Windows Sound System) can provide all of the basic hardware and software for enhancing your 386-or-faster PC with sound and video capabilities. Note that stereo speakers are generally a separate purchase.

If you're still convinced that graphics and multimedia files are exotic, the information in this chapter can help you put matters in perspective. You'll see that much of the territory is already familiar—for example, you've probably been using, or at least eyeing, Paintbrush (a Windows accessory) for some time. And sound and video clips are easy to add and to play in your documents; the overview of Sound Recorder and Media Player in this chapter will explain how straightforward they are to use.

Creating Graphics

Within the Office suite, you have a number of options for creating graphics. Each major Office application provides a set of drawing tools, including some that are unique to the application in some small or large way. We'll touch on many of these drawing tools in the following sections. Windows provides shared applications, such as Paintbrush, which creates bitmapped images. We'll explore Paintbrush to see how it fits in—but first, a little background.

As you learn to work with graphics, you should understand the distinction between drawings and bitmaps. Not only do they use different storage formats, but they are also manipulated in different ways. A drawing is often said to be *object-oriented*: You can break it into its component objects—curves, rectangles, and so forth—each of which is described by its own set of properties. As a result, you can layer, shrink, and flip components with relative ease. A bitmap, on the other hand, is simply a set of pixel values: You can move or change blocks or regions of pixels, but moving part of a bitmap generally leaves a hole that you then have to patch. Typically, you can zoom in on a bitmapped image and edit it pixel by pixel.

Paintbrush

If you've been working with Windows for a while, you've probably wandered through the Accessories program group and launched Paintbrush. The basic drawing tools in Paintbrush are arranged along the left side of the window and are easy to identify. You select a tool (by clicking it) and then use it in the drawing area. Paintbrush offers tools for drawing lines (straight, curved, or freehand), drawing basic shapes (filled or unfilled), and adding text and fills.

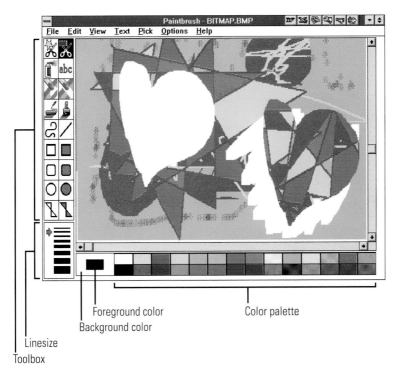

Foreground color
Background color
Color palette
Linesize
Toolbox

In addition to selecting a drawing tool, you can use the controls along the bottom of the Paintbrush window to set the line width, the foreground color, and the background color. To set the foreground color, point to a color in the Color palette and click with the left mouse button. To set the background color, point to a color and click with the right mouse button.

Exploration Ideas   Paintbrush is easy to explore on your own. Here are a few suggestions to help you make use of some of its most attractive features:

- Take advantage of the Undo command on the Edit menu. You can experiment more freely when you can undo mistakes easily. Another repair technique uses the Backspace key. Press it to activate a special eraser that ignores parts of the picture that are aready pasted down.

- Hold down the Shift key while you draw or erase to enforce certain "regularity" rules. Line-drawing movements are restricted to vertical, horizontal, and diagonal; shapes are square or circular (not rectangular or oval).

- Investigate the eraser tools, Eraser and Color Eraser. They're more versatile than you might suppose. The current Linesize setting determines the size of the tool, and the current background color determines the replacement color when you erase. Color Eraser affects only the current foreground color; double-click the Color Eraser icon to execute the replacement throughout the drawing area. You can double-click the Eraser icon to start a new picture.

LESS IS MORE

With the Undo command, less can be more. When you select a new drawing tool or choose a menu command, the items you have drawn are pasted down. Choosing Undo eliminates all of the work that is not pasted down. (Choosing Undo a second time toggles back to the former state.) Before you attempt a risky drawing maneuver or add a fill that might flood your carefully colored page with green, for example, reselect the tool that you are using to paste down your previous work. Then you can undo just the next action.

- Note that the window border defines an unofficial boundary for your drawing. To see what this means, use the Fill tool to flood the drawing area, and then scroll to the right. Notice that the fill stops at the border.

- Activate the Pick menu by using the Pick tool or the Scissors tool to define a cutout. The Pick menu contains nifty commands for flipping the cutout or inverting its colors. (Black becomes white; other colors change to their complements.) Other commands let you create resized or tilted copies of the cutout. You can also clear the original cutout when you create a copy if you've activated the last item on the menu, Clear.

- Hold down the Ctrl key while you drag a cutout if you want to copy the cutout (rather than move the original). Also, the left and right mouse buttons drop slightly different images. Use the left button for a transparent image, the right button for an opaque one. The difference affects the parts of the cutout that match the current background color: A transparent copy

POWER PLAY

Perfect Sizing

After you select an area as a cutout and choose Shrink And Grow from the Pick menu, Paintbrush fits the cutout into the next area you define. If the target area does not have the same proportions as the cutout, the program stretches the original to fit the area. Quick and dirty.

But what if you want to reduce or enlarge a cutout without distorting it? Here are a couple of techniques that work well. One is quick but not too dirty; the second is not as quick, but it's also not at all dirty.

The first technique is to define the cutout and the target area as squares—you hold down the Shift key while you use the selection tool. The square cutout then translates without distortion into the larger or smaller square you define as the target area.

If you cannot define the cutout as a square for some reason, try the second technique: From the View menu, choose Cursor Position to display the location of the cursor in the drawing area (in pixels). Then note the starting and ending positions of the cursor as you define the cutout rectangle. When you define a target area to enlarge or reduce the cutout, be sure that the dimensions of the new area are proportional to those of the cutout.

Displaying the cursor position is a helpful technique for placing objects precisely. (At high resolutions, the cursor position changes rapidly and not always smoothly, so it might be easier to control the cursor position if you use the Del key and the direction keys to move a cutout.)

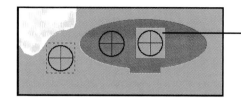

An opaque copy reproduces background-colored elements

reveals any underlying colors through the background-colored parts of the cutout, while an opaque copy shows the background color faithfully (true to the original).

Ins and Outs   When you save an image created in Paintbrush, it is normally stored as a bitmap with a BMP extension. A color picture created with Paintbrush has a maximum of 16 colors, so the default 16 Color BMP format is fine. But other file formats are available—see the Save File as Type drop-down list in the Save As dialog box. If you're working on a file that originated outside Paintbrush, you might need to use the 256 Color BMP format to save the image accurately; you can even exceed the 256-color limit if you save the file using the 24 Bit BMP format.

Paintbrush can also save an image in the PCX format. With some applications that are not Windows-based (such as Microsoft Word for MS-DOS), you can import bitmaps saved in the PCX format but not those in the BMP format. Paintbrush can also open files in the PCX format, which is useful because scanning software is commonly able to generate this format (but not the BMP format).

Besides the BMP and PCX formats, Paintbrush routinely imports only a few other file formats. If you drop down the List Files of Type list box you'll see DIB, a second (older) Windows bitmap format. (Formats for bitmapped images differ in various ways, particularly in the compression schemes they employ.) You'll also see the MSP format, which belongs to the Paint program, a predecessor of Paintbrush that was included with Windows prior to version 3. You can open MSP files, which are all monochrome, and you can save the edited (also monochrome) result in either the PCX or the Monochrome Bitmap (BMP) format.

Why can't you import other formats? Well, you can try, but because Paintbrush is a paint program, which generates bitmaps, it doesn't recognize and manipulate the objects in an image the way that a drawing application does. You'll probably have better luck with most formats if you import them into your Office applications, as described in the next section.

The Drawing Tools

Each major application in the Office suite has a set of drawing tools. Most of the applications (all but Microsoft Access) have dedicated toolbars that include tools for creating lines and shapes, flipping and rotating the lines and shapes, grouping and ungrouping objects, and controlling layers.

HARD FACTS

If your monitor and display adapter or your current display mode limits you to a monochrome display, you cannot create color pictures. Likewise, if you can display only 16 colors, Paintbrush saves only 16-color files, despite the fact that you loaded a 256-color file.

Compared with commercial drawing programs, the drawing tools that accompany the Office applications are modest—far better for making simple diagrams than for creating elaborate artwork. Yet each drawing toolbar has its unique tools, tailored to specific tasks. You can create drawings—labels, diagrams, and doodles—that exist in a layer of their own, distinct from the text of your Microsoft Word document, your Microsoft Excel worksheet or chart, or other objects that occupy your Microsoft PowerPoint slide.

The quickest way to display the Drawing toolbar in Word or Excel is to click the Drawing button on the application's Standard toolbar. In PowerPoint you have the Drawing, Drawing+, and AutoShapes toolbars, which contain drawing tools; in Access, you have the Toolbox and Palette toolbars for drawing.

Before you conclude that the drawing tools are essentially similar from one Office application to another, however, you should note one important qualitative difference: In Word, the Drawing toolbar can create distinct objects—Word Picture objects. In this way, the drawing component in Word functions like shared applications (such as Microsoft WordArt and Equation Editor) to let you create and embed objects. To create a Word Picture object using Word's Drawing toolbar, click the Create Picture button. To create a Word Picture object in another Office application, choose the Insert Object command (the Edit Insert Object command in Access) and select Microsoft Word 6.0 Picture Object in the list of object types.

Let's Draw When you look at a drawing toolbar, such as the one from Word shown in the figures on the facing page, it might not look significantly different from the set of tools in Paintbrush. It includes tools for creating lines and standard shapes, and even though you don't see separate palettes for lines and colors, you can select tools for setting the line style, the line color, and the fill color. The similarities are deceptive, however, as you'll notice soon after you begin to draw.

In the following examples, we'll do some drawing in Word. There are two methods you can use to draw, depending on the result you want. If you want to create drawing objects that can lie on top of or under your text, you can switch to Layout view (Word allows drawing only in Layout view), select a tool from the Drawing toolbar, and start drawing. This technique is useful if you want to create special highlights and effects under and around your text, such as emphasis lines or a watermark.

The second method is to create a Word Picture, which is the technique we'll use in our example. You use the same drawing tools, but when you click the Create Picture toolbar button you work in a special Picture window instead of directly in your document. When you close the Picture window, the picture is placed in your document as an embedded Word Picture object that can be

PALETTE PLEASING
The Drawing Object command on Word's Format menu lets you set the defaults for the weight and color of the line and for the fill color.

moved and sized, but your normal document text flows around the picture rather than over or under it.

Using a tool is simple enough: To use the Ellipse tool, for example, you click the tool's button to select it; you draw an ellipse by dragging to define the shape and size, and then releasing the mouse button.

At this point, the finished ellipse has eight sizing handles arranged in a rectangle around it. Because the ellipse is stored as a distinct object, you can work elsewhere in the drawing or save the file and reopen it, and when you click the ellipse again the sizing handles return. You can move the ellipse or resize it; you can also modify its shape (to make it more or less circular)— something you can do in a drawing program that you can't do in a paint program.

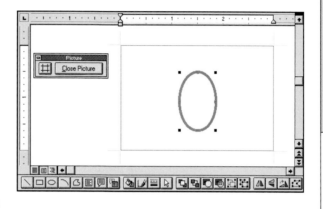

To see another advantage of creating a drawing rather than a bitmapped image, create another shape—a large square that sits squarely in front of the ellipse. Select the rectangle tool, and then hold down the Shift key while you drag from one corner of the square to its opposite corner to create a perfect square. Next, choose a fill color for the square; if it's already filled, choose a different fill color (distinct from the ellipse color). Click the Fill Color button and choose a color from the palette that's different from the square's current fill color.

In a paint program, the ellipse would now be gone (but for the long memory of the Undo command). But the drawn object is still there. You can drag the square aside to prove this to yourself, or better still, you can take advantage of the layering tools to place the ellipse in front of the square. With the square selected (sizing handles visible), choose the Send To Back button. The resulting image resembles the one shown here. Bitmaps don't offer this sort of flexibility.

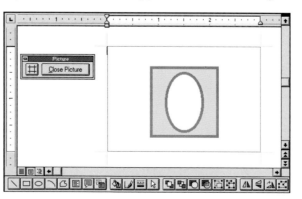

BUTTERFINGERS?

Do you feel like you're dropping your tools after using them? Actually, you're not. The drawing tools do not normally remain selected after you use them once. To avoid having to reselect a tool that you want to use repeatedly, double-click the tool. The tool remains active until you choose another tool or double-click elsewhere in the document.

This ellipse was drawn with a heavy (4-point-wide) line weight. You use the Line Style button to set the line weight.

SQUARE PEG, ROUND HOLE

To draw a rectangle or an ellipse outward from its center, hold down the Ctrl key as you click and drag with the appropriate tool. You can combine this technique with the use of the Shift key to draw circles and squares from their center points.

Now let's try a few transformations. Before we start, let's alter the figure a bit. First, place the mouse pointer on the ellipse (a four-headed arrow is added to the pointer), and drag it to the upper right corner of the square. Next, group the two objects: Select them both and choose the Group button. (To select them both, you can select the first one and then use Shift+click to select the second one; or you can choose the Select Drawing Objects tool and enclose both objects in the selected region.) The two objects become a grouped object with a single set of sizing handles.

In the illustration below, the objects are first grouped, then flipped horizontally, then flipped vertically, and finally rotated 90 degrees to the right.

The toolbar button alongside each image produced the transformation from the previous image.

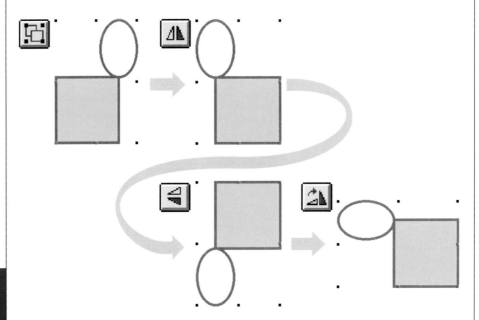

Exploration Ideas   As you explore the sets of drawing tools in the various Office applications, pay attention to the ways in which they differ. The following list offers some suggestions for uncovering unique features and putting them to use:

- Look beyond the default toolbars. In the Customize dialog boxes for the toolbars, you'll find more commands that you can add. For example, Word has layering commands that bring an object forward or backward one layer rather than bringing it all the way to the front or all the way to the back. Furthermore, you might find drawing-related commands in categories other than Draw or Drawing. In PowerPoint, for example, the Draw, Arrange, and AutoShape categories contain commands that directly affect drawing.

- Word and Excel have a Reshape tool for modifying the shapes of polygons. Selecting a polygon enables you to resize it, but you cannot control individual sides and angles. When you choose the Reshape command, however, you can drag any vertex of the polygon.

- PowerPoint has three drawing-related toolbars. The first toolbar, Drawing, offers basic tools. For an extended set of tools, display the Drawing+ toolbar. If you've mastered Word's Drawing toolbar, most of the buttons on these two PowerPoint toolbars will be familiar to you. The third toolbar, AutoShapes, lets you insert not only ellipses and rectangles, but also 15 other simple shapes.

- Experiment with the AutoShapes toolbar in PowerPoint. If it's not displayed, click the AutoShapes button on the Drawing toolbar. Many of the shapes it inserts come with an extra (diamond-shaped) handle to make adjustments that are independent of the overall sizing. You can even change one autoshape to another by choosing the Change AutoShape command from the Draw menu.

- You can rotate native PowerPoint objects—drawings or text objects—using the Free Rotate tool. Unique to PowerPoint, this tool gives you flexibility that's lacking in other applications, which let you rotate objects only in 90-degree increments. You cannot use the Free Rotate tool with imported pictures or OLE objects.

- In PowerPoint, notice the miniature palettes on the Fill Color, Line Color, and Shadow Color buttons. When you choose these buttons, you'll see why the palettes are there: The color scheme determines the available colors for lines, fills, and shadows.

- In Excel, the Color and Font Color tools on the Formatting toolbar and the Pattern tool on the Drawing toolbar drop down palettes that you can drag away from the toolbar. Once you detach one of these palettes, it stays open until you close it (by double-clicking its control box). This persistence is especially handy when you're changing a pattern, which can require a change to the basic pattern (shown in black and white) as well as to the color. One other tip: The image on the toolbar button is variable; it changes to show the current setting.

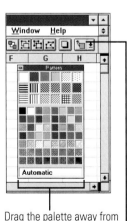

Drag the palette away from the toolbar to keep it open

The button image shows the current setting

- Unlike most paint programs, the drawing features in Office let you edit text that is part of a drawing. (You still cannot edit the text in the document, which is a separate layer from the drawing.) Choose the Text Box button, click and drag to give the text box an initial size, and commence typing. You can edit, resize, and format freely—now or later. Word also has a Callout button for adding labels and a separate button for formatting them.

Inserting Pictures

You can insert a picture in an Office application document in a few different ways. None is difficult, and each has advantages that you should understand. The Microsoft ClipArt Gallery lets you browse through lots of pictures in a quick and purposeful way, but you cannot modify the resulting image easily; for that, you're better off inserting the image in the most editable format available. If the original application is an OLE server, that means linking or embedding an object.

The ClipArt Gallery

Unlike applications that generate electronic images, the ClipArt Gallery is a utility for organizing and previewing graphics that you might want to incorporate in your documents. It presents thumbnail depictions of the images and records the locations of the clip art files.

To use the ClipArt Gallery in Word, Excel, or PowerPoint, choose Object from the application's Insert menu. (PowerPoint also has an Insert Clip Art button on its Standard toolbar to expedite the process of inserting clip art.) To use the ClipArt Gallery in Access, choose Insert Object from the Edit menu. In the Object dialog box (the Insert Object dialog box in PowerPoint and Access), select the Create New tab (or option button). In the Object Type list, select Microsoft ClipArt Gallery and click OK. The first time you use the ClipArt Gallery, it assembles its inventory by constructing thumbnail sketches of the clip art in each Office component that it detects on your disk.

The initial stock of clip art comes presorted into categories, ready for browsing. On your screen, the gallery looks like a photo album that you can page through. You can choose a category to look through images in that category only, or you can browse through all of the gallery's images at once. When you find a piece of clip art that you want to use, select the thumbnail image and click OK. The ClipArt Gallery closes and the contents of the original graphics file are inserted in your document.

You can assign an image to a different category (or a new category) or modify the description of the image. Changing or augmenting the description can help you locate an image later. Choose the Category button or the Description button at the bottom of the window to display the Edit Picture Information

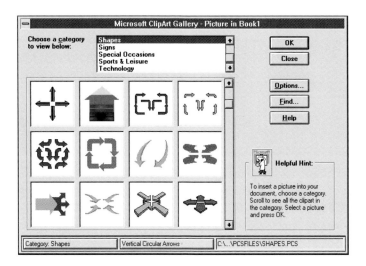

dialog box, where you can edit this information. After modifying the descriptions of some of the pictures, you can use the Find button to search for images by entering keywords in their descriptions. You might, for example, add the word *Business* to the descriptions of certain images—office buildings, businesspeople, and so on; later, you can use the Find button to pull out a selection of business-related images across many categories.

To make other changes to your clip art inventory scheme, choose the Options button. In the Options dialog box you can add a thumbnail picture for a specific graphics file or choose Refresh to have the program review entire drives —local or networked—for appropriate files. The Refresh command lets you preview each item it locates; you can choose to add the image, as well as assign the image a category and a description.

You can also rename or remove categories from the list to tailor the gallery to your purposes. Images that belong to a deleted category remain in the gallery; to see them, choose All Categories and scroll to the end of the sequence.

Linking and Embedding Pictures

If you want the image you insert in a document to be editable, linking and embedding are your best bets. For example, you can link or embed a picture from Paintbrush (an OLE server application) in your Office document. Lo and behold, if you double-click the resulting object, Paintbrush opens in a separate window to edit the picture. You can also embed (but not link) a Word Picture object.

If the picture was created with an OLE server application, such as Paintbrush, linking and embedding are simple enough. Suppose a Word document is the destination. To link a Paintbrush picture, copy it to the Clipboard and then

SCAN GLOBALLY, STORE LOCALLY

If you add an image to the ClipArt Gallery from a source other than a local hard disk, remember that the gallery stores only a thumbnail sketch, not the complete image. You have to use a network connection or insert a floppy disk to insert the actual clip art into a document. To avoid such inconveniences, copy the file to a local hard disk whenever possible (before you add the image).

use Paste Special in the Word document to insert the image as a Paintbrush Picture Object. (Be sure to select the Paste Link option button before you click OK.)

To embed an existing Paintbrush picture, copy it to the Clipboard, switch to your document, and use Paste or Paste Special to embed the Clipboard contents. You can embed a new picture by choosing Object from the Insert menu (in Access, choose Insert Object from the Edit menu), selecting the Create New tab (or option button), and selecting Paintbrush Picture or Microsoft Word 6.0 Picture in the Object Type list.

By far the most flexible way to insert pictures in Word, Excel, and PowerPoint is to choose the Picture command from the Insert menu. The resulting dialog box (shown here, from Word) lets you specify and preview an appropriate

GET THE PICTURE

If you try to embed a Word Picture object, you might find that only one of your drawing objects is copied to the Clipboard. This occurs if you draw your picture and then choose Copy from the Edit menu to transfer the picture to the Clipboard. Unfortunately, only the currently selected drawing object is copied, not the entire picture. To copy the whole picture, select all of the drawing objects by using the Select Drawing Objects tool. Then choose Copy.

graphics file. You can insert pictures in many formats—any format for which Office has the necessary filter. Once inserted, the image is presented as a Windows metafile.

In the Insert Picture dialog box (the Picture dialog box in Excel),

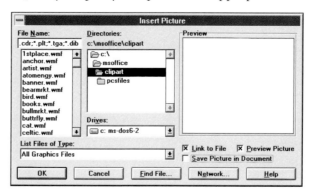

notice that you can select the Link to File check box. If you do so, Word gives you the further option of deselecting the check box below it, Save Picture in Document. Once linked, the picture is updated when the original changes. If you choose not to save the picture in your document, however, it remains static: You cannot double-click it to make editing changes if it's not saved with the document. (There's a way around this, however, as you'll see in the next section.) The benefit of omitting the linked picture from the saved document is a reduction in file size.

NO TWO ALIKE

Only Word and PowerPoint offer the Link to File check box in the Insert Picture dialog box. Only Word adds the option of not saving the linked picture in the document.

Formatting and Editing Pictures

After you insert a picture in a document, the extent to which you can alter it varies widely. In some cases, you can open the picture in its original application and edit it in every way that the application permits; at the other extreme, you might not be able to do anything with the picture beyond resizing it (and sometimes with murky results). Factors to consider include the following:

- The destination document. That is, are you trying to format and edit the picture in an Excel workbook or a PowerPoint presentation (or what)? Each application has its own capabilities. Among the Office applications,

PowerPoint has the best resources for picture editing, closely followed by Word; Excel has considerably fewer capabilities, and Access is a distant fourth.

- The source application. Was the picture created in an application that is available from your computer? Does the application support OLE? If it does, you can insert the object in its native format and edit the picture in the source drawing or editing program.

- How you inserted the picture. Did you link the picture using the Paste Special command? Did you use the Picture command (on the Insert menu)? This determines where and in what format the picture data is stored and what you must do to access the data for editing.

Sizing a Picture In almost every case, you can resize a picture by scaling it. Also, you can usually resize a picture by cropping it. The destination application often determines what you can do.

The size of the picture is the actual dimensions of the picture—its width and height in inches, centimeters, or whatever units you are using. By default, when you change a picture's size, you change the scaling but you do not affect the picture's content. Scaling is expressed in percentages, where 100 percent is the original size, 200 percent is twice as large, and 50 percent is half as large. When you crop a picture, the content and size of the picture change but the scaling does not. You use cropping when you want to change the size of the picture by removing a portion of the picture or adding white space to its edges.

To resize a picture by changing its scaling, click the picture so that the sizing handles appear. Then grab a handle and drag toward or away from the center of the picture. In most situations, dragging a corner handle results in isotonic scaling. That's a plus, because distorting the image is rarely desirable.

In Word and Excel, notice when you're resizing a picture that the status line shows the change in scaling as a percentage of the original dimensions. For fine control over these percentages in Word—especially to restore the original proportions—select the picture and choose Picture from the Format menu.

The resulting Picture dialog box lets you specify cropping, scaling, and sizing information. If the picture has a frame, you can choose the Frame button to modify the format settings for the frame (size, location, and text wrap options).

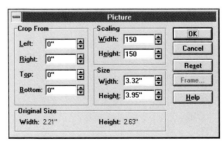

The ability to crop an inserted picture can be a godsend. You can crop the picture in combination with scaling it (isotonically) to make it fit optimally in an available space. You can crop inserted pictures in Word, PowerPoint, and Access; Excel does not let you crop pictures.

Suppose you used the Insert Picture command to insert the clip art Windows metafile SPEAKER.WMF in your document. You'd like to crop the picture to eliminate the audience. (Anything to avoid questions.) If necessary, click the picture to reveal its sizing handles. Move the mouse pointer to the bottom center sizing handle so that it becomes a double-headed arrow, and then press the Shift key. The pointer changes to a cropping tool (a pair of cropping *L*'s). Continue holding down the Shift key and drag the cropping tool upward. As you drag, a dashed line indicates the new border of the picture. (While dragging, you can move the cropping tool away from the sizing handle for a better view and for more control over your cropping.) Release the mouse button to establish the new border. (If you crop too much, hold down the Shift key, grab the handle, and pull it back out to restore as much of the original image as you want.)

This piece of clip art is first scaled using the lower-right sizing handle (top two pictures) and then cropped to eliminate the lower half of the picture (bottom two pictures).

POWER PLAY

Capturing Screen Images As Bitmaps

As you've seen, Paintbrush can open only a limited number of file types. But if you're determined to work with a picture in Paintbrush, you can generally find a way. One method is to display the image in its original application and save it as a bitmap. If that is not possible, or if the application is not available, you can display the picture (or as much of it as you can fit on the screen) and then press the Print Scrn key. This copies the contents of the screen to the Clipboard as a bitmapped image.

Next, start Paintbrush and press Ctrl+V to paste the Clipboard contents into the active window. To avoid cutting off the bitmap or including unnecessary white space in the image, immediately choose Copy To from the Edit menu and copy the (still-selected) image to a file. To edit the image, open the file and do your work there.

If the image is too large to work with at its normal size, use the Zoom Out command on the View menu to display a reduced picture. (You have to zoom in again before you can close the file.)

DRAWN TO EACH OTHER

In Excel, hold down the Alt key while you draw, move, or size a graphic object to have it snap to the nearest gridlines.

Other Than Word   Excel lacks the cropping capability that Word provides. You can, however, resize an object by dragging any of its sizing handles, or you can resize it with isotonic scaling if you hold down the Shift key while resizing with a corner handle.

PowerPoint resizes in the same way that Excel does; in addition, PowerPoint has a cropping feature for pictures. To wield the cropping tool, point to the picture and choose Crop Picture from the shortcut menu. The pointer changes to a cropping tool until you click something other than a sizing handle (or until you press Esc).

In Access, pictures are displayed in bound or unbound object frames in a form or a report. Whether the picture is stretched or clipped (cropped from the right and bottom) to fit in the frame depends on the Size Mode property of the frame, which is set in Design view.

Modifying a Picture   To explore the possibilities for modifying a picture in a document, let's again use Word as the destination application. The options that Word provides are representative of those in the other Office applications, except as noted. Be aware that you can display the Drawing toolbar and make all kinds of shapes and marks on top of a picture that's inserted in a document. These additions will even show up on the printed copy. But they will not alter the picture unless you've opened the picture for editing.

If you cut the picture to the Clipboard, for example, the drawing objects are left behind.

When you're faced with a picture that you'd like to edit, examine its shortcut menu. The commands that you find on the menu tell you what kind of editing you can do.

- Edit *Application* Picture Link. Choose this command, where *Application* is an OLE server application such as Paintbrush, to open and edit the linked source file. You can also avail yourself of the same graphics tools that were used to create the picture.

- Edit *Application* Picture. The availability of this command, where *Application* is an OLE server application, indicates that the picture is embedded (rather than linked) as an object that you can edit using the server application.

- Open Picture or Edit Picture. Choose either command to open the picture in the Word picture editor. By default, this is Word Picture, but if you have an alternative picture editor, you can designate it as the default picture editor by selecting it on the Edit tab of the Options dialog box (choose Options from the Tools menu).

- Format Drawing Object. When this command appears, you've selected a drawing object, not a picture. Recall that a drawing object is not, strictly speaking, a picture. To convert one or more drawing objects to a picture, select the drawing object (or objects) and click the Create Picture button on the Drawing toolbar.

UNSELECTABLE DRAWING

If Word doesn't let you select a drawing object, the object is probably behind the text layer. Click the Select Drawing Object tool on the Drawing toolbar and then try again to select the drawing. Better?

How much of the foregoing scenario applies outside of Word? In Excel and PowerPoint, linked and embedded objects are editable, as described above, although the command names on the shortcut menus are not identical to those in Word. In Excel, for instance, the shortcut menu for an embedded picture names the object and has a cascading menu with Edit and Convert commands.

The big behavioral differences arise when it comes to the pictures you insert that are not linked or embedded. Though Word has a built-in picture editor for the various formats that pass through the graphic filters, Excel does not. Thus, the shortcut menu for a picture might show an Edit Object command, but the command generally displays the Format Object dialog box. In the Format Object dialog box, you can modify the picture by changing the fill and border colors and adding a shadow around the picture, but you cannot edit the contents of the picture directly.

POWER PLAY

Editing the Unsaved

If you choose the Edit Picture command and Word informs you that *You cannot edit a picture that is not saved in the document,* the picture was linked using the Insert Picture command and the Save Picture in Document check box was deselected in the Insert Picture dialog box. The result is an image that is not editable in Word.

Incidentally, the link for this graphic is unusual. The graphic is linked to the saved version of the picture (the graphics file). It is updated each time you open the document, but only manually thereafter, and the update is based solely on the information contained in the graphics file; any unsaved changes that are made to the graphic in the source application are ignored.

If you're determined to edit the picture in Word, you can modify the link so that the picture is saved in the document. You can then edit the picture—but you won't be able to reverse this change. Choose Links from the Edit menu, and in the Links dialog box, select the link you want to edit. (When you do, notice that the Manual and Automatic option buttons are grayed-out.) Select the Save Picture in Document check box and click OK. If you do edit the picture in Word, it becomes an embedded Word Picture and the link to the graphics file is broken.

In PowerPoint, the contents of bitmapped pictures that are not linked or embedded are not editable. You can, however, change any of the colors used in the bitmap using the Recolor command on the shortcut menu, and you can add a border or a shadow using the Format Colors and Lines command. You can edit a picture that is a drawing if you let PowerPoint convert the elements of the drawing (the primitives) to PowerPoint objects. Then you can edit them using PowerPoint's various drawing tools.

Although Access follows its own rules to incorporate pictures (all pictures are placed in an object frame), the procedures for editing linked and embedded OLE picture objects in Access are similar to those in the other major Office applications. To edit an OLE picture object, select the object in the form or the report in Design view and choose the Edit *Application* Object command (where *Application* is the OLE source application); then choose Edit from the submenu. If you use the Edit Paste Special command to insert a picture in Bitmap or Picture format instead of as an OLE object, you will not be able to edit the picture.

Sound, Lies, and Video Clips

Among the object types you can embed in a document using the Insert Object command are multimedia (sound and video) objects. (Okay, so the part about lies was untrue.) You can record a comment to insert in a workbook, record an e-mail message, or record an introduction to a PowerPoint presentation. And you can insert video clips in presentations or in e-mail messages or other documents that you plan to distribute electronically.

Unless you have some other utility for recording and playing sound files, you can use Sound Recorder, a Windows accessory. For embedding multimedia files, Office uses another Windows accessory, Media Player, which can play a video (AVI) file or a sound file—in waveform (WAV) or MIDI (MID or RMI) format.

To play multimedia files, your computer needs the appropriate hardware—commonly a sound card and speakers—and to record files, you also need a microphone. For both recording and playing back the files, you must also install the necessary drivers. Specific capabilities depend a great deal on your hardware and software. Playing MIDI files, for instance, requires specialized hardware and drivers that aren't required for playing waveform files. Likewise, animation is playable, but is less than satisfying, without sufficient processing speed and RAM.

SOUND REASONS

If you want to insert a WAV file that you expect to edit in the destination document, you should link or embed it using Sound Recorder because Media Player has no editing capabilities.

CELL SOUNDS

In Excel, you can use the Note command on the Insert menu to add a recorded note to a cell. The notes are not nearly as conspicuous as an embedded sound object, which is represented as an icon in your worksheet. To play the recorded notes, click the Attach Note button on the Auditing toolbar (or choose Note from the Insert menu) and click Play in the Cell Note dialog box.

Sound Recorder

You can launch Sound Recorder in a couple of different ways. From within an Office application, you can create a new sound object using the Insert Object command. Or you can launch Sound Recorder as a stand-alone application in Program Manager. (It's located in the Accessories program group, unless you've moved it.)

After you launch Sound Recorder, you can record a sound with a microphone (or any standard sound input device) or edit an existing WAV file. The Sound Recorder controls are familiar to anyone who's used a regular cassette tape recorder. To record a sound, click the Record button, which has a microphone depicted on it. Then use the microphone or activate whatever input device you are using. The length of recording that Sound Recorder can handle depends on the amount of memory that is available. To edit an existing sound, choose Insert File from the Edit menu. (You can use the File Open command if you've opened Sound Recorder from Program Manager instead of by choosing the Insert Object command.)

OFF THE RECORDER

If you have another program for recording or playing back sounds, it might supplant Sound Recorder as the utility for embedded sounds. If you want to use Sound Recorder instead, start it from Program Manager.

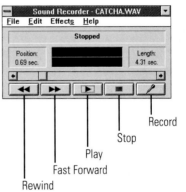

Record
Stop
Play
Fast Forward
Rewind

The editing controls are minimal and straightforward. The Insert File and Mix With File commands on the Edit menu let you introduce another WAV file at your current position in the recording. The contents of an inserted file are added to any existing contents without overlapping; those of a mixed file are combined with the contents they overlap. Other commands do the audio equivalent of picture cropping: You can pause the playback or drag the scroll box to a particular point in the recording and then delete the portion that precedes or comes after that point.

Using the commands on the Effects menu, you can adjust the volume—by increasing or decreasing it in 25 percent increments—and you can increase or decrease the playback speed in 100 percent increments. Other commands add an echo effect or toggle between forward playback and reverse.

After you save a file, the Revert command on the File menu lets you restore the current recording to the form in which it was last saved, discarding any changes you made.

When you finish editing a file, you can insert it in a document very easily. If you started Sound Recorder using the Insert Object command, you need only exit the utility to embed the object in your document. The sound object is embedded as an icon.

If you launched Sound Recorder independently, you can link or embed the contents of the file. Naturally, you must save the file if you want to link to it. To transfer the sound to your document, use the Copy command on the Edit menu to copy it to the Clipboard. Then switch to your destination document, position the insertion point at the appropriate point in the document, and use the Paste command to embed the sound object as an icon.

Linking a Sound File

You can link a sound file using Sound Recorder. Follow these steps:
1. Start Sound Recorder as a stand-alone application in Program Manager.
2. Open a WAV file or record a new sequence. Edit the recording as necessary.
3. Save the file. (This is essential only if you intend to link to the recording.)
4. Choose Copy from the Edit menu.
5. Open or switch to the destination document. Position the insertion point where you want the Sound Recorder icon to appear.
6. From the Edit menu, choose Paste Special. In the Paste Special dialog box, select the Paste Link option button, and be sure that Sound Object is selected in the As list box.
7. Click OK.

Embedding Sound

You can embed sound using Sound Recorder. Follow these steps:
1. Start Sound Recorder as a stand-alone application in Program Manager.
2. Open a WAV file or record a new sequence. Edit the recording as necessary.
3. Choose Copy from the Edit menu.
4. Open or switch to the destination document. Position the insertion point where you want the Sound Recorder icon to appear.
5. From the Edit menu, choose Paste.

To play the recording, double-click the icon. In Word and PowerPoint, you can also play a linked or embedded recording by choosing Play Sound Link or Play Sound from the shortcut menu. In Excel you can play an embedded sound, and in Access you can play a linked or embedded sound, by choosing Sound Object or Linked Sound Object from the shortcut menu and then choosing Play from the submenu that appears. When you play a linked sound file in Excel, Sound Recorder appears on the screen—you can use it to replay the recording or to modify the sound file. To play a linked sound from the shortcut menu, you must choose Edit Object to display Sound Recorder and play back the sound file.

Media Player

Media Player provides a simple standard interface with playback-only capabilities for a number of different sound and animation file formats. You can launch Media Player as a stand-alone program from the Accessories program group, or you can start it from one of the Office applications by choosing the Insert Object command and selecting Media Clip as the object type. The commands and controls that accompany Media Player affect playback, but not the content of the file. (There isn't even a Save command on the File menu.)

POWER PLAY

Quick Recording

If you use Sound Recorder or Media Player frequently, you might consider customizing your Office menu to include a command for launching the application. SOUNDREC.EXE and MPLAYER.EXE are normally located in your Windows directory.

Notice that both accessories have commands on the Edit menu that copy the current recording to the Clipboard. After you've copied the recording, you can switch to a document in an Office application and paste the Clipboard contents as an embedded object (an icon or a representative video frame). In addition, you can drag a multimedia file (a WAV file or an AVI file, for example) from File Manager to an open Word document or Microsoft Mail message to embed it.

After you launch Media Player, choose one of the devices listed in the Device menu. The number of devices you see depends on the hardware and the device drivers you have installed.

Choosing an item from the Device menu causes the Open dialog box to appear with a list of files with the correct format (based on the filename extension). Choose Video For Windows, for example, and the Open dialog box displays filenames with the AVI extension.

Slider

Eject
Stop
Play/Pause

Mark Out
Mark In

Scale

Embedding a Multimedia File

Follow these steps to embed a multimedia file as an object in your Office document:

1. Open Media Player as a stand-alone application.
2. Choose a device from the Device menu.
3. In the Open dialog box, specify the appropriate filename and location, and click OK.
4. Use the Configure command on the Device menu, if necessary, to configure the playback device. Use commands on the Edit menu, especially Options, to set other preferences.
5. For video sequences, drag the slider to the frame that will represent the sequence when the embedded object is inactive.
6. Choose Copy Object from the Edit menu.
7. Open or switch to the destination document. Position the insertion point where you want the Media Clip object to appear and paste the contents of the Clipboard into the document.
8. Switch back to Media Player and close it.

If you then open an AVI file, Media Player selects Video For Windows as the active device and loads the file into memory. Open the Device menu again and choose the Configure command to display a dialog box with appropriate options (scaling, buffering, and so forth) for configuring video playback. Choose the Set Default button if you want the settings you specify to apply to all video sequences you play; otherwise, the settings apply only to the currently opened sequence.

You can also set playback options and edit the appearance and behavior of the embedded object in the destination document. These settings are located in the Options dialog box (choose Options from the Edit menu). Included are a continuous play option (Auto Repeat) and options for specifying a label, removing the border, or displaying a minimal control panel during playback.

After you set any options, you can embed the open file as a Media Clip object. If you're embedding a video file, you might want to drag the slider (or use the small buttons to the right of the slider) to locate a frame that will represent the sequence in the document. You can also drag the slider to points in the sequence that you prefer to use as the starting or ending points. With the slider at such a point, choose the Mark In button or the Mark Out button to specify a start or stop location.

If you started Media Player by selecting Media Clip as the object type in the Object dialog box, you need only exit to return to your document. If you started Media Player as a stand-alone application, choose Copy Object from

The shortcut menu for a Media Clip object lets you play the sequence or set the playback options.

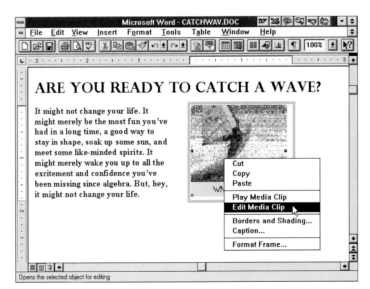

the Edit menu to transfer the sequence to the Clipboard. Then switch to the destination document, position the insertion point, and use Paste or Paste Special to insert the object. If you use Paste Special, you'll notice that linking from Media Player is not an active option.

Although you cannot use the Paste Link command to link to a multimedia file loaded in Media Player, you can create a linked object with the Create from File tab of the Object dialog box (in Word and Excel) or the Create from File option button in the Insert Object dialog box (in Access and PowerPoint): Select the source file, select the Link to File (or Link) check box, and click OK.

To play back a multimedia file, whether it is linked or embedded, you follow the same procedure as when you play back a sound recording: You can double-click the object or use the object's shortcut menu. During playback, you can also open the object's control menu to revisit the Configure dialog box or to close an object that is playing repeatedly.

POWER PLAY

PowerPoint Goes Dynamic

One common vehicle for multimedia objects—sound, video, and animation—is a PowerPoint slide show. After you create the object, embed it as an icon on a slide. Then choose the Play Settings command from the Tools menu to specify how and when the embedded multimedia object should be played during a slide show.

Display the slide that contains the object you want to play, and select the object. Then choose Play Settings from the Tools menu. The option button for the type of object you selected is highlighted under Category in the Play Settings dialog box.

Select one of the following Start Play methods:

- When Click on Object: Choose this method if you want to start

or stop playing the object by clicking the object during a slide show.

- When Transition (Starts): Choose this method if you want the object to start playing automatically when the transition to the current slide begins.

- When Transition (Ends): Choose this method if you want the object to start playing automatically when the transition to the current slide ends (plus the specified number of seconds, if any).

Select the Hide While not Playing check box if you want the object or icon to appear only when it is playing (or not at all, in the case of sound objects). Click OK after you finish.

And Much, Much More

The Office suite includes numerous shared applications that we haven't touched on in this chapter, chief among them being Microsoft Graph, Equation Editor, WordArt, and Microsoft Organization Chart. Buoyed by online Help, you can quickly master the capabilities of any of these. Using Equation Editor, for example, is not much more complicated than playing Minesweeper, but you do have to know when to integrate the intersection of the cube roots.

With each shared application, you can embed objects in your Office documents by choosing the Insert Object command and selecting the corresponding object type in the Object (or Insert Object) dialog box. These shared tools do not run as stand-alone applications; except with Organization Chart, you cannot save the results as separate files, and you cannot link them. You can only embed them in a document created with an OLE client application—any of the major applications in the Office suite.

You'll notice subtle differences as you use the shared applications. Most usurp the destination application window temporarily; others, such as Organization Chart, open their own window. Most will ask if you want to update the document when you close it, while others, such as Equation Editor, update the document automatically (in which case you can re-edit or delete the object).

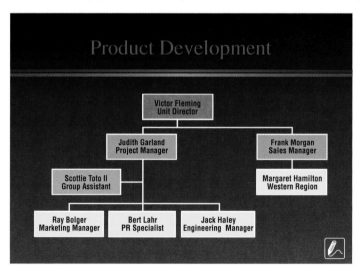

This PowerPoint slide displays a modest sample of the power you can wield with Organization Chart.

⑤ Office Support

Chapter 13

Winning Those Skirmishes with Your Printer

Basic Training

The applications in the Microsoft Office suite rely on Microsoft Windows to handle their printing affairs. And for the most part, you control printing in much the same way in each application. When you use the Print command (or the Print toolbar button) in any of the applications, the contents of your document first go to the printer driver, which translates the characters and formatting codes into instructions for the printer. Files proceed from there to Print Manager, a Windows utility that adds them to the queue for the specified printer.

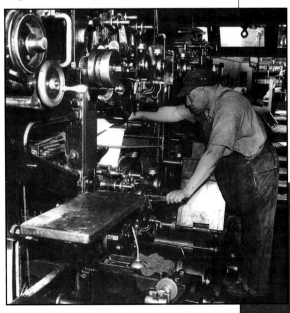

The printer follows the instructions it receives—within the limits of its capabilities. If you've installed the appropriate printer driver, the instructions should correspond to the capabilities of the printer, and the results should match what you intended as closely as the printer can manage. So what can go wrong?

Well, something can go wrong at just about any stage of the process. In this chapter, we'll discuss the steps you should take to get the results you want—and to contend with the obstacles you might encounter. To begin, we'll explore how to use the various settings in your Office applications to specify the results you want. Then we'll look at a few of the difficulties that can arise when you actually engage the printer, and we'll describe a number of factors that can affect the speed and quality of the output. Finally, we'll look at envelope and label printing to head off some common complications.

Plan of Attack

When you click OK in the Print dialog box, your Office application sets to work composing the document that goes to the printer. How is that document different from the file you're viewing on the screen, or the one that's saved on disk? The differences are often subtle, but they can be numerous—and frustrating—if you don't know why they exist. Consider, for instance, the Options dialog box (reached via the Tools menu) in Microsoft Word. Many of the settings on the Print tab of the Options dialog box (shown below) help to determine what data proceeds to the printer.

In the following sections, we'll examine common ways to control printer output, including page setup options and a few easy formatting tricks. Because the settings and their locations differ significantly depending on the application, we'll consider each of the major Office components separately.

Printing from Word

You can examine the Print options in Word by displaying the Print tab of the Options dialog box. (Choose the Options button in the Print dialog box or choose Options from the Tools menu.) With one exception (which is clearly identified), the options on this tab apply to all of your subsequent print jobs—not to the current document alone. Return to this tab of the Options dialog box when you need to make changes.

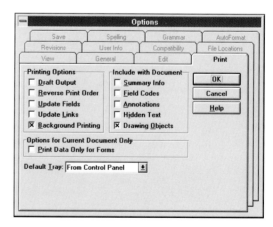

Notice in particular how the Print options can affect OLE objects in your document. By selecting the Update Links check box, you can ensure that Word updates all links to the document before printing. The affected links include those set for either automatic or manual updating, unless they are locked. The Update Fields check box has the same effect on links and also goes a step further by updating all of the fields in the document rather than limiting itself to the LINK fields.

In the Include with Document section, be sure that Field Codes is deselected if you want to see the linked and embedded objects in the printed copy. Remember that both types of objects are inserted in a Word document as fields. When the Field Codes check box is selected, the field codes are printed instead of the results of the fields. Also, note that if the Hidden Text check box is selected, all hidden text prints with your document. If you have used direct formatting to hide any linked or embedded objects (and thereby exclude them from the printed copy), having the Hidden Text check box selected will defeat that scheme. One further point: The Drawing Objects check box controls the printing of the drawing objects in the drawing layer—the ones that become visible only in Layout view—and not the pictures or imported drawings included in the document.

Page Setup   Choose the Page Setup command from the File menu and explore the four tabs of the Page Setup dialog box. Its settings are saved with

POWER PLAY

Both Sides Now

If your printer does not have a double-sided printing capability but does have a good sheet feeder, you can get the same result with a little extra effort and some help from Word. First, print only the odd pages, by selecting Odd Pages in the Print drop-down list at the bottom of the Print dialog box (choose Print from the File menu). Then—that's right—you print the even pages on the backs of the odd ones. But be careful: Know your printer and visualize how the pages will be fed through the printer the second time.

Suppose you're printing a 21-page document. The second time through, page 2 will print on the back of the first sheet, but if you need to turn the stack of odd pages facedown for the second printing, when you put them back in the paper tray the top sheet (with most printers) will be the last page in the odd set—page 21. To accommodate this order and to avoid printing page 2 on the back of page 21, select Even Pages in the Print dialog box, choose the Options button, and then select the Reverse Print Order check box in the Options dialog box. That way, Word prints the even pages in reverse order, starting with page 20.

One last thing. You don't want page 20 to print on the back of page 21. You want it to print on the back of page 19, so take page 21 off the stack. It doesn't need another pass through the printer.

DRAWING A BLANK

If your drawing appears in Layout view but disappears in Print Preview, check the Print tab of the Options dialog box (reached via the Tools menu). Be sure that the Drawing Objects check box is selected. If the drawing is a picture (created with Word Picture or converted to a Picture object), its status is not affected by the Drawing Objects setting. If a Picture object or other inserted graphics file does not show up in Print Preview, you probably need to deselect the Draft Output check box on the Print tab.

UNDER THE TABLE

The dotted on-screen gridlines in Word tables do not print. To print lines between cells, add borders to the table: Place the insertion point anywhere in the table, choose Select Table from the Table menu, and choose Borders And Shading from the Format menu. On the Borders tab of the Table Borders And Shading dialog box, select Grid in the Presets section and click OK.

the current document only, unless you choose the Default button. To support you in creating long, multipart documents, Page Setup gives you the option of assigning settings to a section rather than to the whole document. Document sections, as you'll discover on the Layout tab of the dialog box, can be set up to start on a new page (which can also be specified as an odd or even page), in a new column (select New Column), or immediately below the previous text (select Continuous). In Print Preview, the Multiple Pages command lets you survey your section and page breaks for as many as 21 (8.5-by-11-inch) pages.

I BRAKE FOR...
Use the Break command on the Insert menu to introduce page breaks and section breaks in your document. From Word's Insert menu, choose Page Numbers, and then choose the Format button in the Page Numbers dialog box to specify how page numbering should be handled at section breaks. Default numbering is continuous.

On the Margins tab of the Page Setup dialog box, you can choose to insert gutters to accommodate binding of either single-sided or double-sided pages. You can also specify the positions of headers and footers relative to the top or bottom edge of the

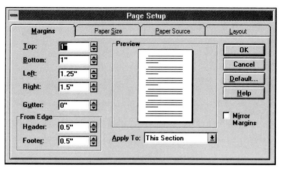

paper. Don't forget that most printers have a nonprinting margin along the page edges (a 0.25-inch margin for most sheet-fed printers).

By default, the paper source is determined by the setting in the Printers dialog box (double-click the Printers icon in Control Panel). You can override that setting in Word by choosing the Print command from the File menu, choosing the Options button in the Print dialog box, and, in the Options dialog box, selecting a different paper source in the Default Tray drop-down list. To specify a different paper source for the first page (for example, to use letterhead for the first page of correspondence or a colored cover page for a report), choose Page Setup from the File menu, select the Paper Source tab of the Page Setup dialog box, and select the paper sources in the First Pages and Other Pages list boxes. If you create an envelope and add it to your document, Word specifies for the first page (the envelope) a paper source that is appropriate for printing envelopes with your printer. We'll look more closely at envelope and label printing later in this chapter.

Text Flow The formatting options for paragraphs include a number of settings that affect where page breaks fall. You can insert this formatting directly, or you can include it as part of a style definition. To see what's available, choose Paragraph from the Format menu and select the Text Flow tab of the Paragraph dialog box, shown at left.

In the Pagination section, you can select the Keep Lines Together check box to keep a paragraph from breaking across pages, or you can select the Widow/ Orphan Control check box to prevent a single line from being stranded on a page—either the last line of a paragraph (a widow) or the first line of a paragraph (an orphan). Select the Keep with Next check box heading to prevent a paragraph from falling at the bottom of a page. Select the Page Break Before check box for a paragraph that should start at the top of a new page.

The remaining check boxes—Suppress Line Numbers and Don't Hyphenate— exempt the paragraph from sectionwide or documentwide line numbering and hyphenation. You apply line numbering (to a section or a document) by choosing Page Setup from the File menu and choosing the Line Numbers button on the Layout tab of the Page Setup dialog box; you apply hyphenation by using the Hyphenation command on the Tools menu.

Background Printing   Among the Office applications, only Word provides a background printing option. It moves the process of sending the document to the printer into the background and reserves the foreground for your ongoing work in Word. Because printing gets less attention in the background, it occurs more slowly; the foreground activity—especially on a slower computer, such as a 386—might also be noticeably impaired until Word hands off the last page. If printing speed is far more important to you than "multitasking," you can turn off background printing by choosing Print from the File menu, choosing the Options button in the Print dialog box, and deselecting the Background Printing check box in the Options dialog box. For more suggestions on speedy printing, see the Power Play titled "Built for Comfort/Built for Speed," later in this chapter.

Printing from Excel

Microsoft Excel workbooks present a number of printing challenges. Many people have their first encounter with landscape printing when they attempt to fit a wide spreadsheet sideways on a page. And on successive pages of a large spreadsheet, the absence of column and row titles can render the spreadsheet figures less than informative. These and other problems can be fixed quite easily.

As in Word, many of the important settings that apply to the current document in Excel are in the Page Setup dialog box (choose Page Setup from the File menu). But unlike in Word, you cannot set default print options in the Options dialog box (reached via the Tools menu). However, you can click the Options button in the Page Setup dialog box to display a dialog box that is specific to the printer model you are using. In this dialog box, you can control some printing features that apply to all of your documents.

EDITING IN PREVIEW

Word's Print Preview screen permits limited editing (at either zoom setting). Before you begin editing, be sure that the magnifier is turned off. (To turn off the magnifier, click the Magnifier button.)

CANCEL IT

To cancel a job during background printing, double-click the printer icon that appears in the status bar (replacing the current time) during the page output process.

LANDSCAPE ORIENTATION

A printed page has a *landscape orientation* if the material to be printed is turned on its side so that the length of the page (its greater dimension) can accommodate the width of the printed material. Landscape is thus the horizontal mode, as opposed to portrait orientation, which is the vertical mode.

When you choose the Print command from Excel's File menu, it prints by default the entire populated region of the current worksheet (and any other sheets you might have selected with it). The Print command breaks large worksheets into page-size regions, dividing them at cell boundaries. That's not what you want? Then take a look at the table below for a few basic techniques for controlling the printing process. You'll find the Print Preview command invaluable as you try out these techniques; it's well integrated with the Page Setup options, and it lets you zoom in if necessary to make the preview readable.

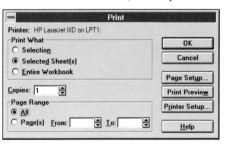

Printing Option	Procedure
Set manual page breaks	Select a cell and choose the Page Break command from the Insert menu to create page boundaries above and to the left of the cell. Select a row or a column and choose Page Break to define only a horizontal or vertical boundary.
Define the print area	On the Sheet tab of the Page Setup dialog box (reached via the File menu), click in the Print Area box; then either enter a range or, on the worksheet, click and drag to define the block of cells you want to print.
Establish the page order	On the Sheet tab of the Page Setup dialog box (reached via the File menu), select the Down, then Across option button or the Across, then Down option button. For more page-order control, consider creating a report.
Select multiple sheets	Hold down the Ctrl key and click each sheet tab that you want to add to the group. To cancel the selection, click the tab of an unselected sheet or point to the tab of a selected sheet, display the shortcut menu, and choose Ungroup Sheets. (On the same menu, also note the Select All Sheets command.)

Heads, Titles, Objects, Grids, and Borders   You probably know that you can freeze the title rows and columns of a worksheet so that they remain visible on your screen while you scroll through other parts of the sheet. This technique can be a lifesaver when you need to scroll to the outer, deeper reaches of the work area. To have the same convenience when you print, you can repeat the title rows and columns on each page of an especially wide or long worksheet.

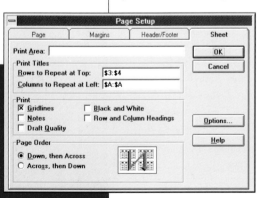

The Page Setup dialog box is the place to go for specifying the rows and columns that contain titles. Choose Page Setup from the File menu, and on the Sheet tab of the resulting dialog box, click in either of the Print Titles text boxes—Rows to Repeat at Top or Columns to Repeat at Left—and then click (and drag, if necessary) across the appropriate rows or columns of the work-sheet. As you do this, the corresponding range notation appears in the Page Setup dialog box.

On the Sheet tab, you can also select the Row and Column Headings check box. The headings (in Excel parlance) are the row and column indicators (by default, row numbers and column letters). Note that these are different from *titles,* which you supply to identify the contents of rows or columns. Also on the Sheet tab, deselect the Gridlines check box if you want to omit gridlines from the printed copy.

As for printing objects—OLE objects, pictures, charts, text boxes, and the like—Excel prints them by default, even though they sometimes overlap and obscure cell contents. If you don't want to print a particular object, select it and choose Object from the Format menu. On the Properties tab of the Format Object dialog box, deselect the Print Object check box; Excel continues to display the object but excludes it from the printed copy. (Instead of printing the object, Excel prints any cell contents that lie behind the object.)

To hide (and thereby exclude from printing) *all* of the objects in a worksheet, choose Options from the Tools menu. On the View tab of the Options dialog box, select the Hide All option button. Another option, Show Placeholders, replaces the objects with gray rectangles. (Note that if you select Hide All, the objects won't be printed, regardless of their Print Object setting in the Format Object dialog box.)

Inserted objects automatically come with a narrow black border. To eliminate the border or to change its weight, style, or color, choose the Format Object command. On the Patterns tab of the Format Object dialog box, select None in the Border section to eliminate the border or choose Custom and then modify the properties of the border.

Landscapes and Other Problems   Specifying landscape page orientation is not difficult: Select the Page tab of the Page Setup dialog box, and in the Orienta-tion section select the Landscape option button. Likewise, if you need to change the paper size—to legal (8.5-by-14-inch), for instance—you can make the change in this dialog box. Just be sure to indicate a different paper tray if that, too, is necessary for your printer: Choose the Options but-ton and select the appropriate paper source. (People using networked printers generally chafe when someone simply switches the paper trays rather than using the Paper Source option.)

LINES THAT CROSS
As you've seen, Page Setup lets you choose whether to print gridlines. De-termining whether gridlines appear on screen is handled separately: Use the Gridlines check box on the View tab of the Options dialog box (choose Options from the Tools menu).

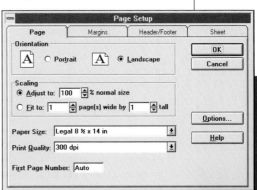

But what do you do when your worksheet is only slightly oversized for its current paper size—just a bit too wide, for example, for portrait orientation but too long for landscape? A few possibilities:

- Use the Scaling adjustments in the Page Setup dialog box to fit the worksheet on the page. You can either specify the percentage (10 through 400) or let Excel do the work by specifying your goal in pages.

- Hide any columns that are unnecessary for your current purpose. For some quick ways to hide and unhide columns and rows, see the Power Play on the facing page.

- If the overflow is slight, adjust the margins to expand the page area. You can drag the margins in Page Preview using the handles that are displayed in Full Page mode.

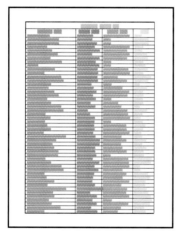 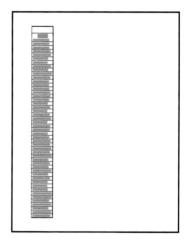

To fit a wide worksheet on a single page you can...

 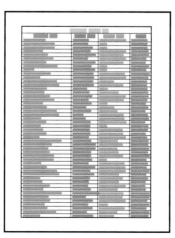 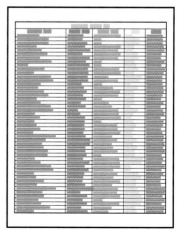

...adjust the scaling...   ...hide unnecessary columns...   ...change the margins...

POWER PLAY

Out of Sight, Out of Print

An easy way to hide rows or columns is to drag their borders together to collapse them to a height or width of zero. To hide a row, drag the bottom border of the row (in the row heading labels) to the top border of the row. To hide a column, drag the right border of the column (in the column heading labels) over to the left border of the column. To hide consecutive rows or columns, start with the last one and keep dragging (up or to the left) across as many borders as necessary. The existence of hidden rows or columns in a datasheet is indicated by a bolder-than-normal border in the heading labels and by a break in consecutive row numbers or column letters.

To restore hidden rows or columns, select the rows or columns that are adjacent to the hidden area, and then choose Row or Column from the Format menu. Choose Unhide from the submenu that appears next to the Row or Column command. You can also reverse the dragging procedure by positioning the mouse below or to the right of the border that conceals the rows or columns. After the pointer icon changes to a double line with arrows in both directions, as shown here, drag the rows and columns out of hiding (one at a time).

Reports Another way to select the components of a workbook that you want to print is to assemble a report. A report consists of a sequence of sheets, each of which can be modified to present a specific view and scenario. In this way, the report can pull together sections of a workbook that are not normally contiguous and, in the process, take advantage of Excel's wide range of display options (including the ones we looked at in the preceding section).

Reports are easy enough to create. But more advanced techniques can come into play if you want to define views and scenarios (both of which are, strictly speaking, optional) to make the report especially impressive. Before you start creating a report, define any views and scenarios that you want to incorporate in it. Then choose the Print Report command from the File menu (even though you're not yet ready to print the report). The resulting dialog boxes make the process easy to complete. To create the report, simply assign it a name and then define each of its sections.

If the Print Report command or the View Manager command does not appear, it means that the corresponding add-ins have not been installed. You can use

---

VIEW

In Excel, a *view* is a set of display options for a worksheet that you can save and reuse. These options can include frozen titles, hidden rows and columns, a zoom percentage, and any defined print area. From the View menu, choose View Manager to create and save a view of the current worksheet.

SCENARIO

For a given Excel worksheet, you can save a set of input values (up to 32 changing cells) and their results as a *scenario*. The changing cells represent your what-if assumptions. To work with scenarios, choose Scenarios from the Tools menu.

the Office Setup and Uninstall command on the Office menu to install missing Add-in components—Report Manager or View Manager.

If you want to rethink the report as you work, you can select a section in the Sections in This Report list and delete it (using the Delete button) or change its position relative to other sections (with the Move Up and Move Down buttons). To have the pages of the report

Creating and Printing a Report in Excel

After you define any views or scenarios, follow these steps to create and print a report in Excel:
1. From the File menu, choose Print Report.
2. In the Print Report dialog box, choose the Add button.
3. In the Add Report dialog box, type a name for the report.
4. For each section of the report, select a sheet and then a view (if any) and a scenario (if any). As you finish each section, add it to the report by choosing the Add button.
5. Click OK.
6. In the Print Report dialog box, click Print.
7. In the Print dialog box, click OK.

numbered consecutively, select the Use Continuous Page Numbers check box.

Printing from PowerPoint

From Microsoft PowerPoint, you can print copies of your presentation slides, or you can print other components of your presentation—speaker's notes, audience handouts, or the outline, for example. In addition, you can print your slides to a PostScript file and then send the file by mail or modem to a service bureau to create 35-mm slides. (See the quick reference card on the facing page.) If you're intent on capturing the colorful on-screen appearance of your presentation by printing slides in color, prepare yourself by reading the upcoming Power Play ("A Color Printing Primer").

Slide Setup   Like the other applications in the Office suite, PowerPoint has a Print command on its File menu. But before we get to it, let's look at the Slide Setup command (also on the File menu), which is PowerPoint's equivalent of the Page Setup command elsewhere in the suite. In the Slide Setup dialog box you can specify dimensions for your slides, including their orientation

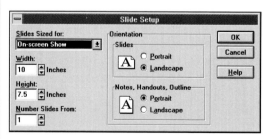

(portrait or landscape), and a second orientation for supplementary materials—speaker's notes, handouts, and the outline.

By default, slides are created in landscape orientation. If you change an existing presentation to portrait orientation, PowerPoint makes the necessary adjustments for the vertical format. Likewise, if you change the output medium (in the Slides Sized for drop-down list box) or modify the dimensions directly, PowerPoint resizes your slide components to fit the new proportions.

Printing Presentations To display the Print dialog box, choose the Print command from the File menu or press Ctrl+P. Don't assume that PowerPoint will print the current view—you could be working in Outline view, but the Print What list box might have a different item selected. In the Print What list box, you have to select the presentation component that you want to print: handouts, slides, notes, or outline. If your presentation contains build slides (in which major points appear successively on the slide), you can choose the Slides (with Builds) option to print each stage of the build.

Other options allow you to print information for the entire presentation or for selected slides. You can specify only the current slide, or you can identify particular slides by selecting the Slides option button and then using commas and hyphens to specify series and ranges. For example, type *1,4,6-9* to print slides 1, 4, 6, 7, 8, and 9.

PowerPoint has no Print Preview command. Generally, the defaults that the application provides work well for most output formats. The Scale to Fit Paper check box in the Print dialog box must be selected if you want the placement on the page to reflect the paper dimensions. (Set the paper size by choosing the Printer button in the Print dialog box and then choosing the Options button in the Print Setup dialog box.)

SHIFT+CLICK

In Slide Sorter view, you can select an assortment of slides by holding down the Shift key and clicking each slide you want to include. To print that assortment, select the Selection option button in the Print dialog box and click OK.

Producing 35-mm Slides

Unless you're equipped to print directly to a slide film recorder, follow these steps to print your PowerPoint slides to a PostScript file that can be sent to a service bureau:

1. With your PowerPoint presentation open, choose Slide Setup from the File menu.
2. In the Slide Setup dialog box, select 35mm Slides in the Slides Sized For drop-down list box. Click OK.
3. Choose the Print command from the File menu.
4. In the Print dialog box, select Slides in the Print What drop-down list box.
5. Choose the Printer button. In the Print Setup dialog box, select the PostScript printer driver supplied by your service bureau. Click OK.
6. In the Print dialog box, click OK again.
7. Follow any further instructions that the driver displays. If you are using the Genigraphics driver supplied with PowerPoint, for example, you are prompted to specify a number of options in a Job Instructions dialog box—mounting preferences, a destination (Modem or Diskette) for the PostScript information, and the like.

POWER PLAY

A Color Printing Primer

PowerPoint supplies a wide variety of colorful templates that you can use for electronic slide shows, overheads, or 35-mm slides. When you print the contents of a colorful presentation—to create your overheads or to produce audience handouts—keep in mind that color brings with it some complications.

First, be aware of your printing options. If you don't have a color printer—or even if you do—you might want to print your slides in black and white. PowerPoint converts the colors to shades of gray, but the results can have a muddy appearance, depending on the color combinations. You can select either the Black & White or the Pure Black & White check box in the Print dialog box to simplify the output and improve the contrast. If you print multiple copies, selecting the Collate Copies option slows down the process significantly.

To compose the colors you see on your screen, PowerPoint (like the other applications in the Office suite) combines red, green, and blue in different proportions. This system, called an RGB system, is also used for developing and printing 35-mm slides, so you can be fairly confident that the presentation colors will be consistent from your screen to the slide. To print color slides on paper, however, color printers typically use a CMYK system, a process that combines percentages of cyan, magenta, yellow, and black. If you want the printed colors to be true to the shades you see on your screen, you might be disappointed. Many shades, especially flesh tones, convert poorly from one color-generating system to the other.

Printer resolution is another factor that affects the accuracy of color reproduction. As the resolution of color-printer output increases—from 300 to 400 to 600 dpi (dots per inch) and beyond—the general appearance of the colors and their faithfulness to the electronic original improve.

WELL-DEFINED ITEMS
In the Database window, you can use the Print Definition command on the File menu to print the definition for any item in your database—a table, a form, a module, or whatever. The contents vary for items of different types, but they include (where applicable) names, properties, permissions, and data types.

Printing from Access

In Microsoft Access, the finer layout controls extend to reports and forms but not to the other database components. This is probably what you'd expect. Tables, queries, macros, and modules serve as the internal components of the database, whereas reports and forms constitute the external components—for gathering and exhibiting information. As a parallel, consider the fact that tables and queries simply list pictures and other OLE objects, while reports and forms display them.

Page Layout To control the basic layout of an Access document, you rely primarily on the Print Setup dialog box. It provides the usual options: printer, page orientation, and paper size and source. You can also get to the Print Setup dialog box by choosing Print from the File menu and choosing the Setup button in the Print dialog box, or by choosing Print Preview from the File menu and clicking the Print Setup button on the Print Preview toolbar. Access saves the Print Setup options you specify for reports and forms, but not those you specify when you print other database components.

DEFAULT MARGINS
You can change the default margin settings for new or existing tables, queries, and modules, or for reports and forms, by choosing Options from the View menu. In the Options dialog box, select Printing in the category list and modify the margin measurements.

When you print forms and reports, Print Setup can make a few additional layout options available. To observe their effects, first choose Print Preview from the File menu for a form or a report, and then click the Print Setup button on the Print Preview toolbar. Choose the More button to extend the dialog box, as shown here.

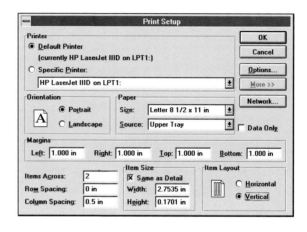

The additional layout options let you consolidate the information on a page by flowing the form or the report in multiple rows or columns. As you might suppose, these techniques work well for layouts that would otherwise be inefficiently narrow or shallow on the page. The Item Layout option becomes active for multicolumn layouts to let you decide whether successive items are placed across the page in successive columns (Horizontal) or whether each column must be completed before moving to the next (Vertical).

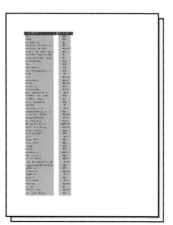
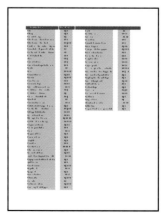

Use the layout options in the Print Setup dialog box to improve the look and readability of your report.

Page Breaks In Design view, you can insert a page break control in a form or a report by clicking the Page Break button in the Toolbox. Insert the page break control above or below other controls, not alongside them (to avoid dividing the information awkwardly). For forms, page break controls affect printouts from Form view but not from Datasheet view.

You can also control page breaks by setting group and section properties in forms and reports. Among the Layout Properties options for forms and reports you'll find Force New Page. It offers the settings None, Before Section, After Section, and Before & After.

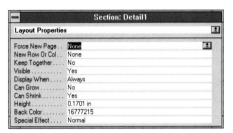

Other properties in the same list include Can Grow, Can Shrink, and Keep Together. Set the first two to Yes if the section contains controls that are permitted to expand or contract. Setting the KeepTogether property for sections forces Access to print a section on a new page if it can't print the entire section on the current page. Setting the KeepTogether property for a group keeps records together on a page and ensures that, on the same page, at least one line of data will follow a group header.

Engaging the Printer

If the proof of the pudding is in the tasting, the proof of a print job is in the printing. A number of surprises can leap out at you, especially if you print to a printer that's different from the one you chose when you created the document. For one thing, all the fonts available for one printer might not be available for another. Likewise, if you used fonts that are not scalable, the screen font might not match the printer font, and the discrepancies can ripple throughout a document in the form of changed alignment, changed pagination, and the like.

NOT INSTALLED?
If the printer you want to use does not appear in the Printers list in the Print Setup dialog box, you can install its printer driver via the Printers option in Control Panel. You must install the driver even if the printer is shared across a network.

Switching Printers

Let's look first at how to switch printers. In any of the Office applications, the Print dialog box (reached via the File menu) identifies the current printer. From the Print dialog box you can switch printers by choosing the Printer button (in Word and PowerPoint), the Printer Setup button (in Excel), or the Setup button (in Access). Select the printer (or driver) in the Printers list in the resulting Print Setup dialog box.

POWER PLAY

Built for Comfort/Built for Speed

Here are five things you can do to increase printing speed. Some of them—the third and fifth items in particular—increase printing speed at the expense of responsiveness in your Windows-based applications.

- Use a printer font instead of a downloadable font. You can replace fonts in your document or (with some printer drivers) you can substitute printer fonts for TrueType fonts in the Advanced Options dialog box of Control Panel's Printers option.

- Be sure that there is a SET TEMP statement in the AUTOEXEC.BAT file to create a directory for the temporary files used in printing. The statement should point to a valid directory on a drive with at least 2 MB of free disk space.

- In Print Manager, choose the High Priority command from the Options menu to allocate more computer processor time to Print Manager. (If you're using Microsoft Windows for Workgroups, choose Background Printing from the Options menu and select the High option button.) At the extreme, you can bypass Print Manager entirely: Close Print Manager, double-click the Printers icon in Control Panel, deselect the Use Print Manager check box, and click OK. Note that you have to reselect the Use Print Manager check box before you can launch Print Manager again.

- Make additional conventional memory available by removing unnecessary device drivers and memory-resident software and by maximizing both the application window and the document window.

- In Word, turn off background printing: From the Tools menu, choose Options; select the Print tab of the Options dialog box, and deselect the Background Printing check box.

In Word, changing printers also changes the default printer for Windows. In the other applications, changing the default printer is optional, if it's available at all. You can, in any event, change the default printer by double-clicking the Printers icon in Control Panel (which is ordinarily in the Main program group of Program Manager).

Font Substitutions and Replacements

The applications in the Office suite make different provisions for situations in which printer fonts are not available. As a rule, you can either specify font substitutions or make replacements in some global way.

Word makes the most elaborate arrangements for substituting fonts. To make a substitution, first open the document. Choose Options from the Tools menu, and on the Compatibility tab of the Options dialog box choose the Font Substitution button. Word checks the file for fonts that you cannot print with the current driver and then lets you match any unavailable font with one that's available.

PowerPoint has a Replace Fonts command on the Tools menu, which provides a quick way to bring a presentation in sync with the fonts available on a system. When you replace one font with another, PowerPoint makes the change throughout the current presentation.

Access makes special provision for one type of font difficulty—when you design a form or a report with one or more screen fonts that are a poor match with the printer fonts. You can avoid this situation by using TrueType fonts, which have matching screen and printer fonts. If you use non-TrueType fonts, set the LayoutForPrint property to Yes so that the controls on the designed form or report will reflect the available printer fonts. By default, LayoutForPrint is set to No for forms and Yes for reports.

Printing to a File

Tired of fighting a printer for the fonts or layout adjustments you need? Can't seem to turn WYS into WYG? Sometimes winning a printer skirmish requires a strategic retreat: Take the job to a different printer—one that has higher resolution or has access to the specialized fonts you need. But how do you take your print job with you without taking along the whole Office? For printing, as you know, involves the source application and the correct printer driver in addition to a printer with the necessary capabilities. The answer is to print to a file.

The print file (the result of printing your document to a file) will be larger—potentially much larger—than the original. Of course, you must create it with the appropriate printer driver—the one that's written for the printer you ultimately want to use. This probably means that you'll install and specify a driver for a printer that is not actually connected to your computer. But the equipment won't hold it against you: The file will contain all of the instructions the printer needs to generate the finished product you're aiming for.

Installing the Driver   When you install a printer driver expressly for printing to files, you can specify a file as the output destination for that driver. That way, you'll print to a file whenever you select that printer. Here's how you do it.

First, you have to have access to your Windows setup or printer setup files (on disks or across a network). Open Control Panel (normally in the Main program group) and double-click the Printers icon. In the Printers dialog box,

EXCEPTIONS
If you normally print directly to a printer but only occasionally send its output to a file for later printing, select the Print to File check box in the application's Print dialog box instead of changing port settings. Note that this is not an option in Excel.

choose the Add button, select the printer in the List of Printers list box, and choose Install. You'll be prompted for the file: Insert the disk or identify the source (on a network share, for example) and click OK.

After you install the driver, select the printer in the Installed Printers list box and choose the Connect button. In the Connect dialog box, select FILE: in the Ports list and click OK. By designating FILE: as the port, rather than a parallel or serial port, you tell Windows to prompt for a filename whenever you print to that printer.

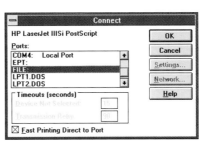

Finally, if you are ready to designate the newly installed printer as the active printer, choose the Set As Default Printer button before you close the Printers dialog box. If you don't activate the printer in the Printers dialog box, you can set it as the default printer from within the application.

Creating Print Files   Once you've installed the driver, creating the print file is no more difficult than coming up with a filename. Of course, you have to specify the appropriate printer as the active printer (either in the application's Print Setup dialog box or through Control Panel). Then, you simply choose the Print command from the File menu and click OK. If you've set up the printer to use FILE: as its printing port, you're all set—you don't have to select the Print to File check box in the Print dialog box. (If you do select Print to File, however, note that it remains selected—even if you change printers—until you turn the option off or end the session.)

After you click OK in the Print dialog box, the program prompts you for a filename. Supply a name for the output file, such as 95THESES.PRN. The extension is largely arbitrary, but it distinguishes the filename from the name of the original document.

Be sure that you also save the contents of your original document. If you need to make corrections, you can make them in your document rather than in your print file.

Copying to a Printer   The scene changes. You've brought the disk with your print file to a machine from which you can send it to a suitable printer. You insert your floppy disk in drive A, and from the MS-DOS prompt you simply copy the file to the port to which the printer is connected.

If Windows is running, double-click the MS-DOS Prompt icon in Program Manager or choose MS-DOS Prompt from the MOM menu. When you are done copying the file, type *exit* at the MS-DOS prompt to return to Windows. Suppose that you have a floppy disk that contains the file 95THESES.PRN.

BAD DRIVER?

Some printer drivers (generally older versions) do not work correctly when you select the Print to File check box in the application's Print dialog box. Change the printer's port connection to FILE: to create a print file with these drivers.

DEEP TROUBLE

When you print to a file in Word, don't specify a file location that is more than two levels deep in a disk's directory tree, and avoid directory names that exceed eight characters. If you ignore this advice, you might find that your print file shows up in the wrong directory with a truncated filename. (The correct filename will also appear in the right location—but with a length of 0 bytes.)

To copy the file to a printer that's connected to the first parallel port, LPT1, enter the following command at your MS-DOS prompt:

```
C:\>copy a:95theses.prn lpt1
```

Printing over a Network

Network printers provide efficient use of resources (and they often provide opportunities for exercise as well). You can connect to a printer that's attached to a server or (with a peer-to-peer system) to a shared printer that's attached to another user's computer. The details depend substantially on the type of network software that your organization uses. In the sections that follow, we'll touch on a few network printing considerations to keep in mind as you use Windows and your Office applications.

Making Connections   With many networks, you can switch among network printers as easily as you can switch among local printers. In the Print Setup dialog box, which you can reach from the Print dialog box (choose Print from the File menu), select a printer to which you are already connected or choose the Networks button (if it is displayed). The resulting dialog box enables you to connect to a network printer by identifying a port and then typing or selecting the appropriate pathname.

If you cannot connect in this way (directly from your Office application), use the Printers option in Control Panel or use Print Manager to make a connection. Be sure that the correct printer driver is installed, and specify the pathname for the network printer accurately.

Printers and Queues   For quick results, Print Manager is normally set up to pass network print jobs directly to the network queue. But it's the usual trade-off: Giving this focus to printing means that your application takes the back seat for a while longer. If you have Print Manager form a local queue of jobs destined for network printers, you'll get more attention sooner for your application, but at some cost in printing speed.

Here's how you initiate local queueing: In Print Manager, choose Network Settings from the Options menu, and in the Network Options dialog box, deselect the Print Net Jobs Direct check box. If you're using Windows for Workgroups, the same option (labeled Send Documents Directly to Network) is located in the Background Printing dialog box (choose Background Printing from the Options menu).

Whether or not it queues the jobs locally, Print Manager can report the status of print jobs in network queues. In addition to showing the status of your own jobs, it can show the status of other jobs in a queue to which you are connected. To see the jobs on the network queue, select the queue and choose Selected Net Queue from the View menu. (Print Manager in Windows for

Workgroups always displays the network queue for any network printer to which it is connected.) You can also display the print queue for network printers to which you are not connected, by choosing Other Net Queue from the View menu and entering the pathname and printer name of the queue.

Special Assignments: Envelopes and Labels

You see it so often, it stops being funny. Organizations produce elaborate printed documents on computers—letters, proposals, printed presentations— but somewhere in the corner of an office, there's a typewriter that everyone uses for typing addresses on envelopes or labels. Milking a printed envelope or a label out of most printers simply seems like too much trouble.

Word offers some relief. You control the process from a well-coordinated set of dialog boxes that lets you create and format the envelope or the label. Then you either print the result or add it to your document. As a further attraction, Word can add those machine-readable codes that speed up mail handling (for envelopes mailed in the United States). Let's step through an example to see how the features work.

If you want to print envelopes or labels by merging address information from another data source, identify the main document as Envelopes or Mailing Labels and insert the necessary name and address fields on a sample form. If you want to include the Delivery Point Bar Code, also identify the field that contains the zip code in the course of setting up the main document. (See Chapter 11, "Mastering Mergers.")

Addressing an Envelope

Suppose you've written a business letter and you're ready to prepare the envelope. Select the mailing address (if your letter includes the recipient's address), and then choose Envelopes and Labels from the Tools menu, as shown on the next page. On the Envelopes tab of the resulting dialog box, you'll see the address you selected, in the Delivery Address text box. If you did not select an address before you chose the command, type it in.

Word supplies a return address from the user information it maintains. If you change or correct the return address, the program asks whether you want the change to be reflected at the source—the User Info tab of the Options dialog box (reached via the Tools menu). Unless you're dealing with a special case, you might as well change the source so that you don't have to answer the same prompt again and again. Select the Omit check box if your envelopes have a preprinted return address or if you want to avoid printing a return address for some other reason.

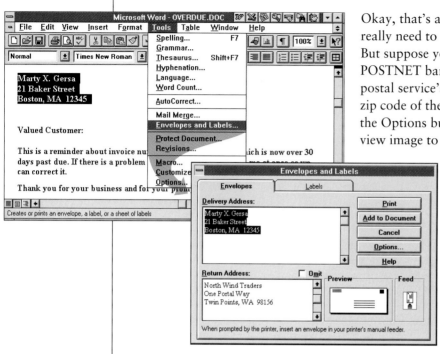

Okay, that's all the information you really need to put on the envelope. But suppose you want to add the POSTNET bar code, which tells the postal service's sorting machine the zip code of the addressee. Choose the Options button or click the Preview image to display the Envelope Options dialog box. Select the Envelope Options tab if it is not already selected, and then select the Delivery Point Bar Code check box. Word places the bar code above the first line of the delivery address. That location suits the post office just fine; the other common location—across the bottom of the envelope—might get cut off by your printer. (Plus, the code generally fits on labels in its top-line location.)

If you select Delivery Point Bar Code, Word activates another check box—FIM-A Courtesy Reply Mail. Select this check box if you want a mark printed on your envelope to identify the front side.

Also on the Envelope Options tab of the Envelope Options dialog box, you can identify the envelope size: Select a standard size in the list or select Custom and type your nonstandard dimensions. When you change the envelope dimensions, Word adjusts the location of the delivery address. To change the preset measurements, modify the From Left and From Top values.

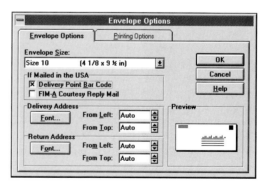

To format either the delivery address or the return address, choose the corresponding Font button. The format options include font styles and font sizes, as well as colors and effects (such as SMALL CAPS). Click OK to apply the font settings.

FIM

The FIM, or facing identification mark, identifies the front side of the envelope for the postal service's sorting equipment. FIM-A is used only on bar-coded mail. It's distinct from FIM-C, which is also used on bar-coded mail but is assigned to a business by the post office for Business Reply Mail (for which the postage is paid by the addressee).

Printing an Envelope

Notice the Feed image at the bottom right of the Envelopes tab of the Envelopes and Labels dialog box: It shows you how Word recommends feeding the envelope into the printer. Pay close attention to the image. It depicts the side that should be facing up, the edge of the envelope that you should feed into the printer, and the position of the envelope (flush left, flush right, or centered).

For details, choose the Options button or click the Feed image to display the Envelope Options dialog box; select the Printing Options tab if it is not already selected. You can select a different paper source and a different orientation for feeding the envelope, but be aware that your printer cannot simply adjust to any option you highlight. Use the recommended feed method unless it produces unsatisfactory results. See your printer documentation for any special instructions on feeding envelopes.

> **BLANK MAIL**
> If the text for your envelopes is not printing or appears in the wrong location, you're probably not positioning the envelope correctly when you feed it into the printer, or else the settings on the Printing Options tab of the Envelope Options dialog box are not correct for your printer.

POWER PLAY

Automating Envelopes

Here are some suggestions for automating the process of creating envelopes:

First, consider adding an Envelope button to one of the Word toolbars you commonly display. The Envelope button is in the Tools category in the Customize dialog box. For an example of toolbar customization, see the Power Play on page 88 ("Adding a Toolbar Button to Embed Objects").

Next, think about using Word bookmarks to identify text to insert automatically on an envelope or a label. You can assign the bookmark names EnvelopeAddress and EnvelopeReturn (with no spaces!) to the delivery address and the return address, respectively. To create a bookmark, select the text, choose Bookmark from the Edit menu, and then type the name. For some reason,

Word's letter-writing templates don't contain these bookmarks. You might want to add them to letter-writing templates you use often.

You can also insert special text and graphics (such as logos and Word-Art) on an envelope by adding the envelope to your document and then editing the new section in Layout view. Note that Word uses a frame for the delivery address to establish its position on the envelope, so editing can be tricky.

To reuse the same enhancements on all of the envelopes that you print (using the current template), select the enhancement, including its position, and create an AutoText entry named EnvelopeExtra1. Word adds the contents of two AutoText entries, EnvelopeExtra1 and EnvelopeExtra2 (again, no spaces!), to all of the envelopes that you print.

Addressing Labels

The procedures for preparing labels for printing are similar to those for pre-paring envelopes. For instance, if you want a label for the delivery address of the current document, select the address (if it's part of the document) and choose the Envelopes and Labels command from the Tools menu. Select the Labels tab of the resulting dialog box; the delivery address should be posi-tioned in the label area, ready for printing. Select the Delivery Point Bar Code check box if you want to include the bar code on the label. The Use Return Address check box permits you to print your return address on the label rather than the delivery address.

Naturally, labels can have many uses besides displaying mailing addresses. You can prepare labels for file folders, floppy disks, test tubes—you name it. The box in the lower right part of the dialog box depicts the label and identi-fies the label type. Click that image or choose the Options button to display the Label Options dialog box, where you can select the label description that matches your label stock.

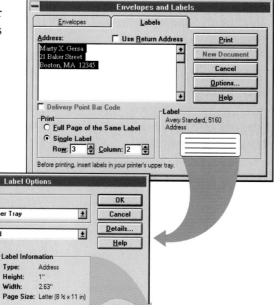

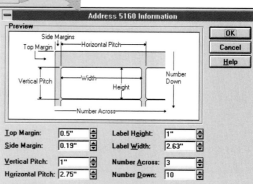

Together, the printer information you provide and the selection you make in the Label Products list box determine the items in the Product Number list.

For each product number you select, the label dimensions are displayed to the right, in the Label Information box. Click the label description or choose the Details button to see a drawing of the label and a list of its dimensions. You can modify the values, such as the margin sizes or the label width, in the boxes below the depiction. The changes you make are not saved as part of the description of the commercial product. Instead, the information is saved as part of the custom label description (Custom Laser or Custom Dot Matrix).

If you want to format the label text, select the text and choose Font from the shortcut menu. You can change font sizes, styles, and colors in the resulting Font dialog box. Choose the Default button if you want the font modifications to become default settings for labels that you create with the current template.

Printing Labels

Display the Envelopes and Labels dialog box when you're ready to print. You can print an entire sheet of the same label—to create a stock of return address labels, for example, or to mail thank-you notes for those lottery payments. Or you can print a single label. If you're printing on a sheet of labels, you can specify which label on the page you want to print on.

Select the Single Label option button to print one label, and then specify by row and column the position of the label on the sheet. The row and column counters are "intelligent," in the sense that you cannot increment them beyond the actual number of rows or columns on the sheet, so be sure that you've identified the correct label stock. After you verify that the labels are properly loaded, choose the Print button to proceed. Happy printing.

Chapter 14

Importing and Exporting

Border Crossing

Chapter 5, "Office Connections," concluded with an overview of importing and exporting within the Microsoft Office suite. In this chapter, we'll push beyond that overview on several fronts.

First, we'll look at some importing and exporting options that you can use with a Microsoft Access database. Then we'll negotiate a few of the issues involved in transferring documents between the Microsoft Windows environment and the Macintosh environment.

We'll also describe the role of Object Packager, which you might already have encountered, intentionally or otherwise. Finally, we'll explore Microsoft Word's file conversion macros.

Importing and Exporting Database Information

You can transfer Access data from one database to another, and you can share the information in Access tables and queries with your Microsoft Excel and Word documents. You can also import and export Access data to and from other database management programs.

With the Database window active in Access, the Import and Export commands are hard to miss. You can find the commands on the File menu and the shortcut menu; the corresponding toolbar buttons are on the Standard toolbar. The Import command copies information to an Access table from a range of sources, including text files, spreadsheets, and databases. If you're transferring information between two Access databases, you can import or export an object of any type. To import an object, choose the Import command, select Microsoft Access as the data source in the Import dialog box,

If the object is a table, the transfer can include the data along with the structure (table definition), or you can import or export only the table structure.

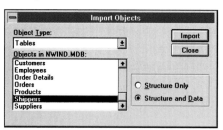

and select the source database file in the Select Microsoft Access Database dialog box. In the Import Objects dialog box, select the object type and then select the object to be imported, as shown in the figure at left. When you choose Import, the object is imported into your open database.

To import an entire Access database (excluding AccessBasic modules, if you'd like), you can use the Import Database add-in. The add-in is easy to launch: Display the Add-ins submenu on the File menu and choose Import Database.

The Export command, like the Import command, can handle a wide range of data conversions. You can export to common text, spreadsheet, and database formats. To export to destinations other than Access itself, you can use a table or a query as the source of the information to export.

If you don't see the specific format for the destination application, you can probably export to a format that the application can import. Word, for example, can import any of the text formats in the list. You can also use the Output To command to transfer information with its formatting intact to an Excel file or a Rich Text Format file.

Let's turn now to a few examples. First, we'll step through a procedure for importing information from an Excel worksheet. Then we'll export a table that can be used in Word as a data source in a mail merge operation. Finally, we'll insert database information into a Word document using the Database command on Word's Insert menu.

Importing Excel Information into Access

Before you begin, be sure that the Excel worksheet that contains the information you want to import is closed. If you don't have an appropriate datasheet available, create a simple datasheet in Excel that has a few rows of data and has column headings in the first row. Don't forget to save the file and close it.

Here are the steps you need to follow:

1. In Access, open the database in which you want to create a new table, or switch to the Database window if the database is already open.

2. From the File menu, choose Import. Access displays the Import dialog box.

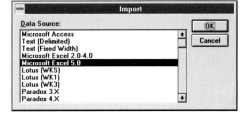

3. In the Data Source list box, select Microsoft Excel 5.0 and click OK.

4. In the Select File dialog box that appears, select the Excel file that contains the information you want to import, and then choose the Import button.

5. Select the import options you want in the Import Spreadsheet Options dialog box. If you want the information in the top row of the spreadsheet (or of the specified range) to serve as field names, select the First Row Contains Field

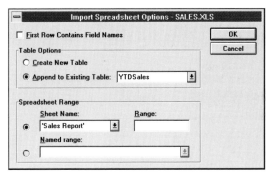

   Names check box. You can add the imported information to an existing table or you can create a new one. Then, because you are not importing an entire workbook, you have to specify a sheet or a named range. If you select a sheet, you can also specify a range by cell coordinates. Click OK to import the information. After the information is added to the database, click Close to close the Select File dialog box.

Don't expect the imported information to retain data formatting. If your spreadsheet shows a column of calculated interest payments rounded off to show dollars and cents, the imported data might consist of decimal numbers with up to 12 places after the decimal point.

TURNING THE TABLES

You can also import information from a Word data source into an Access table. For information about doing this and avoiding formatting snags, see question 41 in Chapter 15, "Real Questions, Real Answers."

Exporting Access Information to a Word Data Source

To demonstrate exporting, let's copy an Access table to a text file that can serve as a data source for a Word mail merge. You might wonder why you'd ever want to do that, since you can link the data directly from Access using the Word Mail Merge Wizard. But let's suppose you want to create a separate file, perhaps to give the file to someone who will perform the mail merge using a different computer—one on which Word is installed, but not Access. We might also assume that the database is updated frequently, so the separate file will serve as a record of the people (and the addresses) to whom the mailing was sent.

For this example, we'll use NWIND.MDB, the sample database that is included with Access.

1. Open the NWIND database (located at the time of installation in the SAMPAPPS subdirectory of your Access directory).

2. With the Database window active, choose the Export command from the File menu (or click the Export button on the Standard toolbar) to display the Export dialog box.

3. Select Word for Windows Merge in the Data Destination list and click OK.

4. The next dialog box, titled Select Microsoft Access Object, lets you select either a table or a query (or both) to export. Select Tables from among the View options, highlight the Customers table, and click OK.

5. In the Export to File dialog box, you can specify a filename and a location for the text file that will contain the exported information. We'll accept the filename CUSTOMER.TXT suggested by Access. Click OK.

6. The program displays a set of options for presenting exported data of different types in the Export Word Merge Options dialog box. Select your preferences for the appearance of dates, times, and decimal numbers in the exported file. When you click OK, Access creates the file.

The result of exporting the Customers table is a text file. If you examine the file in Word, you'll see that the records are separated by paragraph marks, with the first paragraph devoted to the field headings. The tabs indicate the breaks between fields. If you set up a mail merge in which you identify CUSTOMER.TXT as the data source, Word has no problem reading the data and you can insert merge fields in your main document smoothly.

Importing Access Information into Word

Aside from the Export command (with its text-only result), you can use the Output To command in Access to export a table or a query with its formatting as an RTF file, which Word can import. You have yet another option: the Database command on Word's Insert menu. With this command, you can insert the contents of a table or a query as a Word table in your current Word document. Use this option when you want to add the table to an existing document (rather than create a new one) and retain the table format.

As an example, let's insert the contents of a query in the NWIND database. Of course, the source of the data need not be Access; you can also convert information from an Excel worksheet or from files created with another leading database management program, such as Microsoft FoxPro or Paradox.

Before you begin, open a new document in Word. Type some text in the document if you like, and then follow these steps:

1. In your Word document, place the insertion point where you want to insert the table. From the Insert menu, choose Database. The Database dialog box appears, showing the steps in the process.

2. Choose the Get Data button to display the Open Data Source dialog box. Select MS Access Databases (*.mdb) in the List Files of Type list box, and then select NWIND.MDB in the SAMPAPPS subdirectory of your Access directory. Click OK.

3. In the Microsoft Access dialog box, select the Tables tab, highlight the Products table, and click OK.

4. In the Database dialog box, choose the Query Options button. The program displays a three-tabbed dialog box in which you can set filter and sort criteria and select the fields to include in your Word table.

5. On the Select Fields tab of the Query Options dialog box, click Clear All to remove all of the field names in the Selected Fields list. Select Product Name in the Fields in Data Source list, and click Select to add the field name to the Selected Fields list. Continue selecting field names and clicking Select until you have added the field names English Name, Quantity Per Unit, Unit Price, and Category ID to the Selected Fields list. By listing the fields in this order, the resulting Word

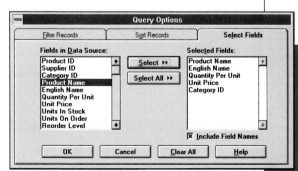

WHO'S DRIVING?
The Insert Database command in Word gathers data from outside sources through the use of ODBC drivers. If you cannot make the connection to the desired database, you might not have the correct drivers installed. Choose the ODBC Drivers option in the Windows Control Panel to display the Data Sources dialog box and see a list of ODBC drivers. You can install additional drivers from this dialog box or you can choose the Office Setup and Uninstall command from the Office menu.

table will have the columns containing the fields in the correct order. On the Sort Records tab, select the Product Name field as the first sort field and select the Ascending option button. On the Filter Records tab, define one filter: Select Category ID as the Field and Equal to as the Comparison, and type 1 for the Compare To value. (The value 1 is the ID number for Beverages.) Click OK.

6. In the Database dialog box, choose the Table AutoFormat button. Select Colorful 1 in the Formats list. Then select the Color check box under Formats to Apply and deselect the First Column check box under Apply Special Formats To. Click OK.

7. Choose the Insert Data button in the Database dialog box. In the Insert Data dialog box, either select the All option button to import the entire table or specify the records to be imported. If you select the Insert Data as Field check box, a DATABASE field will be inserted in the Word

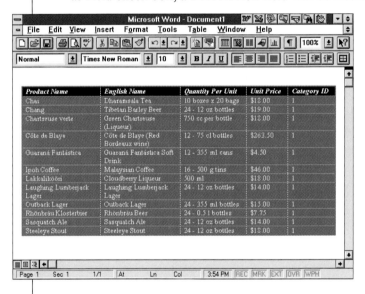

document and the data will be updated from the source database table whenever the field is updated. To insert the table without maintaining a link to the data source, deselect the check box. Click OK. Word adds the contents of the Access table as a Word table, using the formatting options you specified.

Through the Looking Glass

With the exception of Access, all of the major applications in the Office suite are available in versions for both Windows and Macintosh environments. The programs have the necessary converters for importing and exporting files for both platforms. The Open dialog box (reached via the File menu) supplies the converters you need. There are, however, a few hurdles to clear.

Because the Macintosh computer formats disks differently than MS-DOS–based (and Windows-based) computers do, you cannot simply insert a floppy disk with a Word for Macintosh document into your Windows-based computer and expect to open the file in Word for Windows. Nor can you do the reverse—insert an MS-DOS floppy disk into a Macintosh and open a file. No, you have to step through the operating-system looking glass. Fortunately, there are numerous techniques for doing so.

Many networks accommodate both Windows-based and Macintosh computers. If you are connected to such a network, you can transfer a file from one environment to the other by copying it to a network server at a location that gives access to both types of machines. Then you can copy the file to the other machine. You might also take advantage of the network connection to send a file between machines using electronic mail.

If you don't have a suitable network, you can use a (recent vintage) Macintosh and a 3.5-inch MS-DOS floppy disk to effect the transfer. Save the document on its source machine. If that machine is a Windows-based computer, copy the file to a floppy disk and use Apple File Exchange on the Macintosh to transfer the file from the floppy disk to the Macintosh. If the source computer is a Macintosh, use Apple File Exchange to copy the file from the Macintosh to the floppy disk. If Apple File Exchange is not installed, you can install it from the Tidbits disk (System 7) or the Utilities 2 disk (System 6). The floppy disk drive on the Macintosh must be of the high-density variety (termed Super-Drive or HDFD), which is standard nowadays.

Before you attempt a transfer, note that version compatibility between the Windows-based and Macintosh applications can trip you up. The Macintosh

ALTERNATIVE DATING

For compatibility with Excel for the Macintosh, Excel for Windows lets you use the 1904 date system to calculate dates instead of the 1900 date system. If you import into Access a worksheet that employs the 1904 dating system, the date fields will be off by four years. To set the correct dates, you have to deselect the 1904 date system option in Excel and reimport the worksheet into Access. See question 43 in Chapter 15, "Real Questions, Real Answers."

Windows-to-Macintosh Conversion

If you don't have a network (or a modem) for transferring files from a Windows application to a Macintosh application, follow these steps:

1. Save the file in a format that can be read by the Macintosh application. For example, to save a Word document, select Word for Macintosh 6.0 as the file format in the Save As dialog box.
2. Copy the file to a 3.5-inch high-density floppy disk that has been formatted for MS-DOS.
3. On the Macintosh, start Apple File Exchange and insert the floppy disk.
4. Use the Drive buttons to list the Macintosh hard disk contents in the list on the left and the floppy disk contents in the list on the right.
5. Open the destination folder in the list on the left.
6. Select the file to be transferred in the list on the right.
7. Choose Default Translation from the MS-DOS to Mac menu. (Other translation options should be deselected.)
8. Choose the Translate button. A dialog box shows the progress of the translation.
9. From the File menu, choose Quit after the transfer has been completed.
10. On the Macintosh, start the application and load the file as you would any other file.

version of Excel 4, for instance, cannot open a file saved as an Excel 5 for Windows file. Before you transfer an Excel 5 for Windows file to a Macintosh, use the Save As command to convert the file to Excel 4 format.

File naming is more restrictive on the Windows side of the looking glass, so you should assign nicely pruned, MS-DOS–pleasing filenames to the Macintosh files. That way, you'll be sure to recognize the files after they get translated; if you assign the conventional extensions (DOC for Word documents, XLS for Excel workbooks, and so on), the files will even show up in the Open dialog boxes on cue.

Macintosh-to-Windows Conversion

To transfer files from Macintosh applications to Windows-based applications using a floppy disk, follow these steps:

1. Save the file in a format that can be read by the Windows-based application.
2. Start Apple File Exchange and insert a 3.5-inch high-density floppy disk that has been formatted for MS-DOS.
3. Use the Drive buttons to list the Macintosh hard disk contents in the list on the left and the floppy disk contents in the list on the right.
4. Select the file to be transferred in the list on the left.
5. Choose Default Translation from the Mac to MS-DOS menu. (Other translation options should be deselected.)
6. Choose the Translate button. A dialog box shows the progress of the translation.
7. From the File menu, choose Quit after the transfer has been completed, and remove the floppy disk.
8. Load the file from the floppy disk to your Windows-based application as you would any other file. If the file is large, you might want to copy the file to your hard disk before loading it in the application.

POWER PLAY

Win/Mac Word Pictures

To facilitate file transfer, Word documents save imported pictures in two picture formats—one for Windows (WMF) and another for the Macintosh (PICT). The duplication, although it increases file size significantly, preserves the picture quality because you can open the Word document in either platform without converting the picture.

To reduce the file size, you can save a document in only one picture format—the one native to the current platform. To indicate this preference, display the Save tab of the Options dialog box (choose Options from the Tools menu) and select the Save Native Picture Formats Only check box.

Converting Information from Non-Office Applications

Microsoft Office not only provides new ways of using its applications together, but it also provides an open door for non-Office applications. In fact, you can add toolbar buttons and menu commands to Microsoft Office Manager to launch non-Office applications or even non–Windows-based programs.

The Office Setup program installs converters for many non-Office applications. To be sure that all of the available converters are installed, choose the Complete/Custom installation option. You can obtain additional conversion utilities from Microsoft. If you think that a converter might be offered for a non-Office program that you use, contact the Microsoft Support Network as directed in your documentation (or in online Help).

As for compound documents, they can present some interesting combinations. For example, suppose you open a document containing an embedded object that was created with a non-Office application. You can edit the object with its server application—provided, of course, that you have access to the application on your computer. But if you don't have the server application installed, you might be able to skirt the problem by using an Office application to edit the object.

To try this, choose the command from the Edit menu that identifies the object, and then choose Convert from the submenu. In the resulting dialog box, select either the Convert To or the Activate As option button, and then select in the Object Type list an object that you can edit. Converting an object permanently changes the format of the embedded object from its native format to the format of the object you selected in the Object Type list; the object cannot subsequently be edited using its original source application. Activating an object lets you open it for editing in an application different than the source application but preserves it in its original file format so that it can subsequently be edited in its original source application.

If only the original object is listed, you cannot convert the embedded object or activate it in a different application, and you must use the original source application to edit the object. If you need to edit the contents of the embedded object but cannot convert it or activate it, you must either get a copy of the source application or obtain the object's source file separate from the compound document. If the file is saved in a file format that one of your applications can read, you can open the file using any necessary converters, edit the contents, and then reinsert the object.

Inserting Objects from Non-OLE Server Applications

Sounds impossible, but it's actually easy to insert information as an object from an application that is not an OLE server. The result is generally less satisfying than a linked or embedded OLE object, but there are situations in which it's exactly the result you need. The document in which you insert the object must be created by an OLE client application.

To insert these objects in your document, use the Object Packager program. Start this utility program from Program Manager (in the Accessories group) or by selecting Package as the object type when using the Insert Object command. Object Packager also starts automatically when you insert in your document an object that is not from an OLE server.

The visible results of Object Packager are an icon and an identifying label in your document. An icon can be a pretty poor substitute for a document or a picture, so what good does this do you? Remember that the icon is just a representation of the package. The benefits of the package are that you can activate the file (under certain conditions) and you can edit the package and save a copy of the object as a separate file.

PACKAGE

In the world of OLE, a *package* is an object created with Object Packager. A package has two components: its appearance and its content. The appearance consists of an icon and a label and the content consists of a file. (The content can be part of a file if created with an OLE server application, but Object Packager is normally superfluous in such a case.)

What's in the Package?

What you're able to do with a package depends on its content. So let's run through the process of linking or embedding a package in a document. To start in familiar territory, let's suppose you're working on a Word document. Choose Object from the Insert menu, and then select the Create from File tab of the Object dialog box. In your Office directory, select the Office readme file, OFREADME.HLP, and click OK. Your Word document now contains

OFREADME.HLP

the icon shown at left. Because the Help engine is not an OLE server application, Object Packager started automatically and the object was embedded as a package. That the icon represents a package becomes evident if you display its shortcut menu. Choose Activate Contents Package from the shortcut menu or double-click the icon.

Because the file, OFREADME.HLP, is associated with an application, activating the file launches the application (Help) and opens the Office readme file.

To see what happens when you insert a data file that is not associated with a Windows-based application, follow the preceding steps again, this time to insert the ANSI.SYS file from your MS-DOS directory (usually named DOS). The inserted icon is the Object Packager icon, with the name of the embedded file beneath it. If Object Packager cannot acquire an icon from the

ANSI.SYS

POWER PLAY

Packaging Commands

Activating a package might also trigger some sort of playback. If the package contains a sound, a video clip, or a slide presentation, double-clicking the icon plays the recording or starts the slide show. If the package contains an executable file, activating it launches the program or executes the commands (in a batch file).

As an example, consider the manner in which a network administrator might use Microsoft Mail to distribute a setup script for installing Office. The Office online Help describes a process in which the administrator uses Object Packager to create an object that contains the appropriate command line (which points to the network server in which Office has been installed) and includes a parameter to identify the customized setup script.

The instructions, summarized below, demonstrate another way to start Object Packager: by selecting Package in the Insert Object dialog box. Before you update the Mail message, you can add a label to the icon by choosing Label from the Edit menu. This method of distributing the setup icon in Mail does not work if the network server is password-protected.

1. In Mail, compose your message, and then choose Insert Object from the Edit menu.

2. In the Insert Object dialog box, select Package as the object type and then click OK.

3. In Object Packager, choose Command Line from the Edit menu.

4. Type the path to SETUP.EXE on the network server, including the /t switch followed by the filename for the setup script. Click OK. For example, you might type the following command (on one line) to direct the user to the public share of the MYSERVER server:

```
\\myserver\public\msoffice\setup.exe
/t myscript.stf /q
```

The Setup program, installed in the MSOFFICE directory, uses the MYSCRIPT.STF setup script. (If your network does not support UNC pathnames, users who receive the message must connect to the network using the same drive letter you used for Setup before they double-click the icon.)

5. Click OK to return to the Object Packager window.

6. Choose the Insert Icon button.

7. Click the Browse button and locate SETUP.EXE in the shared network directory. Your edited STF file should be located in the same directory. Click OK. In the Insert Icon dialog box, click OK again.

8. In Object Packager, choose the Update command from the File menu and then choose Exit.

associated application (in this case, because there is no associated application), it inserts the Object Packager icon. Double-clicking the icon or choosing Activate Contents Package from its shortcut menu yields the message *No application is associated with this file.*

End of the line? Sort of. If you choose to edit the package—from the shortcut menu or from the submenu alongside Package Object on the Edit menu—you'll see the Object Packager window. This window has two sides, one for each component of the package: appearance and content.

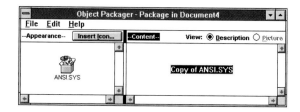

Choose the Insert Icon button if you want to change the icon. Choose Save Contents from the File menu if you want to save ANSI.SYS as a separate file. This feature makes Object Packager a convenient way to convey a file to someone as a component of a compound document. You might, for example, embed a copy of a driver in a Word file that describes the corresponding device.

Batch Conversions in Word

Word supplies two macros to help automate conversions. They are available in the CONVERT.DOT template. (You haven't used a macro before? Don't worry—its easy.) The first macro, BatchConversion, lets you convert a group of files. The second, EditConversionOptions, lets you change conversion settings. What sorts of settings are these? Mostly quite narrow, applicable to special situations. For example, one option for converting files from Word for MS-DOS lets you determine whether chevron characters (« ») should signal a mail merge field (as they do in Word for Windows).

To use the BatchConversion macro, choose Macro from the Tools menu (or from the File menu, if you don't have a document open). In the Macro dialog box, select BatchConversion in the list of available macros, and then choose Run. The macro behaves like a wizard, offering you clear choices as it steps through the procedure: which way to convert, which files to convert, to which destination, and so forth.

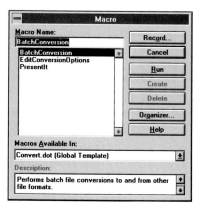

But wait. The BatchConversion macro isn't in your list? Cancel the Macro dialog box. One way to make the macro available is to attach or open the template in which it's saved. Easy enough to do. Choose Templates from the File menu (with any document open), and then choose the Attach button in the resulting dialog box. Select CONVERT.DOT, which is in the MACROS subdirectory, not in the TEMPLATE directory with most of the other templates and wizards. Click OK to close the Attach Template dialog box, and then click it again to close the Templates and Add-ins dialog box. Batch-Conversion will now appear in the list of macro names when you choose the Macro command. (If you want the template to be even more readily accessible, see the Power Play below.)

The EditConversionOptions macro is also available when CONVERT.DOT is attached or open. To use it, simply run the macro; it displays a dialog box in which you select a conversion and then select the conversion option you want to change. The dialog box explains each option and provides a way to change settings for the current option.

POWER PLAY

Global Template

If you want to make the macros in the CONVERT.DOT template (or any template) accessible globally, choose the Templates command from the File menu, and in the Templates and Add-ins dialog box, choose the Add button. In the Add Template dialog box, select CONVERT.DOT (from the MAC-ROS subdirectory of your Word for Windows directory) and click OK.

Back in the Templates and Add-ins dialog box, the template name will show up—with its check box selected—in the Global Templates and Add-ins list. During the rest of the session (after you click OK to close this dialog box), the macros in the template—but none of its styles—will be added to whatever document template you use.

The next time you start Word, CONVERT.DOT will again be among the templates in the list, but the check box will be deselected. Unless you copy CONVERT.DOT to the STARTUP subdirectory, you have to choose the Templates command from the File menu and select the CONVERT.DOT check box for every session in which you want to use it.

Chapter 15

Real Questions, Real Answers

The following questions and answers come hot from the daily info frenzy at Microsoft's Product Support Services (PSS). The entries were compiled by the pros who work there, and reflect the issues that most commonly arise in the daily tide of calls, faxes, letters, and electronic messages from real users with real problems. Some issues involve hard-to-find or hard-to-use features; others reflect problems in the product documentation or the software itself.

The questions are arranged in roughly the same order as the topics in the preceding chapters. If you have a technical question that is not addressed here (or elsewhere in this book or in the documentation), turn to the Microsoft Office online Help. On the Contents screen, go to the Technical Support section and pursue the best course for your situation.

Installation

Question 1: How do I upgrade one of the Office applications on my network installation of Office?

Answer: If you are installing Office for the first time on a workstation, run the Workstation installation from the server, but do not install the application for which you have an upgrade copy. Then run the updated application's Workstation installation.

If you have already run an Administrative installation of Office, all of the individual program executable files and the Office Setup files (SETUP.EXE, SETUP.STF, SETUP.INF, and so forth) are installed in the root directory you specified during setup. When you then run an Administrative installation of an upgrade to an individual Office application (for example, to upgrade from Microsoft Excel 4 to Excel 5), do not install these files in the directory in which you installed Office, because the unique Office Setup files (SETUP.STF and SETUP.INF) will be replaced by the Setup program for the new program upgrade (and when you run the Workstation installation for Office from the network server, the Setup program for the upgrade program will run instead of the Setup program for the integrated Office package). Instead, you should install the program upgrade in a different directory than the one in which you installed Office, by doing the following:

1. Create a subdirectory for the program you're upgrading. For example, if you're upgrading from Excel 4 to Excel 5, you can create an EXCEL5 subdirectory in the MSOFFICE directory (MSOFFICE\EXCEL5).

2. Run the Administrative setup of the new version of the program (setup /a) and place it in the new subdirectory.

3. Run the Workstation installation of the new program by running SETUP.EXE, which is located in the new subdirectory.

Question 2: When I click the Microsoft Office button on the Microsoft Office Manager toolbar and then choose the Office Setup and Uninstall command from the menu, the following error message appears: *Cannot find Microsoft Office Setup. Please start Setup another way.* **Where did my Office Setup go?**

Answer: If you run a Typical or Custom/Complete installation and install all of the components of Office, the Office SETUP.EXE file is installed, along with a Setup icon in Program Manager. But if you run a Workstation, Minimum, or Custom/Complete installation and you don't select the Tools option, the SETUP.EXE file and the Setup icon are not installed. This causes an error message to appear when you choose the Office Setup and Uninstall command from the Office menu.

To run Setup when the SETUP.EXE file is not installed, use the appropriate procedure below.

- If you installed Office from a network server, follow these steps to create a program icon that will run Setup from the server:

1. In Program Manager, switch to the group to which you want to add the icon.

2. Choose New from the File menu. The New Program Object dialog box appears.

3. Select the Program Item option button, and click OK. The Program Item Properties dialog box appears.

4. In the Description text box, type a unique description for the icon.

5. In the Command Line text box, type the server pathname, the program filename, and the full extension using the following syntax:

   serverpath\setup.exe /t *localpath*\setup.stf

   Serverpath is the drive and pathname of the Office network server installation; *localpath* is the drive and pathname of the Setup Table file, SETUP.STF. The *localpath* entry depends on the type of setup you used and any options you selected during setup. If you chose the Workstation or Minimum Installation option, you should type in the Command Line text box something similar to the following:

   L:\MSOFFICE\setup.exe /t C:\MSOFFICE\SETUP\setup.stf

   If you chose the Custom/Complete Installation option without the Tools option, you should type something similar to the following:

   L:\MSOFFICE\setup.exe /t C:\WINDOWS\SYSTEM\setup.stf

   You can determine the pathname for your SETUP.STF file by opening your Windows initialization (WIN.INI) file and finding the MS Setup (ACME) Tables Files section. The pathname is listed in the MSOFFICE.EXE line.

6. Click OK.

You can now run the Office Maintenance Mode Setup from the new Setup icon that you created.

- If you installed Office from a floppy disk drive, rerun Setup from Office disk 1, as follows:

1. Insert the disk labeled Disk 1 Setup in the floppy disk drive.

2. In Program Manager, choose Run from the File menu.

3. In the Command Line text box, type A:\setup or B:\setup and click OK.

4. Choose the Add/Remove button in the Microsoft Office Setup dialog box.

5. In the Maintenance Installation dialog box, select the Tools check box and click Continue. Do not deselect any other check boxes. Deselecting the check boxes for the other options will cause the Maintenance installation to uninstall them.

6. An Office Setup icon appears. You can run Setup from this icon or by using the Office Setup and Uninstall command on the MOM toolbar menu.

Question 3: I ran the Office Setup program to uninstall Excel. In the Maintenance Installation dialog box, I deselected the Microsoft Excel check box and continued with the Setup program. My Excel directory and all the subdirectories are still on my hard drive, even though most of the directories are empty. Why didn't the Setup program remove all of the directories?

Answer: When you run the Setup program and you uninstall an application, not all of the application's files and directories are removed from your hard drive. The Setup program does not remove your data files, of course, but it also does not remove the directories (to avoid removing some of your own files), and it leaves behind some configuration files. For example, Microsoft Word's NORMAL.DOT and WINWORD.OPT files are left, as well as Microsoft PowerPoint's DEFAULT.PPT file. The nice thing about this is that when you install an updated version of the program, it can use these default configuration files.

Question 4: I ran an Administrative installation of Office, and I chose Server as the location to install shared application files. But when I ran the Workstation installation, the shared applications were installed on my local hard drive. Why did this happen, and did I do something wrong?

Answer: There are four circumstances under which the Setup program installs the shared applications on your local hard drive when you run a Workstation installation, even if you choose to have them installed on the server when you run the Administrative installation. They are the following:

- You already have versions of the shared application files on your local hard drive. Setup therefore updates the existing versions.

  To avoid this problem, remove the existing shared applications from your local hard drive, remove any existing references to the MSAPPS directory from your WIN.INI file and REG.DAT file, and then rerun the Setup program on the workstation. (In the WIN.INI file, you can turn the lines into comments. In the REG.DAT file, you must delete them.)

- The Administrative installation was done locally on a nondedicated server.

  If you use the Setup /a command to install Office on the local hard drive of a nondedicated server (such as Microsoft Windows for Workgroups), the Setup program defaults to the following location:

  ```
  MSAPPS Network Server C:
  ```

If the network server is referred to simply as C:, when the Workstation installation is run from another computer, the shared components are installed on the computer's hard disk (the C: drive).

However, if you try to run the Setup program using the Setup /a command to install to the hard drive of the nondedicated server and try to specify its server and share name as the MSAPPS Network Server, you receive an error message indicating that the server and share cannot be found on the network.

To avoid this problem, do the Administrative installation to the nondedicated server from another computer instead of locally. When you run the Setup program using the Setup /a command from another machine, you can specify the server and share name correctly, as follows:

```
MSAPPS Network Server \\servername\sharename
```

- You are using network software that does not support the Universal Naming Convention (UNC).

  Novell NetWare Lite is one example of a network that does not support the UNC. If you try to specify a UNC name when doing an Administrative installation, or if you are not connected to the necessary drive designation on the server when running the Workstation installation, shared components are installed locally.

  If you use this type of network software, you must specify the server and share name as a physical drive letter and directory when you perform the Administrative installation. The drive letter you specify must be the same drive letter that the workstations will use to access the MSAPPS directory from the server. The workstations must be connected to this drive when you run the Workstation installation and when you subsequently try to use any shared application.

- The server, share name, and directory name of the MSAPPS directory on the server exceed 63 characters.

  In this case, the Setup program copies the shared applications to the local hard drive on the workstation to ensure that a valid REG.DAT file is created at the end of setup. This is because the longest line the Setup program can write to the REG.DAT file is 64 characters. To avoid this problem, be sure that your UNC path does not exceed 63 characters.

The MOM Toolbar and Find File

Question 5: When I use the Find File button on the MOM toolbar to locate my files, some of the files don't display a preview. Why is this?

Answer: All of the major applications included in Office, with the exception of Microsoft Access, have a Find File feature. This feature works the same whether you run it from Word, Excel, PowerPoint, or the MOM toolbar. The general rules for the types of files you can preview using Find File are the following:

- To preview a file using Find File from Word, you must have a file converter for that type of file installed on your computer.

- To preview a file using Find File from Excel, PowerPoint, or the MOM toolbar, the file must be saved with summary information. If the file is an Excel file, the first sheet in the workbook must be a worksheet, a chart, or an Excel 4 macro sheet.

The following is a list of the different types of files you can preview using the Find File feature:

From Word	From Excel, PowerPoint, or the MOM Toolbar
Word document	Excel workbook
Excel workbook	PowerPoint presentation
Text files	Text files
Any other file that you can open in Word	

To save a workbook file with summary information in Excel or PowerPoint, choose Summary Info from the File menu in either application, enter your information in the dialog box, and click OK.

Note: You cannot use the Find File feature in any Office application to preview an Access database.

Question 6: Speaking of summary information, I saved my Excel file with a title and some comments by typing them in the Summary Info dialog box, but now I can't see this information when I use the Find File feature in Word. What did I do wrong?

Answer: Nothing! In Word, you cannot view the summary information for an Excel workbook or a PowerPoint presentation.

If you use the Find File feature in Word to find an Excel workbook or a PowerPoint presentation and you select Summary in the View list, the summary information for the workbook or the presentation is not displayed. You can, however, view the Document Size and the Last Saved Date; this information appears correctly for the workbook or the presentation.

Question 7: When I click a button on the MOM toolbar or on the Microsoft toolbar to start an application, I get an error message. I know the application is installed, and I can run it from Program Manager without a problem. Why can't I run it from the toolbar?

Answer: If you get an error message stating that the application you want to start cannot be located or cannot be run, this generally means that the application has not been registered correctly or that something has happened to the registration information.

To fix this problem, start the application by double-clicking its icon in Program Manager. Then click the button for the application on the MOM toolbar or on the Microsoft toolbar. This "teaches" the button where to find the application. You need only do this once—retraining the button on the MOM toolbar also retrains the button on the Microsoft toolbar, and vice versa.

When you click a button on the MOM toolbar or on the Microsoft toolbar to start an application, a path to the application is needed. For applications that support OLE (all of the major Office applications), MOM searches for the path to the application first in the registration file, REG.DAT, and then in the Extensions section of the WIN.INI file.

For applications that do not support OLE, such as Microsoft FoxPro, the path to the application is retrieved from the Extensions section of the WIN.INI file. Once this data is retrieved, it gets written to the MSToolbar section in the REG.DAT file.

Question 8: Can I put an application on the MOM toolbar twice—the same version but different locations?

Answer: The answer is yes, but with one restriction: They cannot share the same toolbar button. The location of the application specified as the current version in the REG.DAT file will use the preinstalled button image for that application, if there is one. If you want to have two different versions of the same application on your toolbar or two locations for the same application (for example, one on the network and one on the local hard drive), you must add another button to the toolbar and assign it to the second instance of the application.

Question 9: I set my working directory for Excel to C:\WKBOOKS, but when I start Excel and choose File Open, the current directory is C:\EXCEL. Why isn't it using the working directory I set using the MOM toolbar?

Answer: Each of the Office applications has two different places where you can set a working directory: Program Manager and MOM. Word and Excel also have their own settings that control the working directory. Because each Program Manager icon or MOM toolbar button or menu item has a setting specifying the application's working directory, and because these settings are independent, it is important to change the working directory in both Program Manager and MOM. Otherwise, you end up with a different working

FOR MOM ONLY

If you run a version of an application that is different from the version registered in the REG.DAT file and the version that MOM would run, and you then click the button on the MOM toolbar for that application, an entry is added to the MSToolbar section of REG.DAT indicating the path of the application that is currently running. That version will be the one that MOM starts or switches to during the same session. But if you close MOM and then start MOM again, it goes back to bringing up the most current version of the application that is registered in the REG.DAT file.

WORKING DIRECTORY

An application's *working directory* is the directory that is active when you choose to save or open a file in the application.

directory when you start the program from Program Manager than when you start it from MOM.

Program Manager   To change the working directory for a Program Manager icon, do the following:

1. Click the icon to select it.

2. From the File menu, choose Properties. The Program Item Properties dialog box appears.

3. In the Working Directory text box, type the path for your working directory.

4. Click OK to save the changes. The changes are permanently stored when you exit Program Manager.

MOM   To change the working directory for a button or a menu item on the MOM toolbar, do the following:

1. On the MOM toolbar, click the Office Manager button (usually the button farthest to the right).

2. Choose the Customize command. The Customize dialog box appears.

3. On either the Menu tab or the Toolbar tab of the dialog box, select the application for which you want to change the working directory. Changing the setting for an application's toolbar button (or menu item) changes the setting for the application's menu item (or toolbar button).

4. Choose the Edit button. The Edit Program Item dialog box appears.

5. In the Working Directory text box, type the name of the working directory.

6. Click OK to accept the changes and to close the Edit Program Item dialog box.

7. Click OK to close the Customize dialog box.

File Locations Tab of the Options Dialog Box   Word 6 and Excel 5 have settings stored in their respective INI files that override the working directory settings in both Program Manager and MOM. To specify the working directory for Word or Excel regardless of how you start the application, do the following:

In Microsoft Word:

1. From the Tools menu, choose Options.

2. Select the File Locations tab of the Options dialog box. Select Documents in the list box and choose Modify.

3. Select a new working directory in the Modify Location dialog box. Click OK.

4. In the Options dialog box, click Close.

In Microsoft Excel:

1. From the Tools menu, choose Options.

2. Select the General tab of the Options dialog box.

3. In the Default File Location text box, type the full pathname to the directory that you want to set as your working directory. Click OK.

Question 10: When I try to obtain information about my system using the Word 6 Help menu (by choosing the System Info button in the About Microsoft Word dialog box), it tells me *Word cannot find or run the application. (MSINFO).* I know it's installed—I chose this option when I ran the Setup program. In fact, I can run it from Excel just fine. What's happening?

Answer: You're probably missing a small piece of information in your WIN.INI file that provides the name and the location of the information-gathering program. To fix this, use Notepad to edit the WIN.INI file and add the Microsoft System Info section; this section should have an MSINFO entry that points to your MSINFO.EXE file. For example, if you used a default setting when you installed the program to your C drive, type

```
[Microsoft System Info]

MSINFO=C:\WINDOWS\MSAPPS\MSINFO\MSINFO.EXE
```

If this entry is missing, one of the following error messages appears when you try to run System Info from an Office application:

Word: *Word cannot find or run the application. (MSINFO).*

PowerPoint: *PowerPoint cannot find or run the application "MSInfo".*

Access: *Can't display system information.*

You can still run the System Info application from Excel without this information in your WIN.INI file. In fact, if System Info runs fine from Excel but not from the other Office applications, you can be pretty sure that your problem is in the WIN.INI file, as described above.

System Info is an application that gives you very detailed and useful information about the way your system is set up, how much memory is available, the versions of various files on your system, the version of MS-DOS you are running, and the amount of available disk space on every drive on your computer. You can run this application by choosing About from the Help menu in any Office application and then choosing the System Info button.

General Interoperability

Question 11: Word 6 runs much slower than earlier versions of Word. How can I get it to run a little faster?

Answer: Word 6 is larger and more robust than previous versions of Word. As a result, performance can slow down simply because your computer is working harder. However, if you optimize the performance of Microsoft Windows, you can also speed up Word's performance.

Optimizing Windows involves both your software and your hardware (for example, processor type and speed, amount of memory, and available hard disk space). Microsoft Product Support Services has an application note, titled "WD1015: How to Optimize the Performance of Word 6.0," that you can use as a checklist to optimize both your software and your hardware configurations for Word and other Windows-based applications running under Windows 3.1 or Windows for Workgroups 3.1. You can obtain this application note from the following sources:

- CompuServe, GEnie, and Microsoft OnLine

- Internet (Microsoft anonymous ftp server)

- Microsoft Product Support Services

- Microsoft Download Service (MSDL)

- Microsoft FastTips Technical Library

Question 12: Why does Word 6 always set the margins to 0 inches when I create a Word 6 document object?

Answer: Word sets the margins at 0 inches in a document object so that you don't wind up with excessive white space around the object—a result of combining two sets of margin settings. If you want specific margins for all document objects, you can set the OLEDOT switch in your WINWORD6.INI file that designates a particular template for Word to use whenever it creates a document object. Here is the syntax of the OLEDOT switch, which goes in the Microsoft Word section of your WINWORD6.INI file (*TEMPLATE* is the name of any existing template):

```
OLEDOT=TEMPLATEPATH\TEMPLATE
```

COMBINED MARGINS

Keep in mind that Word adds the template margins of the document object to the margins of the destination document. For example, if the destination document has left and right margins of 1.25 inches and you use an OLEDOT template to set 1-inch margins in the object, the document object will have left and right margins of 2.25 inches.

And here is an example of the WINWORD6.INI entry:

```
[Microsoft Word]
OLEDOT=C:\WINWORD6\TEMPLATE\FAXCOVR1.DOT
```

Question 13: Some of my Word document objects are cropped when I embed them in another application or in another Word document. How can I get the entire object to show up?

Answer: Embedded Word 6 document objects have default margins of 0 inches and a page size of 6 inches by 9 inches or less. As a result, when you embed a Word document object in another Word document or in another application (such as Microsoft Publisher or PowerPoint), one side of the object might appear cropped. This happens if the page width of the object is greater than 6 inches. When you copy text and paste it as a Word 6 document object into a destination application, it automatically has a page size of 6 inches by 9 inches or less and margins of 0 inches. These settings are applied to every section of the document object. The same thing happens if you create a Word 6 document object using the Object command on the Insert menu.

Word 6 sets the above-mentioned page specifications for its document objects so that each object can be represented at full scale within a standard Word document. Word documents have default left and right margins of 1.25 inches, which leaves 6 inches of horizontal printable space. If you copy and paste text wider than 6 inches as an object, the object will extend past the area of the destination application (and the object page length might also vary) unless you use the workaround described below.

This problem occurs only with objects that are larger than 6 inches by 9 inches. When you paste an object with a narrower page width, it should appear about the same as the original. For example, if you copy text that is 3 inches wide, the width of the object will also be approximately 3 inches.

To work around the problem and preserve the object's margins and page sizes, you must first insert a Word 6 document object and then paste the desired text into the open object. To do so, follow these steps:

1. Select the text for the desired object. Be sure to include all trailing section breaks for text in the selection and the last paragraph mark for text at the end of the document. (Page sizes and margins of sections are stored in trailing section breaks and in the last paragraph mark for the last section of a document.)

2. From the Edit menu, choose Cut or Copy.

3. Switch to the destination application and use the Insert Object command to insert a new Microsoft Word 6.0 document object. The object will have default margins of 0 inches and a page size of approximately 6 inches by 9 inches.

4.   With the insertion point in the open object, choose Paste or Paste Special from the Edit menu to insert the cut or copied text.

Question 14: After I edit a Word 2.*x* document object in Word 6, the object is irretrievably corrupted. The next time I try to edit the object, Word 6 does not recognize the file format, and the Convert File dialog box appears. Why is this happening?

Answer: This can happen when a Word 2.*x* object is embedded in an OLE destination application, such as Word 6, Excel 5, or PowerPoint 4. If, after you open the object for editing in Word 6, you do not save or update the object before you close Word 6, the object becomes corrupted. If you save or update the object in Word 6 before you return to the destination application, the object converts to Word 6 format and does not become corrupted. Microsoft plans to fix this problem, but in the meantime, choose Save or Update from the File menu, even if you do not make a change every time you open a Word 2.*x* document object for editing in Word 6.

Question 15: It seems to take *forever* to save from any Office application to a floppy disk. Sometimes it takes more than 30 seconds to save an average-sized file. How can I speed up the process?

Answer: This happens because OLE applications create files in DOC-File format (not the same as Word's default document format). It takes extra time to write this file format to a floppy disk because it requires many read and write operations. In DOC-File format, objects are saved in "data streams" separate from the main application file stream (similar in concept to subdirectories of main directories in the MS-DOS file model). Other OLE applications (in addition to the application in which a particular document was produced) can read data in the DOC-File format.

To decrease substantially the time required to save OLE files to a floppy disk, you can use the MS-DOS SMARTDrive disk-caching program (SMARTDRV.EXE). With SMARTDrive, you can save files on a floppy disk up to five times more quickly than without it. SMARTDrive creates a cache in your computer's extended memory for rapid processing of disk operations, such as saving to a floppy disk. You can create a SMARTDrive disk cache on your A and B floppy disk drives in either of two ways:

- Add the SMARTDrive command to your AUTOEXEC.BAT file using the following syntax:

```
C:\DOS\SMARTDRV.EXE a+ b+ nnnn
```

where *nnnn* is the cache size, which is between 256 and 2048 bytes. (If you don't want to add this command to your AUTOEXEC.BAT file, you can type the command at the MS-DOS command prompt before starting Windows.)

DISK ERROR!
Never remove the floppy disk from the disk drive while you are saving a file to a floppy disk. If you remove the disk before the operation is complete (before the light on the floppy disk drive turns off and remains off), a serious disk error can occur. If this happens, reinsert the floppy disk and press Enter at the Serious Disk Error screen to finish writing the file.

- Add the SMARTDrive command to your CONFIG.SYS file using the following syntax:

```
Device=C:\DOS\SMARTDRV.SYS a+ b+ nnnn
```

where *nnnn* is the cache size, which is between 256 and 2048 bytes.

Question 16: When I double-click an embedded Excel workbook in a Microsoft Mail message, Excel starts, but it doesn't open the embedded workbook. The same thing happens when I double-click a workbook file in File Manager. My other Office applications open a file this way, so why won't Excel?

Answer: You probably have an option selected that causes Excel to ignore all requests from other applications. If the Ignore Other Applications check box is selected on the General tab of the Options dialog box, Excel does not allow you to access files from any application other than Excel itself. In addition to the problems you described, you also cannot print workbook files by dragging them from File Manager to Print Manager when this option is selected. To fix the situation, do the following:

1. In Excel, choose Options from the Tools menu.

2. Select the General tab of the Options dialog box and deselect the Ignore Other Applications check box. Click OK.

Question 17: I switched to Word and the mouse pointer is stuck in the hour-glass shape. The document seems to be frozen. Is time standing still?

Answer: You're probably running a command (such as Send or Mail Merge) that opens a window in front of the document. You switched out of Word to another application (thanks a lot, MOM) and left that secondary window open. Oddly enough, that window does not reappear when you return to Word, but neither does the command take kindly to your attempts to edit your document behind its back. Press Ctrl+Esc to display Task List, and look for a secondary task that has placed the main application window on hold. Switch to that activity and either complete it or cancel it.

Question 18: When I select text or a graphic in my Word document and then try to drag it to another location, the mouse keeps selecting more information in my document instead of moving what I originally highlighted. What am I doing wrong?

Answer: Assuming that you have the Drag-and-Drop Text Editing check box selected on the Edit tab of the Options dialog box (better check it to be sure!), you might not be waiting long enough for your mouse pointer to change to a drag-and-drop pointer. The drag-and-drop pointer appears after a short pause (approximately half a second). If you attempt to drag your selection before the drag-and-drop pointer appears, the mouse will start selecting more of your document. The half-second delay is meant to prevent you from accidentally dragging information to a new location when you really mean only to select it.

Question 19: I inserted an object in my Word document as an icon. Now I want the document to display the contents of the object instead of the icon. How do I make the change?

Answer: The procedure for displaying the contents of an object that has been inserted as an icon is the same for all of the major Office applications:

1. Select the icon by clicking it once.

2. From the Edit menu, choose the appropriate Object command (Document Object for a Word object) and choose Convert from the submenu that appears.

3. In the Convert dialog box, deselect the Display as Icon check box and click OK.

Question 20: When I run the Spelling utility in Word, a general protection (GP) fault occurs. Help!

Answer: A GP fault may occur in Word if you run the Soft-Art Dictionary spelling checker supplied with Excel, PowerPoint, Publisher, and Mail. Technically, this happens because the Soft-Art shared spelling checker uses a different DLL file (MSSPELL.DLL) from the one used by the International CorrectSpell spelling checker (MSSPEL2.DLL) supplied with Word 6. The Soft-Art DLL file uses MS-DOS file handles, so when Word runs this DLL file, if the FILES setting in your CONFIG.SYS file is too low, a GP fault occurs. You can delay the occurrence of the GP fault by increasing the FILES setting, but the GP fault eventually occurs in Word no matter how much you increase the FILES setting.

Word should be a better neighbor, but for now it isn't, so use one of the following workarounds to avoid this problem:

Method 1 Change the Spelling setting in the Microsoft Word section of your WINWORD6.INI file (located in the Windows program directory) so that it points to the location of the Word 6 spelling checker files. The following is a sample WINWORD6.INI entry that points to the Word 6 spelling checker files. (For Word 6, this setting takes precedence over any other spelling settings in other INI files.)

```
[Microsoft Word]
Spelling 1033,0=C:\WINDOWS\MSAPPS\PROOF\MSSPEL2.DLL,
C:\WINDOWS\MSAPPS\PROOF\MSSP2_EN.LEX
```

Method 2 Change the Spelling setting in the MS Proofing Tools section of the WIN.INI file (located in the Windows program directory) so that it points to the location of the Word 6 spelling checker files. The following is a sample WIN.INI entry that points to the Word 6 spelling checker files. (This setting changes the location of the spelling checker for all applications that share the MS Proofing Tools, including Word, unless you set a different location in WINWORD6.INI, as described in method 1.)

```
[MS Proofing Tools]
Spelling 1033,0=C:\WINDOWS\MSAPPS\PROOF\MSSPEL2.DLL,
C:\WINDOWS\MSAPPS\PROOF\MSSP2_EN.LEX
```

Bringing Information into Word

Question 21: In Word, when I include a date/time field in a database query using ODBC, I get an *ODBC Error* message. What's going on?

Answer: Word passes dates and times to the ODBC drivers in an incorrect format. Use one of the following methods to work around this problem:

- Use Microsoft Query, a tool provided with Excel 5, to perform the query.

- Insert the entire database table in a Word document, save it as a Word document, and then use that document as a data source. You can then perform a query that contains a date field.

- If the database file is from an application that supports DDE, and the database application is available, you might be able to use DDE rather than ODBC to query the database. For example, you can use DDE with Access database files.

Question 22: In Word 6, I can't change the LINK source file to a different Excel spreadsheet. Why not?

Answer: Your Windows REG.DAT file probably doesn't contain a valid path to Excel. Typically, this problem happens with documents you created in Word 2.*x* but not with documents you created in Word 6. The problem occurs when you select a new spreadsheet as a source file in the Change Source dialog box but the original Excel spreadsheet continues to appear in the document. If you reopen the Links dialog box, Word again lists the original Excel spreadsheet as the source file (as if you had never chosen the Change Source button and changed the source file).

To work around this problem, you can choose the Links command from the Edit menu to open the Links dialog box, where you can break the link and then reestablish it to a different Excel spreadsheet. If you want to solve this problem permanently, follow the instructions below to update your REG.DAT file so that it points to the correct location of Excel.

1. In File Manager, select one of the following two files: OLE2.REG (located in your WINDOWS\SYSTEM subdirectory) or WIN-WORD6.REG (located in your Word 6 program directory).

2. From the File menu, choose Associate. *REG* should appear in the Files with Extension box. (If it doesn't appear there, type it in.)

3. In the Associate With list, select Registration Entries (REGEDIT.EXE) and click OK.

4. Double-click the selected file (OLE2.REG or WINWORD6.REG). Click OK when a message appears confirming that the information has been successfully registered in the registration database.

Question 23: I just saved an Excel worksheet in Word, and Word changed my Excel file to the Word format. Now I can't open the file in Excel. Why did Word do this?

Answer: Word can open (import) Excel files, but it can't save (export) in Excel format. If you try to select Microsoft Excel Worksheet in the Save File as Type drop-down list in the Save As dialog box, you get the following error message: *Word cannot save Microsoft Excel Worksheet files. The converter for this format can only open files.*

If, instead, you save the worksheet in Word Document format, Word replaces your Excel file with a Word document file, which Excel can no longer read. If your file was a Microsoft Excel 5 workbook, all of the workbook contents are lost.

If you want to edit and save changes to an Excel worksheet while in Word, open the worksheet via DDE using the Mail Merge Helper (choose the Edit button). Otherwise, open the worksheet file in Excel and work with it there.

Question 24: When I link to an Excel worksheet from a Word document, Word changes the cell references from the A1 method to the R1C1 method. What's going on?

Answer: The information that Excel copies to the Clipboard uses R1C1 cell references, so that's how they appear in Word. Excel does this because many applications support the R1C1 cell references instead of the A1 cell references. Fortunately, Word supports both, so this shouldn't cause any problems in your documents.

Question 25: When I select some text in one instance of Word and drag it to a document in another instance of Word, it is inserted as regular text, not as a Word document object. Why is this happening?

Answer: When you drag selected text in Word to another Word document, whether it is in another window or in another instance of Word, it is always inserted as text. If you want to create a linked or embedded Word object in another Word document, you must first copy the text to the Clipboard and then use the Paste Special command on the Edit menu to paste the data into the destination document.

Question 26: When I paste link an Excel spreadsheet into a Word document, Word inserts an extra paragraph mark above the link. I can't select or delete the paragraph mark, so how can I get rid of it?

Answer: You can't get rid of the extra paragraph mark, unfortunately, but you *can* do the following to reduce the line spacing so that it almost completely disappears:

1. Position the insertion point to the left of the paragraph mark. (You cannot select the mark only.)

2. From the Format menu, choose Paragraph.

3. On the Indents and Spacing tab of the Paragraph dialog box, change the Line Spacing setting to Exactly and the At value to 0.01". Click OK.

Note: The extra paragraph mark does not appear if you paste the spreadsheet instead of paste link it.

Question 27: In Word, when I drag a framed, linked Excel worksheet to another location in the document, it appears twice in my document instead of once. Why?

Answer: This happens if the field result, instead of the field code, is displayed when you frame the LINK field. Word frames the field result (that is, the worksheet) but *not* the LINK field. Consequently, when you drag the framed field result, you drag a *framed picture* of the worksheet but you leave the unframed LINK field behind. If you later update the LINK field, a new, unframed copy of the worksheet appears in the original location. (Are you confused yet?)

If this happens to you, delete the unlinked, framed copy of the worksheet and then use one of the following methods to drag both the LINK field *and* its framed result to a new location:

- Choose the Frame command from the Format menu so that you can position the frame (instead of using the mouse to drag the frame to its new position).

- Take the following steps to make sure that you frame the LINK field when you frame the Excel worksheet:

1. Press Alt+F9 to display all of the field codes in the document, including the LINK field to the Excel worksheet.

2. Select the entire LINK field.

3. From the Insert menu, choose Frame. Click Yes if Word prompts you to switch to Page Layout view.

4. Press Alt+F9 to display the field result. If you drag the framed result to a new location on the page, the field code will be included in the move.

Question 28: Why is the cell alignment wrong in some of the Excel spreadsheets I paste into Word?

Answer: There are a couple of reasons for this. First, when you paste or paste link data from an Excel 3 or Excel 4 spreadsheet into a Word document, the cells are usually right-aligned, which is the default format for numbers in these versions of Excel. Right-alignment can cause alignment problems in Word if tabs are inserted, and data might even be moved into an adjacent cell. If, for example, you insert a decimal tab in the table that you pasted from Excel, the data might become misaligned. These alignment problems do not occur when the copied data is from an Excel 5 spreadsheet.

The second reason for alignment problems is associated with updating an established link. When an Excel spreadsheet is inserted in Word using the LINK field, a formatting switch with the mergeformat option is included by default as part of the field instructions. This switch instructs Word to maintain the formatting of the field result as it was initially inserted or as it was later modified in Word. This prevents any subsequent formatting changes in the spreadsheet from being applied to the field result in Word. Therefore, if you change the alignment of some cells in the spreadsheet and then update the LINK field in Word, the updated field result will not use the new alignment.

The workaround for these problems depends on when and where you want to change the alignment.

- To eliminate alignment problems before inserting data from an Excel 3 or Excel 4 spreadsheet, change the right-alignment of the cells to another alignment.

- To change the alignment of the cells and have the changes included in the Word field result after you link the Excel spreadsheet to Word, delete the formatting switch with the mergeformat option from the LINK field. The alignment in Word will revert to the alignment of the cells in the Excel spreadsheet when the field is updated.

- To change the alignment in Word and have all subsequent link updates retain the alignment set in Word, leave the formatting switch with the mergeformat option in the LINK field and use Word's formatting commands to change the alignment.

- To change the alignment in Excel but preserve any subsequent changes made in Word, delete and then reinsert the LINK field.

Question 29: When I paste an Excel spreadsheet into Word, sometimes it's a tab-delimited text file and sometimes it's a regular Word table. Why don't all of my spreadsheets paste as tables into Word?

Answer: If your Excel spreadsheet is larger than 217 rows long and 8 columns wide, Word converts the data to tab-delimited format when you paste it into a Word document. When this happens, you can convert the data to a Word table by selecting it and choosing Convert Text to Table from the Table menu.

Note: If you paste linked the data from the spreadsheet, you must unlink the LINK field before you can convert the data to a Word table. To unlink the field, select it and press Ctrl+Shift+F9.

Question 30: When I paste a selection of cells from an Excel worksheet into a Word table, an error message appears. What am I doing wrong?

Answer: Word displays the error message *You cannot paste this selection into a table* if you try to paste a selection of cells from an Excel worksheet into a Word table. This happens because Word imports information from Excel in table format, and you cannot insert a table in a table in Word. You have to paste the Excel information into a nontable paragraph in Word.

Question 31: When I try to embed a large Excel worksheet object in Word, I get the following error message: *There is insufficient memory. Save the document now.* I've got plenty of memory, so what's the problem?

Answer: Excel usually cannot embed more than about 66 rows of data in Word. If you attempt to embed a larger selection, a low-memory error will occur. You have to embed a smaller portion of the worksheet or you must link instead of embed the data.

Question 32: The data I paste from an Excel worksheet is always at the top of the table cell in Word. How can I get the data to appear in the center or at the bottom of the cell?

Answer: Word does not support vertical alignment for table cells, so Word does not retain any center or bottom vertical alignment formatting that you may have applied in Excel. (Word *does* retain cell height and horizontal alignment formatting, however.) As a workaround, use Word's paragraph formatting to set the spacing before the paragraph to modify the vertical alignment. You can also paste the worksheet as a picture instead of as formatted text.

Question 33: Why does Word change the font size of the data I paste from Excel?

Answer: Word changes any 10-point text copied from Excel and pasted into Word to the default font size used by Word. It does not change the typeface, nor does it change any text with a font size other than 10-point. (Of course, if the default font size in Word is 10 points, no change in font size is made.)

For example, if your default font (Normal style) in Word is Times New Roman 12-point, all Arial 10-point text in Excel changes to Arial 12-point text when you paste it into a Word document. This change occurs only when you perform a paste operation. It does not occur if you embed or paste link the Excel data.

If you are pasting 10-point text from Excel and want the font size to remain 10 points, change the font size of the Normal style to 10 points in Word (if it is not already 10 points) before you paste the Excel data. After you paste the Excel data, you can change the Normal style font size back to the original setting.

Question 34: When I paste an Excel chart into a Word document and then scale the chart, it never looks right. How can I keep from ruining the chart when I scale it?

Answer: When you scale an Excel chart in Word, one of two things can happen, depending on exactly what you copied and pasted:

Case 1: Excel Chart Object from a Chart Sheet   When you scale a Microsoft Excel 5.0 Chart Object that is embedded in a Word document, the chart plot area might be scaled while the chart text, chart legend, and object frame remain unscaled. This happens if your chart is a separate chart sheet in Excel (instead of an embedded chart object in the Excel worksheet).

Case 1 occurs because the EMBED field in Word contains the \s switch, which returns an embedded object to its original size when you update the field. Word adds the \s switch when you use the Paste command or the Paste Special command and select the Paste option button to embed an Excel chart object. By contrast, Word does not add the \s switch when you embed the chart from an existing file using the Object command on the Insert menu.

Case 2: Excel Chart Object from an Excel Worksheet   If you copy a chart that is embedded in an Excel worksheet, paste it into Word, and then scale the chart object, the chart in the object is displayed off-center, the Excel worksheet cells are visible, and the chart object frame returns to its original size.

This happens partly because of the \s EMBED field switch and partly because, with an embedded chart, you embed Excel worksheet cells as well as the embedded chart. This means that the embedded object behaves more like a

Microsoft Excel 5.0 Worksheet Object than like a chart object. For best results in Word, you should embed a chart sheet rather than an embedded chart whenever possible. (None of the above problems occurs if you create a linked object rather than an embedded object, by selecting the Paste Link option button in the Paste Special dialog box in Word.)

Use one of the following workarounds to embed an Excel chart in Word that you can scale. For best results, use the first method whenever possible.

- Embed a chart that is located in a chart sheet instead of using an embedded chart that is on a datasheet, and then size the chart in Excel before you embed it in Word. In Word, use the following procedure to embed the chart:

    1. From the Insert menu, choose Object. In the Object dialog box, select the Create from File tab.

    2. From the File Name list, select the Excel workbook that contains the chart sheet you want to embed, and then click OK.

    3. If the chart you want to embed is not the active sheet in the workbook, double-click the object and click the sheet tab in Excel for the appropriate chart.

    4. When the chart you want to embed is displayed, scale or crop it as desired, and then click anywhere outside the chart to return to Word.

- When you must use a chart that is embedded in a worksheet instead of one in a chart sheet, you can scale an embedded Excel chart object in Word without distorting the chart object or displaying cells from a worksheet, by taking the following steps:

    1. Insert the chart object in the Word document, and then select the chart object.

    2. Press Shift+F9 to display the field code instead of the object. The field code representing the chart object appears as follows:

        ```
        {EMBED Excel.Chart.5 \s}
        ```

    3. Edit the field code to appear as follows (delete the \s switch):

        ```
        {EMBED Excel.Chart.5}
        ```

    4. Place the insertion point in the field code and press F9 to update the change to the field code.

    5. With the insertion point in the field code, press Shift+F9 to display the chart object.

    6. Size the chart object.

Note: In Word, the \s switch in an EMBED field returns an embedded object to its original size when you update the field. When you embed an Excel chart object in a Word document, this switch is automatically included in the EMBED field for that object. If you remove the \s switch from the EMBED field, Word does not return the chart object to its original size when you update the field.

Question 35: When I link or embed a large range of cells from an Excel worksheet in my Word document, it gets cropped from the right or the bottom. This happens even if there is enough room on the page for the entire range to fit. How can I avoid this?

Answer: Whether you paste link an Excel worksheet as a picture or paste it as an embedded object, you are dealing with a Windows metafile (WMF). Windows limits the height and width of a Windows metafile. Excel sets the height and width of the picture or object presentation by using the Excel page size at 100 percent zoom. If the selection in Excel exceeds approximately 20 columns (the default width) or approximately 75 rows, Word crops the picture when you paste it into the document, even if it appears that there is room on the page to accommodate a larger picture.

To work around this Windows limitation, use one of the following methods:

- Paste or paste link formatted or unformatted text into Word.

- Reduce the font and column size in Excel.

Bringing Information into Excel

Question 36: When I drag and drop a Word table into Excel 5, the first cell in the Word table is deleted in Word. In other words, the first cell in the table is *moved* to Excel, while the remaining table cells are *copied*. Why is this happening?

Answer: This is a problem with the drag-and-drop feature. Another associated problem is that when you drag and drop less than an entire row from a Word table into Excel, the entire row is copied. The smallest table unit you can move using drag and drop is a row. As a result, if you select a single column in a multicolumn table, the entire table is copied. Your best bet for copying a table from Word to Excel is to use the Cut, Copy, and Paste commands on the Edit menu.

Question 37: When I export to Excel 5 an Access table that contains a column of time data values, all of the time values are displayed as the date *1/0/00* when I open the workbook in Excel. How can I correct this?

Answer: This behavior occurs because of the way Excel interprets serial numbers. To display the time correctly in your Excel worksheet, take the following steps:

1. Select the affected values in the worksheet and choose Cells from the Format menu.

2. In the Format Cells dialog box, select the Number tab.

3. In the Category list, select Time. In the Format Codes list, select the time format you want. Click OK.

Excel and Access both use serial numbers to display dates and times. An Access table that is exported to Excel automatically formats all serial numbers as dates. You simply have to change the format of the column of serial numbers on the spreadsheet to a time format.

Bringing Information into PowerPoint

Question 38: I created a table on a PowerPoint slide using the Insert Microsoft Word Table button. In Word, I applied standard black table borders, but when I activated my PowerPoint slide again, the table borders changed to yellow. Why did this happen?

Answer: PowerPoint recolors the object to maintain the color scheme definitions used in your slide show. PowerPoint behaves this way so that if you change the color scheme of your slide, you won't suddenly have an unreadable table.

To override this behavior, and to prevent the table formatting from changing when you change the colors on your slide, follow these steps:

1. Select the table object whose colors were remapped.

2. From the Tools menu, choose Recolor. A dialog box appears that has a swatch of each original color in the Word table. Each color that PowerPoint has changed will have the check box to the left of that color selected. Deselect all of the check boxes and click OK.

Your Word table will now appear in PowerPoint with the original coloring.

Question 39: When I embed a chart or a selection of cells from Excel in Power-Point, the background is solid and completely covers a portion of my slide. How can I insert the chart or cells in my slide so that the background is transparent and lets the colors on my slide show through?

Answer: The background pattern/fill color is controlled by a combination of settings in Excel and PowerPoint. In Excel, the setting is the area or cell pattern. In PowerPoint, the setting is the object fill.

Ordinarily, an Excel object pastes with an opaque white background when the setting for the area or cell pattern is Automatic. When the pattern is set to Automatic (or any color) in Excel, you cannot override that color with a fill in PowerPoint. (The Recolor command is effective, however.)

To make the Excel object (chart or cells) paste with a clear background, or to preserve the option to fill the object in PowerPoint, set its area or cell pattern in Excel to None by following the appropriate procedure below.

- To set the background pattern of an Excel 5 chart:

    1. In PowerPoint, double-click the embedded chart to activate it in Excel.

    2. Point to the chart (not its frame) and open the shortcut menu. The contents of the menu depend on the type of chart. If the chart was created in a chart sheet, choose the Format Plot Area command; if the chart was created as an embedded object in a worksheet, choose the Format Object command.

    3. The Format Plot Area dialog box or the Format Object dialog box appears, with the Patterns tab active.

    4. In the Area or Fill section, select None. Click OK.

The chart should now have a transparent background, allowing the Power-Point slide background to show through.

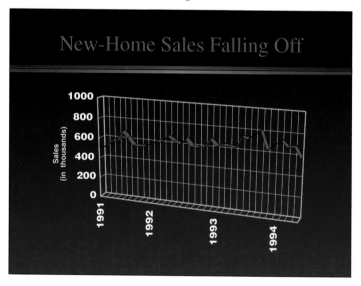

Note: If you are editing an Excel 5 chart that has already been embedded in PowerPoint 4, you might have to click outside the object to exit from Excel before the slide background will show through.

- To set the cell pattern (background) in Excel:

  1. In Excel, select a range of cells.

  2. From the Format menu, choose Cells. In the Format Cells dialog box that appears, select the Patterns tab.

  3. In the Cell Shading section, select None as the Color option. Click OK.

Question 40: In Word, where is the Present It button that I can use to copy a Word outline to a PowerPoint presentation?

Answer: Word supplies the PresentIt macro, which exports the outline information in the current Word document to PowerPoint. In Word 6.0, the PresentIt macro is located in the CONVERT.DOT template. In Word 6.0a, it is also located in the PRESENT.DOT template. The CONVERT.DOT template provides a separate Present It toolbar, while the PRESENT.DOT template adds the Present It button to the Microsoft toolbar.

If you have Word 6.0, use method 1; if you have Word 6.0a, use method 2.

Method 1: Copy Present It from CONVERT.DOT to NORMAL.DOT
Word 6.0 supplies the PresentIt macro and the Present It toolbar as part of the CONVERT.DOT template file. You can copy them from CONVERT.DOT to your Normal template by taking the following steps. (If you want to copy the Present It button to your Microsoft toolbar, use the instructions below and then follow the procedure in method 2.)

  1. In Word, create a new document based on the Normal template (by clicking the New button on the Standard toolbar).

  2. From the File menu, choose Templates.

  3. Choose the Organizer button, and then select the Macros tab of the Organizer dialog box.

  4. Choose the left Close File button. (The button changes to an Open File button.)

  5. Choose the left Open File button.

  6. Select CONVERT.DOT, which is located in the MACROS subdirectory of your Word 6 program directory, and then click OK.

  7. Select PresentIt in the In CONVERT.DOT list box, and then choose the Copy button. PresentIt should now appear in the To NORMAL.DOT list box on the right.

  8. Select the Toolbars tab of the Organizer dialog box.

WHICH VERSION?
To determine which version of Word you have, choose the About command from the Help menu.

9. In the In CONVERT.DOT box, select Present It, and then choose the Copy button. Present It should now appear in the To NORMAL.DOT box on the right.

10. Click Close to exit the Organizer dialog box.

11. To display the Present It toolbar, choose Toolbars from the View menu. The Toolbars dialog box appears. From the Toolbars list in the dialog box, select the Present It check box. Click OK.

Method 2: Attach PRESENT.DOT to a Word Document When you attach PRESENT.DOT to a Word document (using the Templates command on the File menu), the PresentIt macro becomes globally available. You can then add a button for it to your toolbar. Simply follow these steps:

1. Copy the PresentIt macro from PRESENT.DOT to your Normal template by following the instructions in method 1.

2. Open or create a document based on the Normal template.

3. If the toolbar you want the Present It button to be located on is not displayed, use the View Toolbars command to display it.

4. From the Tools menu, choose Customize, and select the Toolbars tab of the Customize dialog box.

5. In the Categories list box, select Macros.

6. In the Macros list box, select PresentIt.

7. Drag the PresentIt macro and drop it at the location on the toolbar where you want the Present It button to reside. (Notice that the mouse pointer changes to a gray-outlined square.) When you drop the macro, the Custom Button dialog box appears.

8. In the Custom Button dialog box, select the PowerPoint button (the seventh button in the fourth row), and then choose the Assign button. You should now see the PowerPoint button on the toolbar.

9. In the Customize dialog box, select Normal.dot in the Save Changes In drop-down list, and then click Close.

Bringing Information into Access

Question 41: I know how to import data from a table in an Access database into Word for a mail merge, but how do I import data from a Word document that is a Word mail merge data source into Access?

PATCHWORK PIECES

The Word 6.0a for Windows patch supplies a new template file, PRESENT.DOT, but depending on the configuration of Office and Power-Point, the template file might remain in the directory where you originally placed the patch files instead of being copied to the TEMPLATE or MACROS subdirec-tory of your Word 6 program directory. If this happens, you can copy the PRESENT.DOT file from the loca-tion where you expanded your Word 6.0a patch files to your TEMPLATE subdirectory.

Answer: To use data from a Word mail merge data file in Access, you must save a copy of the file as a comma-delimited or tab-delimited unformatted text file.

A Word mail merge data file can be formatted with comma-delimited or tab-delimited data, or the data can be contained in a table. If the data is already comma-delimited or tab-delimited, you need only save the file as unformatted text for it to be ready for Access.

If the data is in a table, you must convert the table to a tab-delimited format before saving it as a text file. Because you can create multiple lines of information in a table cell using carriage returns (paragraph marks), you must remove the carriage returns before you convert the table to a tab-delimited format to bring it into Access.

To prepare a mail merge data source in Word for use in Access, use the following procedures to modify the data file into an appropriate form:

Removing Unwanted Carriage Returns from a Table-Formatted Data File

1. Open the data document in Word.

2. From the Edit menu, choose Replace.

3. In the Replace dialog box, with the insertion point in the Find What text box, choose the Special button. Choose Paragraph Mark from the menu that appears.

4. In the Replace With text box, press Spacebar once to insert a single space.

5. Choose the Replace All button to replace each paragraph mark (carriage return) with a space.

6. Choose the Close button to close the Replace dialog box.

Converting Data from a Table to a Tab-Delimited Format

1. Position the insertion point anywhere inside the table.

2. From the Table menu, choose Select Table.

3. From the Table menu, choose Convert Table to Text.

4. In the Separate Text With section of the Convert Table To Text dialog box, select the Tabs option button. Click OK.

Saving a Copy of a Data File as an Unformatted Text File

1. From the File menu, choose Save As, and in the File Name text box, type a unique filename.

2. In the Save File as Type list box, select Text Only. Click OK.

Importing a Text Data File into Access

1. With a new or existing database open, select the Table tab of the Database window.

2. From the File menu, choose Import.

3. In the Data Source list, select Text (Delimited). Click OK.

4. In the Select File dialog box, select the directory in which you saved the text file from the Directories list, and select the Word text file to import from the File Name list. Choose the Import button.

5. In the Import Text Options dialog box, select the First Row Contains Field Names check box if the first row in the Word data file contains field names.

6. Choose the Options button.

7. In the Field Separator list, select {tab}. Click OK to begin the import.

8. Close the Select File dialog box.

Question 42: I inserted a Microsoft Excel 5.0 Worksheet Object in my Access form, edited the object, and then minimized Excel to do some other work on the form. When I closed the form in Access, Excel was still running. Why?

Answer: Access does not close some OLE servers when you close a form while the OLE object is still open for editing. The same behavior occurs when you embed an object in an Access table or report. Because a Multiple Document Interface (MDI) application can have multiple documents open at the same time, Access does not close an MDI application, even if it was started as an OLE server for an object stored in Access. This prevents the closing of an application that you might also be using for other purposes. Word 6 and Excel 5 are examples of applications that are left running if you double-click an existing embedded object in Access and then switch back to Access and close the form without closing the embedded object.

To be sure that the application in which you created the embedded object is closed when you close the form in which you embedded the object, close the application for the embedded object when you finish editing.

If you close a table, form, or report while you still have an open embedded object that you created in an application such as Paintbrush, Microsoft Draw, or Equation Editor (these are not MDI applications), the application closes when you close the table, form, or report.

Question 43: When I import an Excel spreadsheet into an Access database, the date fields are all off by four years. What is going on, and how can I fix this?

Answer: If date fields imported from an Excel spreadsheet are off by four years, the 1904 date system was used in the workbook containing your spreadsheet. This setting can be verified in Excel by opening the workbook in question, choosing Tools from the Options menu, and selecting the Calculation tab of the Options dialog box. In the Workbook Options section, if the 1904 Date System check box is selected, the spreadsheet is based on the 1904 date system. If the check box is not selected, the spreadsheet is based on the 1900 date system.

By default, Excel starts its dates at January 1, 1900. A serial number of 1 in Excel represents January 1, 1900. Excel can also be set to start on January 1, 1904. This option was included to make Excel for Windows compatible with Excel for the Macintosh, which starts its dates on January 1, 1904. The starting serial numbers are also different. A serial number of 0 (zero) in Excel for the Macintosh represents January 1, 1904.

To fix the spreadsheet that you want to import into Access if it was based on the 1904 date system, follow these steps before importing the spreadsheet into Access:

1. Open the Excel workbook that contains the spreadsheet.

2. From the Tools menu, choose Options.

3. Select the Calculation tab of the Options dialog box.

4. In the Workbook Options section, deselect the 1904 Date System check box. Click OK.

5. Save and close the workbook.

The spreadsheet is now ready to be imported into Access.

Mail Merge and Printing

Question 44: Word seems to constantly access my mail merge data source. How can I decrease the time Word spends doing this?

Answer: When you activate a mail merge main document, Word maintains a constant reference to the most recently used record in the data source, which requires Word to access the data file frequently. Word does this so that the most up-to-date values are always displayed. This means that if someone changes the data file record in the source application, Word automatically displays the new information in your main document.

The following measures can minimize the time you have to wait for Word to access your data source:

- Avoid unnecessarily switching from one document to another. This decreases the number of times Word accesses the data source.

- If you anticipate frequent switching from one document to another, activate record 1 in your main document. This eliminates the time you have to wait for Word to go from record 1 to the active record.

- Temporarily restore your main document to a normal Word document while you do tasks that require you to switch from one application to another or from one document to another. In this way, Word no longer spends time accessing the data source. After you finish the tasks that require frequent switching, you can reattach the data source.

To restore your main document to a normal Word document, do the following:

1. From the Tools menu, choose Mail Merge.

2. In the Mail Merge Helper dialog box, choose the Create button.

3. In the list that appears, select Return to Normal Word Document.

4. In the message box that informs you of the consequences of the change, choose Yes.

5. Close the Mail Merge Helper dialog box.

To reattach the main document to the data file, do the following:

1. From the Tools menu, choose Mail Merge.

2. In the Mail Merge Helper dialog box, choose the Create button.

3. In the list that appears, select the type of mail merge document you are creating.

4. In the message box that appears, choose the Active Window button.

5. In the Mail Merge Helper dialog box, choose the Get Data button.

6. From the menu that appears, choose Open Data Source.

7. In the Open Data Source dialog box, select the data source file and click OK. The data file is reattached to your main document.

Note: If Word is accessing your data source using DDE, leave the data source application open. This eliminates the time you have to wait for the application to open each time Word accesses the data source.

Question 45: When I attach an Excel or Access file as a mail merge data file, Word automatically uses DDE to start the source application and get the data. How can I get Word to use ODBC or a converter instead so that the source application does not need to be started?

Answer: When you open a database file or attach a data file for a mail merge in Word, Word uses DDE by default to gather the information. The following methods let you use ODBC or an appropriate file converter to access the data file directly.

Method 1 Select the Confirm Conversions option when you specify which database to use. With this option, Word opens the Confirm Data Source dialog box each time you open a data source so that you can select the OBDC driver or converter you want to use each time you attach a data source.

1. From the Tools menu, choose Mail Merge.

2. In the Mail Merge Helper dialog box, choose the Get Data button.

3. From the menu that appears, choose Open Data Source.

4. In the Open Data Source dialog box, select the data file in the File Name list box and select the Confirm Conversions check box. Click OK.

5. In the Confirm Data Source dialog box that appears, select the data source that uses ODBC or a converter. Click OK.

Method 2 If the filename extension for your database is listed in the Extensions section of the WIN.INI file, commenting (by inserting an apostrophe at the beginning of the line) or removing the line forces Word to use ODBC or the appropriate converter to access the database. Here's how the modified lines for Excel and Access might appear in your WIN.INI file.

```
[Extensions]
xlw=C:\WINDOWS\WINAPPS\EXCEL\EXCEL.EXE ^.xlw
'MDB=C:\WINDOWS\WINAPPS\ACCESS\MSACCESS.EXE ^.MDB
```

Question 46: When I try to use an Access database file as a mail merge data source in Word by means of ODBC, the Queries tab is not available (as shown on page 678 of the *Microsoft Word User's Guide*). The same thing happens when I try to use an Access database file in a Word DATABASE field. What should I do?

Answer: Access must be running to generate a query result. ODBC drivers do not activate the source application; they access the data file created by the application. That means you need to open the file using DDE instead of ODBC when you want to use an Access query as a data source. If DDE is not available, be sure that the Confirm Conversions option is selected in the Open Data Source dialog box. Also, verify that the following line is in the Extensions section of your WIN.INI file:

```
MDB=path\MSACCESS.EXE ^.MDB
```

where *path* is the location of the Access program directory. For example:

```
MDB=C:\ACCESS\MSACCESS.EXE ^.MDB
```

Question 47: Why do I get a mail merge error when my data file is in Excel CSV or Text format?

Answer: In Word, if you use an Excel file saved in the CSV or text format for the data file in a mail merge, the following error message might appear during the merge if the last column in the data file does not contain data in at least every 16th record:

> *There are fewer fields in data record* record name *than there are field names in the header record. Do you want to continue with the mail merge?*

Record name is the number of the first record of a 16-row block of records in which the last column contains no data.

In Excel, if you save a file in CSV or text format, Excel places tabs or commas between each column of the worksheet. However, if the cells in the last column contain no data, the extra tab or comma indicating the blank field for that record is stripped off when the file is saved. Excel saves text files in 16-row blocks. Therefore, if all the cells in the last column in a 16-row block are empty, Excel saves that area as if the column did not exist. No tabs or commas are saved for that 16-row block of cells.

To work around this problem, do one of the following:

• If you do not need to use the CSV or text format (in order to avoid errors due to commas within the data, for example), save the Excel file in the Excel file format.

• If you must use the CSV or text format, verify that the last column in the file contains some input at least every 16 rows throughout the file. (If necessary, you can add spaces or other characters in every 16th cell, or you can reorder the columns in the worksheet so that the last column in the worksheet always contains information.)

Question 48: When I try to print, nothing happens. What should I do?

Answer: First, be sure that your printer is turned on and that it is on line. Verify that both ends of your printer cable are making tight connections. In the Print dialog box, be sure that the page-range setting corresponds to the pages you want to print, and verify that the selected printer matches the printer you are using. If you still can't print, use the following additional troubleshooting steps:

• Check the status of your print job in Print Manager. If the print job is stalled, choose the Resume button.

• Try printing a file supplied by Word, such as README.DOC. If the file prints, the problem might be related to your document. To rule out this possibility, save your document in Rich Text Format before printing it.

Converting the document to Rich Text Format should remove any part of the document that is not compatible with printing. To save the document in Rich Text Format and test its printability, follow these steps:

1. From the File menu, choose Save As.

2. In the Save As dialog box, select Rich Text Format in the Save File as Type drop-down list, type a new name with an RTF extension in the File Name text box, and click OK.

3. From the File menu, choose Close.

4. From the File menu, choose Open. The Open dialog box appears.

5. In the Open dialog box, select Rich Text Format in the Save File as Type drop-down list. In the File Name list, select the RTF file you saved in step 2 and click OK.

6. Try printing the document.

- If you are printing over a network, be sure your network connection is intact. Check with your network administrator for assistance.

- If you still can't print, try printing a file from the Write program. If you cannot print from Write, the problem is probably affecting all of your Windows-based applications. Consider contacting Product Support Services.

Question 49: What can I do if my envelopes are printing blank or if the text is printing in the wrong location?

Answer: The settings in the Envelope Printing Options dialog box might not be correct for your printer. To change these settings, do the following:

1. From the Tools menu, choose Envelopes and Labels. The Envelopes and Labels dialog box appears.

2. In the dialog box, choose the Options button.

3. In the Envelope Options dialog box that appears, select the Printing Options tab.

4. Select the feed method that matches the envelope-feeding direction your printer uses.

   Change the other settings if necessary and then click OK.

5. Print your envelope or add it to your document.

Question 50: When I print a Word document that contains an embedded OLE object, the object prints at a very low resolution—it's grainy and ugly. How can I get my OLE objects to look better when I print them?

Answer: If your Word document contains an OLE object that you print while it is being edited in situ (while the server application's menus and toolbars temporarily replace those of Word), the object might print at a low resolution. Lines in the object might be jagged or incomplete, shading or patterns might appear incorrectly, or text might be compressed or missing. This happens because while you are editing an OLE object in situ, Word prints a bitmap of the object—as it appears on screen—instead of the actual object. The object prints correctly if you return to Word to print.

Index

D

Q

R

Eric Stroo

Lured to the Northwest in 1987, Eric Stroo observes the evolving world of computer software from Duvall, Washington. A onetime instructor of English literature and composition, he has for the past decade edited and written books and documentation on computer hardware, programming languages, and applications. He is currently employed by Microsoft Corporation, where his duties include writing, managing, and some light weeding.

The manuscript for this book was prepared and submitted to Microsoft Press in electronic form. Text files were prepared using Microsoft Word 2.0 for Windows. Pages were composed by Microsoft Press using Aldus PageMaker 5.0 for Windows, with text in Sabon and display type in Univers Condensed.

Cover Graphic Designer
Rebecca Geisler

Interior Graphic Designers
Hansen Design Company
Kim Eggleston

Interior Illustrators
David Holter
Mark Monlux

Typographers
Brett Polonsky
John Callan

Principal Compositor
John Sugg

Principal Proofreader/Copy Editor
Sally Anderson

Indexer
Shane-Armstrong Information Systems